P9-CEB-739

KOSSUTH

KOSSUTH IN AMERICA

OTTO ZAREK

KOSSUTH

Translated from the German by
LYNTON HUDSON

With 9 illustrations & a map

KENNIKAT PRESS
Port Washington, N. Y./London

KOSSUTH

First published in 1937
Reissued in 1970 by Kennikat Press
Library of Congress Catalog Card No: 78-112823
ISBN 0-8046-1090-8

Manufactured by Taylor Publishing Company Dallas, Texas

Contents

Part One

PRIDE

Part Two

A WEAPON: A PEN

Part Three

INSURRECTION

Part Four

A SECOND LIFE

List of Illustrations

PART ONE

PRIDE

I

Portrait and Prophecy

LAJOS KOSSUTH WAS HANDSOME. ALL THE PORTRAITS OF HIM in his manhood, the photographs of him in his old age, show a virile head, clearly the head of a clever, good, imaginative man. Each of these ennobling characteristics are written unmistakably in Kossuth's face. The human face, particularly if it be a man's, however beautiful it may have been in youth, loses, if it is not marked by struggle and experience in maturity, mellowed by the lines and wrinkles of development. The face should be a mirror of a man's life, showing whether that life was rich and full, whether it was well and truly lived; whether the person—as is permissible to every man—has by his work and his experience succeeded in enhancing and enriching his individuality. If facial beauty is the adequate expression of character, it cannot fail to be arresting, and some deep instinct prompts the feeling that "manly beauty" is the reflection of superhuman greatness, genius. Hence the reverential awe with which we contemplate the portrait of a Goethe, a Byron or a Stefan George.

But Kossuth was not a poet. His genius was not creative. He was, taken all in all, a man: the highest expression of his race, the prophet of his people. Whether he was a leader, or still more a hero, whether he deserved the nimbus legendary hero-worship has given him, must be judged impartially. We cannot read it from his face. Cleverness, goodness and imagination, the three qualities that are immediately revealed, are written perceptibly in the lines of a symmetrical, almost noble physiognomy. He has the high, blameless forehead of a daring thinker; but it is evident that his mind is not the exact mind of the mathematician of which the classical instance is angular skull of Archimedes with its salient temples, applicable to a whole category of intellectual faces, Newton, Gauss and Darwin. His wide, well-arched, high forehead is not so much the independent superstructure of an insignificant face; the intellect is closely correlated with the senses. This is no abstract thinker, searching the infinite; this is a man whose eyes are fixed upon the ground, whose way of thinking, close to reality, is more excogitation than investigation. His eye reveals the latent fire of passionate enthusiasm. Photographs of Kossuth, taken when he was very old, bear a striking resemblance to the well-known picture of the grand old man who, like him, was a prophet and an enthusiast; the American poet, Walt Whitman. He, too, was the prophet of the birth of a new race, he, too, proclaimed his faith in a new order of things, in the equality of man and universal brotherhood. Only the strong and prominent chin betrays the man of action. Otherwise the lines of his face might almost be called soft. One who knew him best, Endre Horn, the author of his first biography, wrote in 1851: "Who would have recognised in the slim, almost slender, figure of the new agitator with his Western rather than Eastern European features, the chestnut hair, the gentle blue eyes, the finely chiselled mouth: who would have recognised in Lajos Kossuth the descendant of the conquering hordes of Attila?" The soft, visionary, melancholy type of a young Werther. Indeed his earliest portraits remind one of Byron; none of them have anything in common with a Cæsar or a Cromwell, or whoever else may be chosen as the archetype of the revolutionary or the dictator. Was Kossuth really the hero of the Magyar nation, as his people think to-day, or was he rather, as the study of his portraits would lead us to believe, Hungary's prophet, the poet of a new future for this isolated, strongly individual and favoured nation?

Kossuth's biography laid stress upon the fact that there was nothing typically Eastern European in his features; that is to say, nothing typically Hungarian. Possibly, when Horn wrote this, the fringe of Grecian beard hiding the salient cheekbones—vide his portraits from the age of fifty—concealed this characteristically Magyar feature. His fair hair and blue eyes were clearly inherited from his mother who was German. His "chestnut locks" must have been quite fair, even golden, when he was a child. It is a pity that we have no likeness of his childhood. We only learn that, as a boy, he was remarkable for his looks. But who would have dreamt of having a portrait painted of a boy, unless he were the son of a magnate or some wealthy merchant of Pest or Pressburg ? Certainly no one in the little village of Monók.

For Lajos Kossuth was country-born. He grew up among the sunny, vine-clad hills of Tokaj. Here, on the Southern slopes of the East Carpathian mountains, a thousand years before, the young warrior hordes that emigrated from their old home in the plains north of the Crimea had halted. Here they pitched their tents. When Prince Arpad led his people south to settle in the friendly plains of Hungary, he left behind a rearguard in this town of tents. The people who remained behind called the place: New Tent Place; in their language: Sátoralja-Ujhely.

Here, in the village of Monôk, near Sátoralja-Ujhely, one of the oldest towns of the thousand-year-old kingdom, Kossuth was born in September, 1802.

The village of Monók belonged to the county of Zemplén of which Sátoralja-Ujhely was the capital. His father, Lászlo Kossuth, belonged to the untitled aristocracy, the gentry. He was poor. But he had not, like many of his status, relapsed into the condition of a peasant. He belonged to the family of the de Udvards, whose patent of nobility had been renewed by King Béla IV, in the year 1242, the year of the Tartar invasion. But Lászlo Kossuth owned no paternal acres; he was a lawyer. Like many members of the Kossuth family, he had left the family home in Kossuthfalva in the county of Turócz. It was one of the oldest families in the land, but it had produced no great men. The only one who had ever held an official position—for such appointments were only given by the Hapsburgs—had been a vice-governor of the fortress of Turócz. The Kossuths had never inherited nor being given land, yet they had always kept their family estate in Kossuthfalva.

Lászlo Kossuth, the village lawyer of Monôk, owned no land; only a porticoed, high-roomed, one-storey manor house. The lofty windows overlooked a wide expanse of green. When Kossuth senior moved to Zemplén, he had not, like so many of his family who had changed their domicile, gone over to Catholicism. Lászlo remained a Protestant. His wife Charlotte, the daughter of the postmaster of the Slovak village of Liszka, came of an old German Lutheran family which had emigrated to this Hungarian frontier district before the Reformation. Both father and mother therefore came of deeply religious, ardent Protestant families. The Reformation had been the protest against the oppression of the individual and his liberties in bygone centuries; the protest of the new era was not religious, but political. Lászlo Kossuth in his village retirement learnt of the great ideas of enlightenment and the French Revolution. He discussed them with his neighbours, he read and listened to the exposition of the ideas of Rousseau, Mirabeau and the Abbé

Lamennais. But he did not change his views: he was a devout Protestant, but nothing else.

Kossuth's father recognised the duty of bringing up his son in the faith of his ancesotrs, and so he insisted on the Sabbath being kept holy. Parents and children—Lajos and his four sisters—gathered in the high-ceilinged drawing-room, and the father, following time-honoured custom, brought out the large family bible and in a loud and reverent voice read the lessons of the Holy Scriptures, in Károlyi's Lutheran Hungarian. In 1874, when Lajos Kossuth was seventy-two, he wrote, in a letter to a priest: "I can still remember the huge bible with its gilt brass clasp from which my father used to read us a few chapters every Sunday, and in it the dates on which I and my sisters were born and christened were entered in the old tradition. If I still had this bible with its brass clasp I should cherish it as a sacred relic out of piety towards my parents. But it is lost. It was lost in the storms of my tempestuous life, like so many things I valued."

Incidentally, owing to the loss of the family bible, the exact date of Lajos Kossuth's birth cannot be determined. He himself goes on to say in this letter: "I have an idea that I was born between the 16th and the 19th September; I think on the 19th."

This date, the 19th September, was afterwards fixed as his birthday by the Hungarian people; but it is by no means certain.

Kossuth's father read to his family from the Hungarian bible; at home he spoke Hungarian to the children, German to his wife, Slovak to the servants. And so the boy grew up trilingual, talking Hungarian to his father, German to his mother, and Slovak in the fields. His German was as fluent as his Hungarian, for his mother was the one who bothered most about her children. She told him German fairy tales and later, when he was bigger, the half-true legends of her ancestors. The pretty fair-haired boy sat at her feet and listened with glowing cheeks. The long, frosty winter evenings were not dark or cold, because his mother told him stories. He never tired of hearing the story of his ancestor Andreas Weber who had died a martyr's death. In the year of Our Lord, 1687, the Emperor Leopold I had sent his murderous henchman Caraffa to Hungary, to wipe out its God-fearing people who believed in the message of the Gospel. Andreas Weber has been executed. To his religious mother whose piety Kossuth always emphasised this terrible—historical —"massacre of Eperjes" represented the tragic fate of Protestantism in a land under Hapsburg rule. And indeed this year 1687, the year in which Prince Eugene of Savoy freed Buda from the domination of the Turks, was propitious to the anti-Reformation in Hungary. But her simple mind only saw the legendary horror of the story, although she knew that the tale which had been handed down from grandfather to grandson in the Weber family tallied with the accounts of history books. To her the massacre of Eperjes was an instance of the test of faith which God imposes upon all true believers. She taught her son to be in constant readiness to obey the will of God, as Andreas Weber had been: to live truthfully, never to deny his faith and to be true only to himself.

This story of his mother's made a deep impression on the boy. It is as well not to overestimate the influence of, more or less accidentally, recorded episodes in the childhood of a great man on his development; still the Caraffa legend was a decisive influence on the young mind of the boy Kossuth. His pride—the pride of the Kossuths allied to the pride of the Webers—was a fundamental trait of Lajos' character.

Even in those days he pondered; his thoughts strayed further than those of his religious mother. The boy asked his first teacher how it was possible that an "Italian scoundrel" like Caraffa had been allowed to shed good Hungarian blood in a good Hungarian town. The answer taught him that Hungary was not governed by Hungarians, but ruled by a foreign, powerful domination: the House of Hapsburg. And that the Emperor in Vienna, all-powerful "by the grace of God," had often in the course of centuries sent wicked hirelings from his wide provinces into Hungary to subjugate the Magyars. The story of the massacre of Eperjes discovered the elements which formed in the awakening mind of the boy the picture of the historical situation of Hungary. It is worth noting that in later life Kossuth studied the historical sources and then wrote the story of the " Slaughterhouse of Eperjes."

Then, after a long life, he saw clearly what he had only dimly guessed as a child: that the political background of history is stronger than the religious. His ancestor had been the victim, not of anti-Reformation, but of anti-national tendencies, in other words of Hapsburg absolutism. But the dramatic core of the story remained as his mother told it him. Kossuth wrote: "From the day that Protestantism first took root in Hungary, the Jesuits who already held in their hands the reins of Hungary's government made Hungary's subjection their chief aim. It was their counsel in the main which incited the Hapsburg to the most bloodthirsty acts of cruelty. Rákóczi was the first to raise the flag of Protestantism alongside the banner of revolution and to lead his followers against the imperial armies. . . . When the Turks were driven out of Hungary, Austria began a punishment such as history had never seen before." And he describes the cruelties of the Italian who, for the wholesale execution of innocents, including nobles of ancient lineage, such as Gottfried von Windischgrätz, was promoted to the rank of imperial general.

The boy bore himself with a defiant pride worthy of his martyred ancestor. It was natural that he should become the ringleader of the boys of Monók.

Lászlo Kossuth was a stern father, concealing his affection for his son, his first-born, behind a brusque reserve. Kossuth later describes him: "My father was violent, hot-tempered, but of an unflinching honesty. In his heart dwelt a warm sympathy for the independence of his fellows which only bows the knee to God. From him I learned the incorruptibility that refuses to accept a present even from a friend." This father, proud and unbending, like all the Kossuths, once ran across his twelve-year-old son playing with the boys of the village; he was not pleased and forbade him to associate with them. Lajos obeyed. He hovered sadly near the playground, enviously watching the other boys at play, but he respected his father's wishes. By chance his father passed as he was standing there. Thinking that the boy had disobeyed his orders, he flew at him in a rage and gave him a thrashing. For the father that was an end of the matter; but not for the son. Nothing would induce the boy to come to meals. He avoided his father. He resisted all his mother's entreaties that he should apologise. "I would rather die," he said, "than apologise to him for something that I have not done." And his father had to give in; he had to apologise to his son. He did so with a grin, proud that his son had inherited his pride.

The boy's earliest education was entrusted to the school teacher of the neighbouring village of Tallya. This excellent young man threw himself heart and soul into his work; he considered the lad precocious and intelligent. The teacher and the boy became fast friends. When the teacher was transferred, Lajos' father decided to send him to the grammar school at Sátoralja-Ujhely, the county town. The school was a Catholic foundation and was governed by the Piarists; but Kossuth was not intolerant. The school at Sárospatak was nearer, but his father hated the bigotry of that institution. The boy was happy at the school; the priests who taught there grew to love him, as the young teacher at Tallya had. His quick intelligence and eagerness to learn roused their interest. He remained there several years and every year he was the *primus eminens* of his class. Afterwards Kossuth praised the tact with which his teachers refrained from trying to influence him with Catholic precept. But he learned to understand the Catholic mentality, an invaluable experience for later life.

His teacher in Tallya had often taken the boy for rambles in the country; he taught him to recognise plants and animals, to botanise, and finally to understand the cultivation of the vine. For Tallya lies among the vineyards of Tokaj. Lajos loved nature; the landscape of the first home of the Magyars, in all its seasons, its teeming spring, its scorching summer, its melancholy autumn, and its bitter winter.

The boy was a Romantic. He would roam about the countryside, lying on the red earth among the vineyards and playing the flute. For he saved up the pocket money his parents gave him to buy fruit and secretly bought a flute. He learned to play it perfectly. On one of these solitary rambles in the country the boy was caught in a thunderstorm. He was now fourteen. He was in the middle of a forest. He ran and ran. The thunder crashed overhead. In a clearing he saw a gipsy cabin, such as are often to be found hidden in the woods, and ran in. The cabin was not empty, as he had expected, for gipsies spend their days wandering round the villages and only return to their huts at nightfall. Instead a band of gipsies was gathered round the hearth. The boy had never spoken to a gipsy; he did not know whether to accost them in Hungarian or Slovak. But in reply to his greeting in Hungarian the chief of the band invited him amicably to sit down. Lajos squatted beside the fire. The men smoked in silence. Suddenly an old crone, the mother of the chief, approached the boy. He sprang to his feet and shrank away from her. But the old woman, grinning, seized his arm. A young gipsy picked up a burning log. For three minutes a reddish glow fell on the boy's slim and delicate hand. The flame flickered and went out. The old woman released his hand. "Listen," she said and her voice had that commanding pathos which very old women's voices sometimes have; it seemed to Lajos as if it came out of the bowels of the earth. The boy shivered. But his curiosity was greater than his fright. Like Luther when confronted with the devil, he stood his ground.

"Listen," croaked the old woman, "you will become a great man. Soon the time will come when you will be famous and looked up to. You will be the liberator of your country."

The boy listened. His heart thumped. Did the cabin vanish? Like Macbeth's witches to a clap of thunder? The thunderstorm continued, the lightning flashed, but the old crone was still there before his eyes, a corporeal being, and presently the voices of the men chanting a sad and weary song proved to the boy that he was awake and not living in a fairy tale.

The boy who had expected something great and wonderful to happen in this tempest took the prophecy with all seriousness. Kossuth mentions this episode in his memoirs: "I do not know what influence brought about this prophecy; but this prophecy was really decisive for my future. I was not superstitious, but this hour made me aware of my impulse to freedom which had been kindled by the independence of my father and which led me through the study of history and law to the democratic conviction that guided all my steps."

His pride was now offset by this new impulse to freedom. It soon landed him in conflict. It was felt in the school that one of the teachers was tyrannising over the boys. All of them trembled before the tyrant, all except Kossuth who refused to tolerate this despotism. He got out of hand. Naturally the bullying teacher replied with a more vigorous attack: he was the master. And as it was the cleverest and most popular boy who offended the despot in his belief in his infallibility, he set him a humiliating punishment. The moment he heard the sentence, Kossuth rushed out of the classroom and tore out of the school. No one tried to stop him. And yet there must have been a threatening fire in his eyes, a deathly pallor in his cheeks, for the dumbfounded teacher sent two other boys to fetch him back. They caught up with him on the bridge over the torrent of the Bodrog. Lajos was in the act of throwing himself in the river. He was ready to die for his wounded pride. At twelve he had made this threat to his father, at fourteen he was capable of carrying it out.

A boy, pre-eminent among his schoolfellows, a born leader—a Coriolanus with the traits of a Hamlet? A daredevil, a fanatic, hating compromise and severe with himself, but with the sensibility of a young Werther? Fearlessness of death, or perhaps even the desire to die? From this moment those who loved him were anxious for this proud and sensitive boy, concerned for this life which was to last ninety-two years, almost a century. Such pride is to be found in men capable of giving their lives for an idea.

His school-mates who had saved him in the nick of time persuaded him to come back with them to the school, but he only returned to pack up his belongings. He refused to stay longer in a school where he had been insulted. He went home to his parents.

II

Dominus Kossuth

KOSSUTH WAS NOW TURNED SEVENTEEN. HE NEEDED ONLY A short preparation before he was ready for the University. The question what he was to be was never raised: it was taken for granted that he would be what his father was. His career was mapped out for him; he would study law, and then become a lawyer. It was no less clear that he would practise in Monók. The son inherited his father's office. Gradually Lászlo Kossuth would retire and leave his son his modest practice.

Lajos raised no objection to this choice of subject which was no choice at all. His abilities fitted him in every way for a legal career: he was quick-witted, inventive, logical. His written essays showed a startling eloquence—the Piarist fathers called him a "master of style." His elocution was superb. He not only spoke his native language, Hungarian, and also German, and moderately good Slovak—though this latter seemed superfluous—but, most important, the language of science, Latin. He was fascinated by the eloquence of the ancient Roman stylists, the intoxicating eloquence of Cicero; and while his friends were working off their high spirits in some wild escapade, Kossuth would be trying to write prose as forcible and rhythmically beautiful as the Catiline Oration. Once when he had to make a speech in Latin, his teacher criticised him with the remark: "You speak Latin better than any one in the Hungarian Diet."

The Piarist did not know that this sarcastic comment on the efforts of the country squires who attended the parliament of nobles in Pressburg awoke a curious echo in the lad's mind. He was a first-rate Latinist, a Latin orator! Really it would not be a bad thing to sit in Pressburg, a magnificent city, people said, so near to Vienna, the imperial capital. Lajos built castles in the air. Here he had no scope: Monók, Sátoralja-Ujhely, the whole county of Zemplén were too small for him.

With feverish excitement he waited for his father to decide

upon a university. Debrecen was not far away: Debrecen, the "Rome of Calvinism," the stronghold of the reformed faith. Better Debrecen, thought Lajos, than this backwater. But still better would be Pest. He longed to go to Pest, the big and beautiful city on the left bank of the Danube, joined by a pontoon bridge to the rock of Buda where were the imperial government offices, the headquarters of the army corps, the seat of the Palatine. The university of Pest was famous. The choice lay between Pest and Debrecen. As a matter of fact Sárospatak near by had a Law Academy, and it had to be admitted that its legal faculty was reputed to be better than either of the universities. Kövy, the great commentator on the Hungarian *corpus juris*, the Bible of the hereditary rights of the nobility, was a professor here. A generation of brilliant lawyers owed their education to this famous man. But his father's objection to the bigotry of Sárospatak still prevailed.

But to his astonishment his father decided for Sárospatak after all: the fees were less; the life of a student in a big city, if he were to keep up appearances, would be expensive. And so Kossuth had to remain in this provincial backwater. Naturally he obeyed.

Kossuth was now eighteen. The impressions he received from his new life at the Law Academy were stronger than he had expected. He attended Kövy's lectures on political law. The constitution of Hungary was difficult; but more difficult was to understand the historical events which led to continual disrespect and alteration of the constitution. What was the meaning of the word: constitution? Was it a lifeless formula, a piece of paper written with legal paragraphs? Or was it not rather a living thing? The fundament of justice? The ultimate and sacred security of the nation? How differently this pathetic word "nation" sounded when Kövy uttered it! Yes, these law school students were Hungarians—Magyars. In their midst dwelt strangers: belonging to other nationalities; Slovaks who had once been conquered, but who had since recovered certain liberties; Germans who were full citizens, but who stood closer to the House of Hapsburg; Croats, living in a land that Hungary had ruled for centuries. This was the picture of the Hungarian nation: a conglomeration of races, a reproduction *in petto* of the great Hapsburg empire, with its welter of nationalities.

Kossuth learned a great deal from Kövy. At the same time his history lectures gave him a survey of the development of Hungary and its cultural, religious and political relationship to the other states of Europe. But this was not sufficient. Kossuth pursued his studies independently. His knowledge of German opened to him the German intellectual world. He read Goethe; he read the early Romantics; he read Herder; and, first and foremost, he read Schiller, the awakener of the national spirit, the prophet of liberty.

He devoured all the contemporary German literature he could find and soon there was a little group of youthful enthusiasts who shared his reading. For youth set its hopes on Germany. German was synonymous with liberal. This was the year of the Wartburg festival, the solemn manifestation of young liberal Germany, the challenge of the German spirit to Metternich.

The Calvinist college had no objection to its students occupying themselves with the spirit of enlightenment and the theoreticians of the Great Revolution. Hungary looked to her young men; there would be a day of reckoning with the Hapsburgs yet. And so the reading of Rosseau was permitted, even recommended. To Kossuth he became an inspiration. He dreamed of being the champion of the oppressed: the people, and the nobles who were largely impoverished and fallen below their status, would yet wrest a constitution from the ruling house. The state was no longer a superimposed structure and citizens merely subjects—the state was born of the *contrat social* and the citizen was the guarantor of the contract, not the chattel of the government.

Kossuth's parents had removed to Sátoralja-Ujhely and he often went there on a Sunday. He found his father's house full of friends discussing politics. His knowledge of political ramifications surprised his father's friends. In the evening, when the golden wine of Tokaj had loosened their tongues, the handsome youth stood up in the room thick with tobacco smoke and recited the verses of Hungary's first poet of freedom which he had learnt by heart.

The men rose, one after the other, and wrung his hand. At nineteen he had won his initiation to the Sunday circle of his elders. He was there when the news of Napoleon's death arrived in 1821. A friend of his father's asked him if he knew the appeal that Napoleon had made to the nobility of Hungary after the battle of Wagram, in 1809. Of course Napoleon's message had shown his extraordinary historical acumen. But what concern was Hungary's internal quarrel with the House of Austria of this foreign usurper? What impudence to suborn the nobility of Hungary from their allegiance to their elected king! Kossuth was naturally indignant at this characteristically Napoleonic game of incitement to rebellion. But nevertheless he read the text of this appeal :

"Hungary! The moment has arrived; you can regain your original independence. Accept the peace I offer you. Your country and your liberties shall remain intact, as also the constitution of your country: either in its present form; or else make such changes in it as you consider right. I want nothing else of you; I wish you to become a free and independent people.

The union with Austria is the main cause of your misfortune. For Austria you have shed your blood in distant lands, your rights have been sacrificed in the interests of the crown lands. Your country was the fairest part of the empire, and yet you have been ruled by principles which are completely alien to you.

You have your national character, your national language, you can boast a noble past. Win back now your national integrity; choose yourselves a king who will live in your midst, surrounded by your soldiers and your citizens. Hungary! This is what is demanded of you by Europe whose eyes are fixed on you in expectation. I too wish this of you: an assured and lasting peace, complete independence, and a new courage. This is the reward that awaits you, if you are ready to prove yourselves worthy of your ancestors. Assemble on the field of Rákos, according to the tradition of your ancestors; hold council there and inform me of your decisions."

Certainly the young Kossuth felt that with this cunningly conceived appeal Napoleon recommended the Hungarian nobility a dangerous step: a crime against the sacred spirit of the ancient constitution, for the king who wore the crown of St. Stephen was sacrosanct. But here for the first time he heard the voice of rebellion, the plain, outspoken incitement to defection from the Hapsburgs.

In the Law Academy at Sárospatak the new tendencies were tolerated—in theory. In practice they were very strict. Particularly Kövy. Kövy was feared and respected, but it sometimes happened that the students, tired after a night of conviviality, lolled on their worm-eaten benches with their attention only half-awake. Kövy stormed. He threatened to plough every one of them who dared to come to his lectures half-asleep. The effect was different from what Kövy had anticipated. The students rebelled. They had been hearing of the liberty of the individual, the rights of man. They were not going to be tyrannised by Kövy. And, most astonishingly, Kossuth, the one who had least participated in his fellow-students' excesses, summoned a protest meeting of Kövy's class. He delivered a mutinous harangue. "It is an insult to our pride," he said, referring to the old tyrant's encroachment on their liberties.

He was cheered. His first speech—his first success! A deputation was elected with Kossuth as the spokesman. They went to Kövy to inform him that his whole class had decided to go on strike unless he apologised.

A Kövy apologise! To these young jackanapses! The old man glared at the deputation and turned his back on it. But the ringleader of the students, Kövy's best pupil, was not to be rebuffed. "With all due respect, sir," declared Kossuth, "unless you apologise, none of us will return to class."

It was not the words that nonplussed Kövy, but the tone. A tone he had never heard before. Not impudent—overpowering. The lad who spoke like this was capable of dying for his pride. Such pride was dangerous, but it was imposing.

Kövy turned and looked hard at the young Kossuth. Perhaps as he stared into Kossuth's blazing pale blue eyes, he realised that he was looking into the eyes of a new generation.

Then, turning to the students who were waiting in fear and trembling, for their great teacher's answer, Kövy said: "Very well then, I apologise."

The tension was broken. The lads were speechless with astonishment. The dreaded, unapproachable Kövy had surrendered.

Kossuth's knees were shaking. The first tyrant had been overthrown—by him! His face relaxed into a smile.

The deputation bowed. Their mission was fulfilled; they moved towards the door. Then Professor Kövy turned to them once more and in his old cracked voice remarked: "Dominus Ludovicus Kossuth, unless he takes counsel with himself, will yet become a great rebel—*maximus perturbator*."

A year later, at Easter, 1823, Lajos Kossuth was passed in his law examination by the self-same Professor Kövy.

III

Sentimental Interlude

EPERJES, THE FINAL STAGE OF EDUCATION. THE GRADUATED LAW student must spend a year here practising in court. As he drives into the little town in the jolting coach, excitement takes possession of him: he is about to see the place linked with the infamous name of Caraffa. As a boy he had pictured the scene in detail to himself: would the reality contradict his imagination?

Yes, it did. In the summer heat of the narrow streets of the old town there was no smell of blood, only the aromatic scent of lush meadows, and wine. Gay crowds filled the taverns. The young lawyer, assessor is now his proper title, sits at the table reserved for regular customers and joins the party when his colleagues and superiors pass the evening over their cups. Otherwise the place is half asleep; the gaiety of Sárospatak now seems like the vanished carelessness of boyhood. Life is beginning and it is a serious business.

This is not his sphere. He is passionately determined to get away from this atmosphere of vegetation, and when at last, a year later, in 1824, he is able to leave Eperjes a fully qualified lawyer, he goes at once to Pest.

Equipped with the good wishes of his parents, some money and friendly letters of introduction from those gentlemen who are well disposed towards his father, Baron Vécsey in particular, Lajos Kossuth arrived in the capital. In those days Pest was a fairly extensive industrial city, spreading far over the plain on the left bank of the Danube. Opposite it lay proudly Buda, stretching a long way into the country behind the high rock that rises steeply from the right bank of the river. The town, and especially the promenade along the Danube, presented an animated picture. Kossuth stared in amazement at the elegance of the women; this was what he had imagined Paris or the Glacis in Vienna to be like. The men, too, were dressed differently from what he had been accustomed to, in English fashion.

Kossuth was anxious to do something to make himself look a little less provincial, and as he noticed that the people whom he saw strolling in the Hatvani utca—which was later to bear his name—wore flowers in their buttonholes, he went into a flower shop and bought himself a dark red carnation. The ladies of Pest saw a dark, handsome young man with a strikingly high forehead, who bore himself with a natural grace which made up for his lack of style. He was alone in wearing a red carnation in his buttonhole; his example was to create a fashion. People smiled at him. Already on his first day Pest seemed to bow to him like his schoolfellows at school, as even Kövy had had to bow to him. This was dangerous. In pride lurks the danger of vanity. The proud boy risked his life, the proud student his career; the proud man did not guess the danger which is born of pride. He looked triumphantly about him, dark eyes smiled at him. Life flattered him, a loose and pretty woman for a young man of twenty-one to flirt with. He meant to make the most of life; to enjoy it, to succeed. But he must make haste—he had lost too much time already.

The best and quickest method of making one's way in society is to be taken up by those who matter. The House of Austria, the "system," the masters of Austria, these held the key to success; the thing to do was to gain their favour, to become one of their protégés.

Kossuth counted his letters of recommendation. Five good letters. They would open to him the doors of the fortress.

He climbed the hill to the palace of Buda. He knew that he had a right to offer himself; his diploma vouched for him as being a qualified lawyer, an original thinker, unusually talented. And so he applied for an appointment in the court chancellery: that was the first step, afterwards he could rely upon himself to make a career.

From the top of the palace hill he looked down over the city of Pest and the country stretching away beyond. Here, in the palace and the ministries, sat the real rulers: Hapsburg's loyal servants. They were Hungarians, like himself. He knew that from their names. Hungarians who kept Hungary in subjection. He was suddenly filled with melancholy; anger; glowing hatred. He was no longer the young coxcomb; there was a challenge in his earnest face. He thought of Eperjes; of his ancestor Andreas who died a martyr's death; he thought of the gipsy woman's prophecy and Kövey's warning voice: "Dominus Kossuth . . ." He would be a "perturbator."

He would drive out the taskmasters and create an independent Hungary.

What business had he here? Did he hope to open the door from inside? The doors of the Buda palace?—He knocked. . . .

He was not admitted. A Mr. Kossuth from Monók, a De Udvard, of an unknown and unlanded genteel family, had the presumption to desire to adopt a career as government official! He wished to serve the emperor, in other words Metternich. What qualifications had he? A diploma? That was not much. Let him become a lawyer. Whose protégé was he? Who recommended him? Baron Pál Vécsey of Zemplén, a man of influence no doubt. But the authorities of Buda had a retentive memory. This Vécsey on whose recommendation Kossuth relied had been in league with the refractory Hungarians who had been imprisoned for anti-constitutional propaganda. And this man had the impudence to give an introduction to an unknown Hungarian? The recommendation sufficed to settle Kossuth's application: they were not such fools as to ask for trouble. Let this provincial become a provincial lawyer. There was no room for him in Buda.

The first rebuff: the first defeat. The House of Hapsburg rejected the man who was to become its most dangerous adversary. It had no suspicion of his genius. Perhaps Kossuth might have used in the service of the Hapsburgs the pen and the sword which he learnt to use against them. That is the fate of autocrats: they breed their enemies themselves. In their blindness they scorn budding genius, instead of harnessing and developing it. Louis XIV laughed at Prince Eugene of Savoy when he asked him for a company. The House of Hapsburg, Metternich's creatures in Buda, shut the door in Kossuth's face.

This rebuff was a crushing blow to the young man. He guessed that he would have to give up more than the hope of an official position: he had lost his chance of getting on the right side of the government. He had wanted to range himself on the side of legality; he had hoped to climb to the top of the ladder where a man with talent, industry and luck could make a great career. These hopes were dashed. Good-bye to the hope of living in Budapest. The pretty women whose glances had encouraged the young man in the Hatvani utca would see him no more. Not for some time. "When? When?" asked Kossuth with a pang. He departed sadly; he had breathed the air of the great world, if only for a few days, but he never forgot the sweetness of that taste of life. His fancy had new stuff to play with, his ambition a concrete goal: this city which had so long fired his imagination closed its doors to him.

Back to the provinces! Back home to the county of Zemplén, to his father's house. To work in his office. He settled down in Sátoralja-Ujhely. But now he saw the little town with other eyes. Was this a town? No Korso, no promenade, no Hatvani utca? But there were pretty women here nevertheless. No palace, no government offices. But there was the county assembly —the rendezvous of the local nobility of Zemplén. For what they were worth there were the administrative services, the courts of justice. The political intelligence of the budding lawyer docketed the results of his reflections: there were two possible ways of getting on in Zemplén: the social, and the political.

But he very soon discovered that in the narrow confines of the county which was as shut off and as independent as an island these two ways were inseparable. The thorny path of a political career ended in the same *salon* as the rose-walk of social dalliance.

It was essential to get accepted by the nobility, then one had a future. Kossuth was young, extremely handsome, quite sufficiently smart—he had not failed to profit by his short stay in Budapest—a certain note of fashion, a red carnation in the buttonhole for instance, transformed the raw youth of Monók into a man of the world. It was also a good thing that the old custom prescribed the wearing of uniform for a gentleman: in a tight-fitting, richly braided, green tunic, or in a black "Atilla," with the little dagger on the hip, the latest acquisition to the legal fraternity of Sátoralja-Ujhely, Kossuth junior, looked very fetching.

Now open Sesame! Open, drawing-rooms of titled ladies! Surely there will be one ready to take this passionate, ambitious Julien Sorel under her wing. She will polish the rough edges of his manners, she will teach him to make conversation so that the astonished provincial squires will ask where this young man acquired his remarkable knowledge. And finally, when those who frequent this lady's house have grown accustomed to seeing him there, she will pull the wires for him. And if he is not a fool and minds his p's and q's, later, if His Majesty shall be pleased to convene the Diet, he may perhaps be sent there as the representative of some magnate, as "ablegatus absentium." This is the third decade of the nineteenth century.

It is not to no purpose that the provincial aristocracy spend the winter in imperial Vienna, with an occasional jaunt to the Paris of Balzac's *Comédie humaine.* Even under the strictly moral rule of Franz I, Vienna secretly apes the characters of Balzac. *La Femme de trente ans* has already been written. The lonely life on the immense estates, in the days when roads were bad, was only tolerable to the Hungarian magnates in the summer, until the end of the shooting season. They had their agents who managed their estates; and, as the Russian landed aristocracy spent their winters in Baden-Baden, so the Hungarian nobility moved to their palaces in Vienna.

The summer was the time for the introduction of young Kossuth into the houses of the county families, the Vécseys, the Töröks, the Andrássys and the Szápárys. Lászlo Kossuth senior had been for years the family solicitor of a wealthy countess whose country house lay on the outskirts of Ujhely. He introduced his son to her, too. Countess Etelka Andrássy lived alone at Terebes, managing her estate, even in the winter when her neighbours went to Vienna to enjoy the gaieties of the life about the court. When a lively and intelligent young man enters this melancholy, cloistered world, is it surprising that this Madame de Rênal succumbs to the attraction of this Julien Sorel? Etelka's husband, Karl Andrássy, judged the social claims which Vienna had upon a Hungarian magnate of more importance than the unseasonable claims of a wife who asked only to lead a simple, homely life. The young Countess had already borne him three children and now the Count felt that he could justifiably leave her alone during the winter months and devote himself to the gaieties and pleasures of the capital.

But Etelka remained alone on the estate, now a woman approaching thirty, "la femme de trente ans," still too young to be inconsolable. When the young Kossuth entered her service as his father's proxy, she soon relieved him of the realistic duties of a family solicitor and let him assume the more romantic role of family friend. Kossuth was still very young. He was dazzled by her beauty which she bequeathed to her youngest son Julius—who afterwards became Kossuth's friend and adversary—and her position tempted him. Ambition catches fire as easily as passion.

This liaison was no mere adventure. It was a formative influence in Kossuth's life for many years. Like Thomas the Rhymer, he served his Queen of Elfland seven years. He transacted her legal business, he mediated in her quarrels with her tenants and the peasantry, he dealt with poachers and the silly, awkward cases of drunkenness or brawling among the farmhands with a severity worthy of the master whom he represented; but his ear was also open to the rhythm of village life. He wandered over the fields, he visited the poor; he talked with old and young, to ploughman and to shepherd. He gained the confidence of the army of peasant serfs of the Andrássy estates. And this at bottom may have been the reason why even the Count's agent praised him to the Countess.

But Etelka required no outside encomiums of his usefulness. His abilities mattered less to her than his affection, and she even forgave his tentative efforts to break down the rigid barriers that separated master and serf. Lajos could do just as he liked. And so Kossuth roamed the fields and chatted with the men that worked in them. This was a new, a second education: a training in human sympathy. Not only the *éducation sentimentale* imparted to every young man by the riper wisdom of a loving woman, but at the same time a reassorting of ideas which communion with nature and easy contact with simple people teaches to a sensitive mind. Little everyday experiences became symbolical. The idyllic world captured Kossuth, as it captured the young Goethe and the Romantics.

Did no echo of the disturbances in the Pressburg Diet in 1825 penetrate this idyllic solitude during these years at Terebes? Did Kossuth hear nothing of Count István Széchényi's campaign against the government? Did he not hear the tocsin that announced the dawn of a new era?

Kossuth roamed the fields. He was in love. And so the years went by. But as every year and every day diminishes the radial energy of every love, and as even this romance of Terebes was slowly growing cold, he was driven to seek some new adventure to supplement the cloying sensations of a languishing passion. He began playing cards. On certain evenings he was glad to exchange the perfumed luxury of Etelka's drawing-room for the frowzy atmosphere of the village tavern; after being closeted in the charming, but monotonous company of this one woman, he longed for the easy, unpretentious naturalness of male society. He found companions who ignored his position and his rise into a higher world with a tolerant smile. They gossiped over the scraps of news that reached them in this remote corner of Slovakia. And now for the first time he realised that the years had rolled by relentlessly, like the stream that rushes past some sylvan solitude.

But what were these companions with whom he spent occasional evenings? What was this circle of noisy fellows who sang and squatted round a table playing cards? Etelka, who was now in the early thirties, clung to him and as she had, in her opinion, elevated him from his lowly status she had no intention of letting him relapse. She gave him company, she took him with her when she visited the country houses of relations in the county, she forced supercilious aristocrats to accept him as their equal. One day when she found out that he was putting in an appearance almost regularly at the card parties in the local sheriff's house, she lost patience with him. She overwhelmed him with reproaches. She remonstrated that he was reserved for something better, for a career which might lead him, perhaps to court, certainly to some high office. But Kossuth did not wish to be her protégé. He had been her lover, that was all. And so at last the hour drew near in which Octavian in the *Rosenkavalier* bids the Feldmarshallin good-bye.

The idyll was not ended. This sentimental intermezzo still lasted for a long period of Kossuth's life. When we look back on it to-day, it seems like an interval of repose before the bursting of the storm. Fate has a wise plan of giving certain men the instinctive certainty of a long life before them. For such it is a right or a necessity to pause and to recuperate their strength. There are other lives of short duration, flickering, hectic lives which must cram all their work and all their sufferings into their short span, dimly aware that no time will be allotted them: such were the lives of Byron, Grabbe and Arthur Rimbaud. Lajos Kossuth's life was granted the proud curve of reposeful development. The third decade in such a far-seeing scheme of life is spent in self-forgetfulness; the man is waiting in the ante-chamber of his epoch, at the disposition of history. At the same age Bismarck was the extravagant Junker, Frederick the Great the indolent æsthete, Leo Tolstoi the most dissolute of all Russian officers. Kossuth was the sentimental lover. But the man of action in him watched and waited. It only needed the alarum to rouse him from his seven years' slumber, from dalliance to reality.

IV

Hungary's Eyes are Opened

METTERNICH, AT THE HEAD OF AN ENORMOUS EMPIRE, A LOOSE construction of groups of nationalities, knew how to retranslate the Roman maxim *divide et impera* into: "Lull to sleep and govern." Joseph II on his deathbed had abjured the liberal ideas that he had fostered. The Emperor Franz I autocratically tightened the links of his empire, saved from dissolution by the battle of Leipzig. What did he care that ancient rights and decaying constitutions raised a feeble voice of protest? The malcontents did not understand that he was welding the Danubian monarchy into a solid structure. Let the eternal grumblers croak and mutter in the remote counties. He had the power, and where there is power, there is splendour; and splendour attracts the pampered and the pretentious, the proud nobility and all those who are powerful in their own sphere. Power loves power: the splendour of the imperial city, Vienna, drew the aristocracy from the succession states and the magnates of Hungary once more opened their winter palaces. Whoever wished to be master in his own country, on his own estates, had to renew his dusty privileges: he had to be near the court in order to confirm his chartered prerogatives. Hungary could go to sleep; it slept. The wise and smiling Prince Metternich might well say: "The syncope of the provinces is Austria's safeguard."

In this lasting sleep the country lost its individual consciousness. It lost those things which characterise the individual: its language and its personal aspect. In Vienna the magnates spoke German, and only Hungarian when they were at home; the towns were German, and the serfs in the villages spoke Slovak or Roumanian, and only the gentry stuck to Hungarian. But when the Hungarian nation appeared as an entity, at the Diet which sat in Pressburg, quite near to Vienna, the magnates, the clergy, the deputies of the counties of Hungary and Croatia which belonged to it, all spoke Latin. But what is a country that has been robbed of that which makes it alive, its language?

Since the unfortunate days of the rebellion under Rákóczi Hungary had abandoned itself to its helplessness. But in the humble closets of the poet and the thinker the longing stirred to give the nation back its original self. The poets began the fight for the Hungarian language.

Every usurpation has its origin in might, every regeneration in the spirit. From the Cæsars to Louis XIV, from the condottieri of the Italian republics to Napoleon the lust of power and political ambition have laid waste the fields of Europe. From Erasmus to Rousseau the downtrodden, defenceless peoples have answered the advancing regiments with the weapons of the spirit. Might can build strongholds, dams to hold in check the natural growth of the organism; but sooner or later the body will burst the dykes—or it will perish. Hungary had been denied its natural development for centuries; it had never become a nation, it lay in medieval twilight. But now, while might was celebrating its triumphs, the poets began gently to disturb this age-long sleep.

But it was not the soft aubades of poets that awoke the nation, but the ringing challenge of a single man.

In this year 1825 the Diet sat again in Pressburg. Now in this body, which had been actually convened as legislator of the land, but in reality could do no more than voice its protest against the arbitrary acts of the Vienna government, for the first time the new spirit of a young literary national movement made itself heard. But now, awakened by the invigorating voice of a national literature, the members of the Diet rose from this humiliating business of uttering negative complaints to the active work of systematic nationalisation. The first firecracker was the "language question." At last a desire showed itself in this the most dignified assembly in the country to speak Hungarian instead of Latin. Let the representatives of the Vienna central government, the "royal personnel," translate their elaborate, ambiguous, incomprehensible declarations from the artificial construction of a diplomatic and accommodating Ciceronian into the more forceful, clearer language of the country. Opposition was to be expected: first and foremost from the magnates themselves. Long stays in Vienna and a pretentious education had left them neither the wish nor the ability to speak their native tongue. Secondly, from the Croats who, after centuries of common history under the rule of the kings of Hungary, were beginning to boast their racial difference and their own language. Any one with political vision could foresee that the language question would develop into a political, a national question. Latin had helped to conceal the racial disparity of the peoples living side by side. By introducing Magyar as a compulsory official language the ruling Hungarians would arouse the contrariness of the alien races. But the new-born patriotism overshouted the warning voices of discretion. Yet it was clear that the enthronement of the Magyar language was the first step in the process of becoming a nation. The motion to promote Hungarian to be the language of the Diet and to obtain the king's sanction therefore was carried. The "new spirit" was progressing. Animated by this flash of national feeling a Count Apponyi made a present of his valuable library to the town of Pressburg. The idea of founding a Hungarian academy was revived. Nothing was lacking save money.

Now something unexpected happened. From one of the back benches of the assembly rose a figure whose appearance alone was cause for wonder. A captain in hussar uniform had stood up, a young man with a pale bewhiskered face. Although, as his uniform showed, he was not a member of the Diet, he asked permission to speak. Everybody knew him, and a wave of curiosity and astonishment ran through the hall: Count István Széchényi bore an illustrious and familiar name. What had this young officer to say?

Count Széchényi spoke in Hungarian, but he spoke it badly. Nevertheless he held the assembly from the first. What poise! He began: "It is not my business to speak in this assembly. I am not a member of the house. But I am a landowner and if an institute is to be founded for the cultivation of the Hungarian language, with a view to promote the Hungarian education of our fellow-countrymen, I will devote to this enterprise the revenues of all my estates for one year."

The effect of this announcement was indescribable. The house gazed spell-bound at the young hussar and cheered him to the echo. With his few short sentences the Count had unleashed the nationalist attack. He was now followed by the greatest in the land, the Andrássys and the Károlyis, the Batthyányis and the Eszterházys, and in the shortest possible time a quarter of a million had been offered for the foundation of the future academy. One sceptic asked the count what he intended to live on, if he made a present of his revenues for one year, 60,000 gulden. "My friends will keep me," replied the count.

History is fond of employing these surprise effects in order to contrive a dramatic entrance for a new character upon the stage. With the sure technique of a daring playwright she made the little known Monsieur Desmoulins spring up from his table in a café in the Palais Royal—and the entrance of this new character ushered in the great scene of the taking of the Bastille. Captain Count Széchényi was able in a brief attack to flutter an irresolute and indifferent assembly—and from this moment no one in the land was to resume his comfortable slumber. Great orators have often faced a mob with destiny; but Count Széchényi had not won his audience by his rhetoric. His weapon was an idea. An idea has an explosive force, an idea makes history.

The previous life of this young man who was not yet thirty was as remarkable as this first appearance in the Diet. There are men who are early marked out for great deeds. Széchényi was one of these. Many brave men distinguished themselves in the Napoleonic wars; their deeds remained anonymous. But the young ensign Széchényi's "dare-devil ride" became a byword; he had ridden through the fire of the enemy's guns and carried an important despatch to Blücher's headquarters. The old marshal had decorated him. When he entered Paris with the allied army he made use of the occupation to study the spirit and the life of the French capital. The young magnate's first experience of Western culture made a deep impression on him. Even at that date he was stirred with the desire to open its beauties to his country and the twin cities, Pest and Buda. The conclusion of peace sent him to a provincial garrison town. Soon he asked for leave to travel to France and England to make a thorough study of conditions there. "He brought back with him as the fruits of his journey the cult of English jockeys and a predilection for loud suitings and an extravagant cut of clothes. He could not be absolved from the weakness of exaggerated aping of foreign customs and habits" (A. Springer). When he rode along the Danube promenade, his yellow check breeches betrayed him from a distance. But the dandified, provocatively dressed cavalier did not return the astonished, admiring glances of the promenaders. His face was sad, his jet black hair and beard made his yellow-complexioned face seem even paler. The most friendly of contemporary portraits is: "His face reveals charity, enthusiasm and coldness all together; he has a dignified, earnest, English-oligarchical face, he is powerful and wiry."

Széchényi's first appearance had been significant and opportune. His next step was as eagerly awaited as the second book of an author who has become famous overnight. The years 1825–1830 were to be for him a period of intense activity. The great were not spared in his attack; with breathless energy he hurled himself upon the foe without, as well as on the foe within. Wherever his keen eye perceived the crumbling, antiquated barriers of medievalism, he charged, and one act followed another at breakneck speed. For Hungary, he thought, must shake off its Eastern torpor under the influence of changing actuality and be transfused with Western blood. He was essentially a founder; he was the architect of a new era, but he had to be himself the builder too; at least he must get together a small enterprising group to raise the capital needed for his plans. He fired the Diet with his academy proposition, he set the example of a free-will offering, with the result he had foreseen. Now, with England as his model, he founded a club, to be the home of the progressively minded of his class; he called it the National Club. He found accommodation for it in Pest, he equipped it with all the comfort of the best London clubs, and soon magnates and landowners on business visits to Pest found a home in the club rooms of the Nemzeti Kaszino. Here politics were discussed. Here was evolved the programme of the future. Széchényi, always on the spot, personally interested and roping in his fellow-aristocrats, infecting them with his spirit and animating them with his convictions. And so the club which was apparently a social rendezvous with no particular purpose became the school of a new phalanx of men pursuing a common object. Even the proud magnates of Transylvania now came to Pest; one of them, a Baron Wesselényi, allied himself to Széchényi as his disciple, and Széchényi who had an inkling of Wesselényi's remarkable gifts took him with him on his next journey to England, in order to show the destined leader of Transylvanian regeneration the picture of West European civilisation. For England was to Széchényi at once pattern and criterion. He was determined to westernise Hungary. He had no time to lose in breaking up the soil of his half-oriental country. He had not the patience of the gardener, leisurely waiting for his plants to grow organically; he wanted fruit-bearing trees at once. Thus many of his sallies were adjudged ridiculous; it was said that he wanted to make every one wear loud-coloured and Tartan plaid breeches. He actually set himself to give this peasant people whose middle class consisted almost exclusively of German or Jewish tradesmen the pleasures of the sport of kings: he introduced horse racing, he imported English stallions, built stables and engaged jockeys, he felt himself a Hungarian Lord Derby. When he was ridiculed, he replied with the pique of an eccentric prima donna and the prolixity of a Schopenhauer defending his philosophy by writing a witty, cutting pamphlet, like an offended dandy, but with such profound wisdom in it that the captain of hussars was forgiven his extravagances and his genius was recognised. Heedless of ridicule and gossip, Széchényi forged ahead. Pest and Buda were only joined by a pontoon bridge across the river. Széchényi was aghast. He had seen the Tower Bridge in London; to him the Danube was as important as the Thames to Englishmen. From now on he was plagued with the idea of building the first solid bridge between the twin towns of Buda-Pest. But there is always an *arrière-pensée* behind every one of Széchényi's ideas. The bridge—the suspension bridge—which is to replace this contraption of the Middle Ages will not only enable traffic to cross the Danube at a Western pace; it will break down the isolation of Buda where Hungary's German masters hold the fort. There are difficulties. He recognises them and promptly gets to work to overcome them: the æsthete becomes an architect, the architect must study national economy. For a suspension bridge costs money; later the bridge toll can be used to liquidate a loan. But where is he to find capital, where credit? Is there such a thing as credit in Hungary? And now he is absorbed in economic problems. He devotes months to an untiring study of the physiocrats, free trade, the doctrines of Adam Smith and Bentham; at the same time he studies with the precision of a statistician the economic situation of the country; and suddenly the man who had been laughed at as a dandy, and smiled at as an æsthete, surprises the public with a thrillingly written monumental work "Credit" ("Hitel").

The tone in which he writes is arrogant and condescending. He never loses sight of two facts: that he must hedge in his dignity, and yet, in order that his words may have effect, stoop to the level of the vulgar. He is ready to give, he wants to educate, to build, but he refuses to sit at the same table as those who are not his equals. He is like the lord canvassing for votes who deigns to shake hands with his gardener, but uses the protection of a glove, as in a later age Lassalle, the labour leader, used to do. In order to disarm the suspicion that he was trying to be a Mirabeau, Széchényi who considered himself to be the peer of any English high Tory threw the crumbs of popular ideas to the people with a nonchalant hauteur. Here, too, there is the same contradiction of coldness and enthusiasm. There is no spate of fire inspiring his words and work.

To reach the man himself, it is necessary to look beneath this pose. Suddenly in the structure of a purple patch one finds a sudden gleam of passion. At first in *Hitel* he tried to gloss over real problems with a literary veneer, as if they were unseemly, so that his argument only just remains discernible, in a manner reminiscent of the budget speeches of Disraeli. He pillories the antiquated credit system of the country which, owing to the privileged position of the magnates, keeps their money out of a healthy circulation, thereby atrophying huge parts of the land, and its resources. The national regeneration in which Széchényi believes, by whatever means it is accomplished, must be his work. Hungary is to spring out of his head, fully equipped, a new, a powerful, a splendid Hungary. And he declares with a Promethean pride: "There has been no Hungary, but there shall be one."

V

Kossuth Enters the Arena

KOSSUTH COULD HARDLY HELP FINDING HIS PROLONGED STAY at Terebes, with its daily meetings with Etelka, tedious. And yet he remained. The environment was not without its charms. For it is just the man who is destined for great things who, growing to awareness of his powers, but not yet conscious of his mission, gladly accepts any gift which fate seems to offer him as corroboration that he is one of the elect. And what was it but predetermination that he, a Kossuth de Udvard, should be a privileged person in the house of Count Andrássy? A *persona grata* in the best Hungarian society?

It may seem an enigma that Kossuth, the man of the people, should so early have lost contact with real life, and have shut himself up for seven years in the feudal atmosphere of this idyllic isolation. But there are many parallels. Did not Rousseau through Madame de Varennes seek an *entrée* to the very court society that he desired to destroy. And even the first great leader of the lowest classes in Germany, the real proletariat, which was much further removed from the feudal world than the gentry and the middle-class world to which Kossuth belonged, owed his advancement to the love of Countess Hatzfeld. But whereas later Lassalle found in Countess Hatzfeld a wise helpmate and an unprejudiced critic of his plans, Kossuth was forced to recognise that Etelka was no companion for his thoughts. Count Széchényi's attacks, the sensation caused by *Hitel*, the first signs of national regeneration were to Etelka matters not worth discussing. In order to escape the boredom of her repeated demonstrations of affection, Kossuth sought the company of casual companions at cards. Where was he to turn to flee the narcotic of their indifference to what was happening in the world? There were two avenues open: the one led into the realm of fantasy, the other was the highroad of reality. And Kossuth took them both. Groping and uncertain, he tried both ways of escape from the narrowing restraint of Terebes.

The more comfortable way was to seek refuge in imagination. No one in the little town suspected that Lajos Kossuth, shut off from contact with the times, had discovered a new approach to actuality. He wrote poetry.

The resultant effort was—one might almost say: of course—a drama, *Crown and Sword*. His choice of subject showed no great originality. The early history of his country has furnished every dramatic adept with the material for his apprentice play. How many before him, and how many after him have used this theme, sure of the theatrical effect of one great scene. King Andreas lets his brother Béla, to whom he had promised the throne before the birth of his son Salomon, choose between the crown and the sword, the latter symbolising the service of his country. Béla naturally elects for power, but a loyal friend warns him that if he chooses the crown he will be murdered. And so he chooses the sword and flees the country, only to return with an army and to conquer with the sword—the crown! Every novice playwright, like Ibsen in his *Catilina*, begins by searching the dramatic book of history for theatrical effects. But Kossuth was more attracted to his subject by its contrast of ideas. To him the brother who bore the sword was greater than the king, because he chose service to the crown. By dramatising his ideas in the night hours of his seclusion Kossuth prepared his way towards the second avenue of escape which led to actuality.

The constitution gave every member of the nation, every man of gentle birth, the right to attend the county assembly, and there to vote on all political questions. Now, as the third decade of the century was drawing to an end, a lull had succeeded the stormy ebullition of political interest that marked the session of the Diet in the years 1825–27. The aristocracy had soon tired of Széchényi's alarums. Life in the provincial towns and on the great estates had relapsed into a comfortable lethargy. Kossuth's entrance into the arena coincided with this period of exhaustion. His first appearance at the county assembly, a tyro, like Széchényi on his first appearance in the Diet, must be considered as a signal to a new awakening. What had this romantic lover, this man of no experience, to say? What interest had he in the debate, the tedious question whether the two delegates which the county had sent as its representatives to the Diet recently gone into recess had acted counter to their authority by sanctioning an increase in the contingent of Hungarian troops doing service with the Austrian army, against the wishes, and without the approval of, the nobility? Once again Austria had cunningly

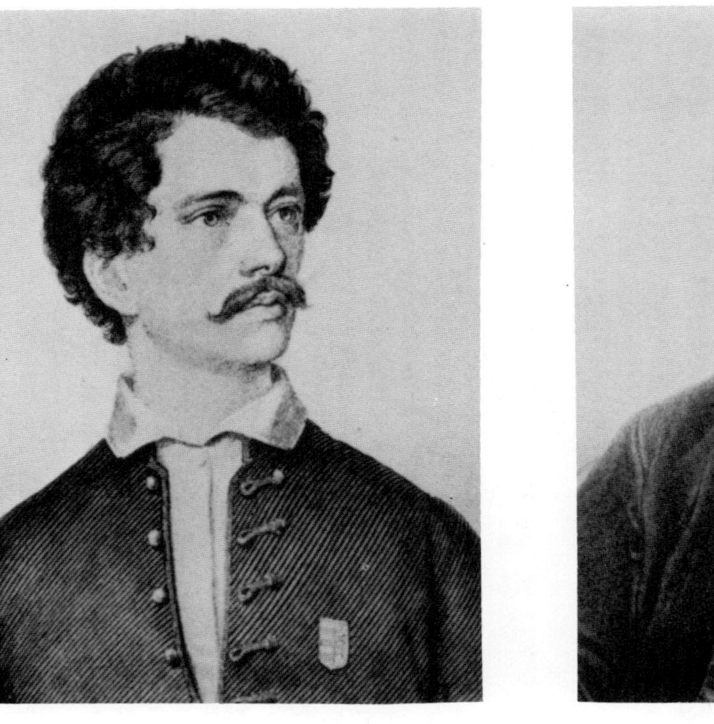

THE POET, SÁNDOR PETÖFI

COUNT ISTVAN SZÉCHÉNYI

From the Portrait Collection of the National Library, Vienna

laid new burdens on Hungary, without any compensation, and, moreover, without even respecting the charter of the constitution. Countless protests had remained unanswered and ineffectual; and in spite of this the two delegates had grovelled to the House of Hapsburg?

The dispute in the county assembly was very tame. The magnates who had taken the trouble to turn up defended the policy of Vienna and the delegates. Particularly Count György Andrássy, Etelka's nephew, spoke condescendingly and with a scarcely restrained contempt to the gentry who deplored this new burden. The opposition was tepid. And then Kossuth rose.

His audience smiled and whispered. They knew the history of this upstart. But suddenly everyone was silent. They were listening to such language as they had never heard before. Mastery of words, declamatory power, perfect elocution. The assembly listened in amazement. Even the pro-Austrian party was nonplussed by the unexpected attack. Despite the unimportance of his subject Kossuth made it an excuse to outline the political problems and to paint a lurid picture of the situation of Hungary. What was the sense in lecturing this comatose provincial audience in the county of Zemplén, on the northern edge of the Carpathians? But Kossuth must have felt that even this restricted platform might be the springboard that would lift him over the walls that hemmed him in.

The effect of his address was indescribable. His audience cheered the man who had aroused them from their slumber. The most reliable witness of the scene, Kazinczy, said in describing it: "His speech seemed to me like the torch of insurrection." The young Kossuth had flung the torch of insurrection into the county; his maiden speech had earned him the reputation of being an orator. As he left the scene of his triumph, with the cheers ringing in his ears, must he not have been reminded of the prophecy which had foretold his career? Now he felt that the county was too narrow for him. Now he longed to get away. He returned a few times to the assembly meetings, but only for the sake of practice as a speaker. It was for him what the bar is to the budding politician in France, a training ground. And so in this year in which he graduated from the school of susceptibility he also matriculated in the school of rhetoric. But every time of schooling had its end; the pupil feels himself a master. It is time to enter the arena of the world.

VI

The Plague

BUT KOSSUTH'S DAYS AT TEREBES WERE NOT YET NUMBERED. HE hunted bear, he dissipated over cards, and when the county assembly made no call upon his leisure, he led the healthy, quiet, unexciting life of a country gentleman in a village cut off from the world. And then a disaster which men have always feared, as they fear war and famine, terrified the county: the plague. In those days it made very little difference which kind of plague it was: bubonic, typhoid or cholera. Humanity was scarcely less helpless in the face of these death-bringing pestilences in the first decades of the nineteenth century than it had been in the Middle Ages. The times when those infected with the plague were walled in in their houses lay nearer the year 1830 than 1870, when Robert Kock and other scientists of genius discovered bacteria and robbed this phantom of much of its pristine terror. When the Asiatic cholera appeared, towards the end of the summer of 1831, in the frontier counties of Upper Hungary, no one knew what this unknown pestilence was. The pious called it a visitation of God; they prayed, flocked to the churches and did penance.

The cholera epidemic of 1831 was particularly virulent. What was the cause of it? It may be termed a punishment of charity. Never had fate so punished a people for its altruism. There is no doubt that the disease was brought in by the refugees from Poland who fled across the Carpathians after their revolt against the tyranny of Russia and their defeat at Ostrolenka. This insurrection of its downtrodden neighbour aroused an enthusiastic echo in Hungary. Oppression made the nations kin. The Poles had risen to overthrow the domination of the Czar; their aim was to set up their own national state. What else did the Magyar patriot want, as he dreamed of the regeneration of the splendour of St. Stephen's crown? Certainly there was no one who contemplated snatching this crown from the House of Hapsburg. But the Hungarian desired to be free under the rule of his crowned king, with the freedom his constitution guaranteed him. And were not the Poles fighting against the Czar, the ally of the Emperor Franz? If they defeated him they would destroy one of the two strongholds of absolutism. If they could drive him out of Poland, they would undermine his power in the European field. They would weaken the Holy Alliance through which Austria secured her domination and the whole edifice erected by the Vienna Congress would begin to crumble. Therefore, the insurrection in Poland was followed with breathless interest and unconcealed sympathy in Hungary. The Hungarians would have liked to help the Poles. But only the king could mobilise the army and declare war. All that could be done was to petition the king. As the Diet was not in session, the initiative had to come from the counties. The addresses sent by the individual counties to the Emperor Franz are evidence of the readiness of the Hungarian nation to sacrifice itself. In order to aid those fighting for the cause of liberty in their hour of need, Hungary pressed for war with Russia.

It must be admitted that never was a more worthily inspired appeal addressed to a monarch to save from annihilation by an imperialist enemy a nation fighting for its existence. Hungary asked nothing for herself; but she was ready to hasten to the help of a nation in distress. How was this? Is not Europe divided into states that have nothing to do with one another—except it be that their governments should have contracted alliances and military conventions? What was the explanation of this spontaneous desire of the people to consider a foreign nation as a brother community? And this feeling actually transcended frontiers? How strong must the spirit of humanity have dwelt in this people, if they could think in this manner! Perhaps misfortune teaches compassion. Perhaps the hard school which Hungary had had to go through under Hapsburg rule was the best teacher of charitableness. In any case, Hungary's intercession for the threatened Poles showed for the first time in history that the solidarity of oppressed peoples is stronger than despotism, and that ethics in political conflicts are a factor never to be underrated.

The Vienna court, that is to say, Metternich, ignored these appeals. Perhaps there were moments when Metternich, the sworn enemy of all revolutions, felt a certain measure of sympathy with the Polish insurrection, not from any humane promptings, but for purely political reasons. Under the Czar Alexander Russia had often enough shown her greed to her ally of 1815 and frustrated Austria's plans. Alexander's successor, Nicholas, showed himself openly Austria's enemy. It could only be convenient to have an independent Poland as a buffer state between Austria and Russia. But tactical considerations weighed less with Metternich than those of principle. His anxiety for the continuance of the *status quo* outweighed every other consideration. He felt himself to be the defender of all thrones. His conservatism even went so far that he was prepared to put Austria's armed forces at the disposition of Russia. His plan of armed intervention in favour of Russia was only frustrated by the stubbornness of the Archduke Karl. By the time the counties of Hungary made their appeal to the King-emperor, Metternich had long since dismissed the Polish question as "closed."

In the autumn, as it had been feared would happen, the Polish insurgents fled across the Carpathians into Hungary. The sacrifice of the Magyars who had sent them money and supplies had been in vain. In vain countless Hungarians had slipped across the frontier to fight in the ranks of "heroic Poland," as Lord Byron had fought for the independence of Greece. The new Russian Marshal Paskiewitch had annihilated the Polish army and put an end to Poland's independence almost for a century to come. Now the Hungarians, particularly the gentry, vied with one another in offering hospitality to the refugees and helping them in their distress. If they had failed to help them in the field, they could at least aid them in defeat. When Metternich's spies arrived in search of the hated refugees who might infect the country with the spirit of rebellion, the gentry appealed to their ancient privilege of *salva guardia*. Kossuth's father, now aged and impoverished, took two Polish fugitives into his house as guests, sharing with them his meagre fare and chatting in the evenings over the battles of the past and the battles that were still to come. The words "liberty" and "independence" were often spoken there and in every house in Upper Hungary that sheltered a Polish soldier. The idea of freedom was a bond between these neighbouring peoples; and hospitality, a sacred tradition in Hungary, was offered more sincerely for this fact. But with the foreign guests came the cholera; its ravages spread through the county, just as Pressburg had predicted.

The story of the cholera epidemic in the remoter peasant districts of Upper Hungary is a catalogue of horrors. The aftermath was even ghastlier than the plague itself. Medical science was still in its infancy. The doctors were helpless. There was no sanitation fit to speak of. And there was one dreadful, murderous ally of the pestilence: stupidity.

This was the revenge for having kept the labouring peasantry, the alien conglomeration of Slovak farm hands in a state of total unenlightenment. There is no educational sin which is not a political mistake, just as there is no political progress without educational progress. The peasant farm labourers were literally robots; they spoke a different language from the foreign masters whom they served, they lived in a primitive and semi-savage ignorance. It was no wonder that their minds worked like those of primitive races and that they found the absurdest explanations for natural phenomena. It had happened in the Middle Ages that epidemics had been attributed to the Jews who were accused of poisoning the wells. But this was a delusion consciously fostered from above by avaricious princes or unscrupulous Jesuits, and originating in religious fanaticism. But what happened here was that the downtrodden agricultural labourers—for it is impossible to call these serfs peasants—created a legend to explain the causes of the epidemic: not the Jews, but the nobles were accused of having poisoned the wells in order to exterminate them, the serfs.

It did not occur to these illogical, deluded creatures that it was an absurdity to suppose that the landowners would deprive themselves of slaves who tilled their fields. Were not the nobles dying too, magnates and gentry? Did not the death-roll include priests and officials, the people in the towns, and even in some cases the doctors and the nurses too?

But it is the nature of madness to be impervious to common sense. The accumulated hatred born of centuries of humiliation, the endless misery of a slave existence, identifies the evil with those who for generations had held them in subjection. A cry went through the land: "Down with the nobles. Let us kill those who are trying to kill us." The people banded together, armed themselves, and marched against the castles and country houses. What had they to fear? With death before their eyes, death already in their entrails, they were resolved to profit by the time still left them to deal death.

The cholera revolt was not an echo of the French revolution; the idea of liberty, the belief in the rights of man which had driven the peasants of South Germany in 1525, and the people of France in 1789, to take up arms, had touched the Slovak peasants of the

Hungarian counties less than the negroes of San Domingo. They had never heard of them. They were merely following their instincts. Their vengeance on the landowners was no more than the hatred of a caged tiger. The fear of death maddened them, and hounded them against their tyrants. This was no guerilla warfare, for the landowners were totally unprepared. They had scarcely any possibility of defending themselves. They were overwhelmed by an infuriated, bloodthirsty mob. Nobles were roasted alive on spits, ladies were horribly mutilated, high officials were buried alive or starved to death. Not content with this and drunk with vengeance, the rabble turned against the towns, bent on slaughtering the rich, for to the peasant mind every town is rich.

The towns, unprotected and unarmed, were in terrible danger. The menace swept towards Sátoralja-Ujhely. So did the cholera.

Kossuth's three sisters had volunteered as nurses at the commencement of the outbreak. The news of the approaching Slovaks threw the little town into a panic. After the atrocities they had committed in the country houses they were spoken of as the "maniacs." The county of Zemplén was the most threatened, for it had harboured the greatest number of Poles and the cholera was rifest there.

When the "maniacs" entered the town of Sátoralja-Ujhely, they were joined by a cheering rabble from the poorer quarters. This raving mob, now composed of beggars as well as cholera-stricken serfs, armed with scythes, guns and flails, marched through the streets. Kossuth, after assuring the safety of the Countess Etelka, hurried from Terebes to the town. What steps had been taken by the municipal council, by the county sheriff, or the magnates to save the townsfolk? None. Every one of them who had been able to escape had fled. But the townspeople cowered in their houses, hale and sick alike, paralysed with fear, waiting resignedly for the moment when these lunatics should break into the house and wreak their fiendish revenge. Kossuth was horrified at this supineness of his fellow-townsmen in the face of the danger. No one did anything. And so he who held no official position in the town, the family solicitor of Countess Andrássy, made up his mind to save the situation.

The astounding thing is that Kossuth actually did. In the face of a crisis there are many who say: "We should," "We must." Between thought and action there is only the brief moment of decision. The man who takes it must be adjudged a leader.

Swiftly and confidently Kossuth set about the work of organising a defence. He did so in the simplest way: by mounting the steps of the church and rallying the running townsfolk. In a few hours the town was under arms. But when the hastily organised militia begged him to take over the command, Kossuth refused. He found a retired officer, a captain, and handed over the command to him.

This is significant. It shows the character of the man. Kossuth entrusts the military command to a military leader. He recognises that leadership is a thing that must be learnt. He accepts the responsibility for the idea of resistance, but not for its success.

The insurgent mob were surprised to find themselves up against an armed, and a well-armed, resistance. The captain of the volunteer militia gave the order to fire. But Kossuth intervened. He advanced towards the rabble and spoke to them. He spoke in Hungarian and then translated his short and pointed sentences into Slovak. "The cholera," he said, "is a plague of heaven. Not wicked men have brought this plague upon us, but God. The disease takes every one, as God wills. Do you not see that towns, the landlords and the nobles die of it as you do? Go home, trust your doctors and wait."

The mob laid down their weapons and went home ashamed. Kossuth's first incursion into the history of his country was as a pacifier of rebels. His name soon became known in every part of Hungary. "Kossuth?" people said. "The young lawyer who quieted the bands of murderers? We shall hear more of him." Presently the epidemic ran its course. The cholera plague was over.

But this gruesome episode which interrupted the idyl of Terebes left on Kossuth a deeper and decisive impression: he had seen for the first time human misery in all its ghastliness. And, more than that, he had seen misery great and menacing. The poor, the slaves, the robots: threatening. A picture in miniature of the dreadful power of a people that has broken its chains, the power that stormed the Tuileries and overthrew a dynasty.

VII

Release

KOSSUTH'S TRIUMPH AS CHOLERA COMMISSIONER OUTSHONE EVEN his reputation as an orator in the county. Resolution and determined action is always more impressive than thinking and word-weaving. Now he had established connections with the outside world more happily than he had dreamed. Would not his budding fame be a recommendation to the politicians in Pressburg and Pest? If he were to go to Pest now, would his prospects be as black as when he had vainly knocked at the doors of the Buda palace? He was surely justified in thinking that he had paved the way for a career. But he was still a long way from his goal. His father would persuade him not to give up his good position with the Countess Andrássy. There was always a chance that the reputation he had won might convince the county assembly that he was the best man to send as delegate to Pressburg. For the Emperor Franz had condescended to convoke the Diet for the end of the year.

Kossuth longed to get away from Zemplén. He was on the verge of thirty, an age when a man wishes to shape his destiny to some purpose. Thirty! "*Trente ans, comme le bon sans-culottes Jésu Christ,*" as Camille Desmoulins said before the National Convention.

Cautiously he hinted at his plans to Etelka. He mentioned that he would like to go to Pressburg for the opening of the Diet. But she entreated him to stay with all the vehemence of a clinging love that is ever reluctant to surrender a lover. He resigned himself and stayed. He had not the courage to be cruel. He was afraid of hurting her. His sensibility clipped his wings.

But Kossuth was waiting for this waning love to die a natural death. Etelka still thought she could escape the inevitable. She behaved discreetly. She shut her eyes to his more frequent visits to political meetings. When he stayed out half the night drinking in the village or playing cards at the vice-sheriff's house, she never said a word. All she asked was that he should stay with her, that he should come back to her.

And he came back and waited, hoping for some word that would give him an excuse to bid her good-bye and part as friends. But this was not to be the case.

In this year 1831 it often happened that Kossuth had to rise early after a long night of gambling or carousal to collect rents or to go on some errand as the Countess' attorney; on these occasions he took with him a little book which transported him into the world of ideas. He read Lamennais. This daily, intimate intercourse with the ideas of the great Abbé completed Kossuth's education. Driven in desperation to seek escape from boredom in dissipation, he yet found his deepest solace in these faith-inspired works.

Before Kossuth completed his training for politics, after his sentimental education and the perfecting of his oratorical style, he passed through the highest stage of human culture: he reconciled the religious demands of his being with all new ideas, he founded his political judgments on a Christian basis.

The revolt of the poor wretches whom he had been instrumental in pacifying had opened Kossuth's eyes. The daily spectacle of need and suffering that he encountered on his wanderings made him realise before any one else that there was such a thing as a social question. The nobles, living a life of leisure on their estates, were disinclined for any serious thinking. Even Széchényi's *Hitel* was laid aside or rejected as pretentious and heavy reading. Those on the other hand who reacted to the stirrings of awakening Hungary, and listened to Kossuth's electrifying speeches in the county assembly, were not disposed to tackle the difficult question of a readjustment of relations to the dynasty, nor yet that other difficult, unfamiliar problem, the social question. They had a suspicion that this was playing with fire: prudence counselled them to leave these things alone. Why meddle with conditions which had stood the test of a thousand years, at least in so far as the upper classes were concerned? Kossuth could find no one willing to be companion to him on his visits to this poverty and misery, on his rambles in the fields or in his communion with Lamennais. He went his way alone; alone he wrestled with ideas. He read: "The number of the poor will always grow less, because little by little servitude will vanish from society." And: "Every man has the right to earn by his labour the things he lacks, for otherwise poverty would be eternal." Did this mean that the poor who, like maniacs, had wickedly taken vengeance on their innocent masters for the misfortune of the plague had just reason for their despair? The words of a priest justified them and contrasted the sins of the ruling classes with their need. How startling this sounded: "There are dumb creatures which are shut up in pens, fed so that they may work, and then when they are old fattened to provide meat for human food. There are others that run free in the fields which cannot be harnessed to servitude." The kernel of Kossuth's character was pride: who was more likely to understand the humiliation of the under-dog. He appreciated human dignity, the unalienable possession of the very lowest; Christian faith in the brotherhood of man compelled him to. And so he committed the solecism of not addressing farm hands in the second person singular, but with the courtesy usual in conversation with a stranger. The serfs were puzzled and grateful; they felt that here was one soul that sympathised with them. And now, as afterwards in Tinye, it was whispered of Kossuth that he was fraternising with the lowest, the people.

For it is this conviction that was taking shape in his mind—at first with the vague uncertainty of an emotional experience, then given fuel by Lamennais and finally by earnest thinking and a rational examination of the conditions of society—the conviction that every man in Hungary had the right to live the life of a human being, as a member of one brotherhood, the nation. Now Kossuth understood how retrograde and unjust was Verböcsy's theory, this mythical doctrine of the omnipotence of St. Stephen's crown, this constitution in which there was no mention of the word "people." Another term, "the nation," was substituted for it. But nation excluded people. "Qu'est-ce que c'est que le peuple? Une grande amitié!"

Thus in this year, after the suppression of the serf rebellion, a great change took place in Kossuth. He recognised his mission: to become the liberator of his people—recognised it in the same words in which the gipsy woman had told his fortune. The "democratic conviction" that was growing in him, the origin of the fanaticism with which he afterwards fought to make his nation a people, was at bottom a religious conviction. Lamennais' words were coined for him: "I go to fight, to free my brothers from oppression, to break their fetters and the fetters of the world." And in the solitude of the fields he heard the answer: "A blessing on your arms, young soldier!"

Disgusted by the emptiness of his idle existence, but deterred by the imposing luxury of the life at Terebes, he throws himself with less and less restraint into the dangerous adventures of nightly dissipation. It almost seems as if he were purposely wallowing, before becoming the prophet of his ideas, so as to free himself, definitely and for good, of all sensual entanglement. For similarly the other great prophet of Christian brotherhood, Leo Tolstoi, was at the same age too much the slave of his passions. Kossuth knows but one way of escape: he seizes every occasion to flee to nature. When his work does not take him into the fields, he accepts invitations to shooting parties because they promise him the solitude of the woods. But once he found in the Terebes library a volume of Firdausi. The Persian poet spoke of the sanctity of life and included animals. Kossuth was staggered. He took an oath that from that moment he would never again take a gun in his hand. The words of the poet had the power to kill his passion for the chase. Who would cure him of his more dangerous passion, gambling?

Etelka felt clearly that she had lost her lover. Now the moment had arrived for the woman to show her character. She might have let him go, calmly and with her blessing, and kept her tears for after his departure. But this was not the stuff that Etelka was made of. Kossuth was hers, she meant to keep him. And woe betide him, if he slipped away from her.

For several evenings Kossuth had not come to her. He had been gambling, and losing heavily. And then an incredible thing happened: György Andrássy, Etelka's nephew, called Kossuth to account. He cast aspersions on his honesty; he even went so far as to spread the story in the county that Kossuth had gambled away money entrusted to him.

There were quite a number of people in the county who had not listened to Kossuth's inflammatory speeches with approval. Something about him seemed suspicious: the magnates were not slow to sense the menace of his genius. These noble gentlemen were not at all pleased to see the infiltration into the county of Zemplén of those ideas of which Count Széchényi—a renegade in their opinion—was so energetic an exponent. This subversive propaganda must be nipped in the bud, before this young hothead became an agitator. Count Andrássy's open insinuations afforded a welcome opportunity. Kossuth had to vindicate himself before a tribunal of the county aristocracy.

His exoneration was an easy matter. He had only to produce his books. The charge collapsed. But painful as was this denouement which finally absolved him from his obligation to

Etelka, it also had a very important result. His immediate reply to the accusations made against him was, in conformity with his character, a stand upon morality. And, just as he had laid aside his gun under the influence of a stanza of Firdausi, so now under the influence of this trial he took an oath never to touch a card again. And he kept his oath.

Thus ends the sentimental interlude with Etelka. The year 1831 writes finis to the chapter of flirtation with Romanticism and marks Kossuth's entrance into the political arena.

The rupture was now complete. It was impossible for a man of Kossuth's pride to remain in Zemplén after these proceedings. His acquittal gave him his release; the world lay open, the prisoner of Terebes was free.

VIII

Commencement

HOW THE WORLD HAD CHANGED! THE TIDE OF GREAT EVENTS of European history had lapped the shores of Hungary, this country "sunk in medieval slumber." In the towns the hearts of an awakening generation throbbed with new ideas. Kossuth turned his steps to Pest. But the city spoke different language from that of ten years ago. He felt the change at once. The National Club which Széchényi had founded welcomed liberal ideas. Soon the Count's mania for reform attracted a following of the more enlightened spirits of the aristocracy. The conservative magnates, friendly to the Hapsburgs and loyal to Metternich, looked askance at this Tory who had departed from tradition and had brought back from his travels a wealth of European ideas which could not be confiscated. What was to be done with him? Already the whole people were at his beck and call. With lightning swiftness the brain of this one man conceived one project of reform after another. Wherever Kossuth went in Pest he heard the name of Széchényi. Wandering about this eager, aspiring city, in search of a sphere where he could make his presence felt, he realised with a painful shock that others had forestalled him. Others had been working in the spirit of his ideas. The principal parts in the drama of history had already been distributed while he had been content to play a walking-on part in a provincial masque. Even the hero had been cast.

"The Count"—by which abbreviation Széchényi was generally spoken of—stood at the head of the growing movement, pressing for reforms. The Count's popularity in the capital was enormous. Kossuth was forced to admit that accident of birth had provided Széchényi with all the advantages that had been denied him, the village lawyer. The authority of a magnate, wealth, a splendid education, the culture acquired in his travels abroad, elevated him to a position no one could hope to reach. Kossuth recognised this, and at this first moment, as he walked the pavements of the unfamiliar city, an unknown nobody, he had to admit, when he compared himself to Széchényi, that he had a harder task than the Count. Perhaps in setting out to be the leader in the fight for liberty, he had proposed himself a goal impossible of attainment.

The great event of the epoch, the July revolution in France, had not failed to make a strong impression in the towns of Hungary. The middle classes of Buda and of Pest in whose hands lay practically the whole of Hungary's trade, hailed the revolution with delight. Merchants love freedom and hate frontiers; they despise the legislator and the rules and regulations that hamper trade. And the middle classes consisted almost exclusively of Germans and Jews. They did the work of which the true Magyar was ashamed. Therefore the middle classes were German and liberal in their views, because they were influenced by economic considerations. In Count Széchényi they found the noble champion of their practical economical aspirations. Like Bentham in England, Széchényi was for Hungary the pioneer of economic liberalism. Kossuth on the other hand had reached a democratic conviction through a theological perception: he had read Lamennais. Now he had to learn to combine ideal liberalism with the doctrines of the economical.

He began to read up in the back numbers of the most important newspaper, the *Augsburger Allgemeine Zeitung*, the chronicle of the events that had convulsed France. Who had emerged victorious in Paris? A Lafitte, a middle-class banker? A Thiers, a small provincial lawyer? The age was dawning in which men of the middle class were climbing into power. Why should not he, the Monók lawyer, emulate this Thiers and reach the top?

It seemed as if the times were his ally. They wanted such a man as he was. The door was open—and yet he could not see the way to enter it. In what direction should he look? What was he to do? He had come to Pest, a lawyer without a livelihood. This was his second visit to Pest and once again he stood there without position, occupation, or means of subsistence. No one wanted him, no one was interested in him.

Kossuth hugged his dream, but immediate worries were of more importance. His pride sagged, his self-confidence evaporated. In September of this year, 1832, he was thirty. His youth was over, it had slipped away.

He sat in his lonely room on this, his thirtieth birthday,

anxious and dispirited. The September day was drawing to its close; the streets of Pest still sweltered in the sultry air; at home they would be gathering the fruit, the grapes would still be hanging, in their heavy clusters, in the vineyards of Tokay; soon would be the vintage festival and dancing round the wine-presses and in the barns. The Countess too, Etelka. . . .

Someone knocked at Kossuth's door. In the shadow of the half-opened door he saw a hussar. He thought he recognised him. This uniformed messenger might well belong to the manor of Terebes. The hussar bowed and handed him a letter. Kossuth tore it open, he recognised the writing—it was hers.

No present could have made him happier at that moment: this note put an end to his self-torture, restored his threatened pride. Etelka begged his forgiveness. In her pique she had been capable of a stupid revenge. But the consequence that she had brought upon herself, their separation, had brought her to her senses by the pain it caused her. Now she was anxious about him, she was sorry for him. He was no longer her lover, he no longer handled her affairs, but she wished to give him back her confidence. She rehabilitated him. She had, in her motherly concern, got him a mandate as representative of a relative who was a member of the Diet. He would have to attend as *ablegatus absentis* during the coming session; this would insure him for some time at any rate. He could stay in Pressburg. The way was open.

Kossuth seized the chance. He accepted the mandate. He left at once for Pressburg. The world was his oyster.

This was the last echo of their lost love: reconciliation and understanding. Countess Etelka Andrássy introduced Kossuth to his future, she sponsored him to history.

PART TWO

A WEAPON: A PEN

I

Light and Shadow

LAJOS KOSSUTH CAME TO THE DIET A NAMELESS, UNCONSIDERED nobody, the delegate of some obscure baron. He took his place on the side benches reserved for those who had a seat, but not a voice. He could listen but he might not speak. Of what use now were his gifts of oratory, the ephemeral reputation he had won in Zemplén?

At first Kossuth was satisfied to listen to the great men who spoke here in the name of Hungary. He experienced for the first time the shock that awaits every one who has had reason to imagine himself a leader within the restricted confines of his own home: he was forced to recognise that there were many others like himself, pushing, talented and self-assured. And what an array of powerful personalities surrounded him, against whose knowledge, gifts and quality he felt the urge to match his own! The youthful dream of every man conscious of a mission, the dream of rising to the top, faded and a sense of ineptitude stole over him, the nameless watcher in the background. Those others made speeches: their words possibly even reached the State offices in Vienna. But Kossuth was an outsider, an ambitious lieutenant in the company of generals. It had needed an upheaval of the existing order of things for a young subaltern, barely passed out of St. Cyr, to be given the command of an army. But the prevailing order stood firm and the leaders showed no sign of taking the offensive beyond these interminable debates.

Condemned to silence, Kossuth sat following every word that echoed from the tribune, familiarising himself with every speaker's face, voice and mode of thought. He began, at first as a kind of game, to group and criticise. It amused him to fit people into categories, lukewarm and courageous, cautious and fanatical, hedgers and die-hards, hypocrites and honest men. Among the leaders of the *avant-garde* he saw the poet Ferenc Kölcsey who had been fired by Széchényi's work to stake his genius for the revival of the Magyar language. He saw Jànos Balogh, the hero of the younger members: he heard him mention in a brief argument a name which he had never forgotten. Balogh told how he had drilled into his son a short political catechism: "Who was the first man?"—"George Washington." "What is the best form of government?"—"A republic." "What are you?"—"A democrat." So there were other democrats beside himself in this assembly. And their star was George Washington. Would they ever emerge from their democratic convictions into action? Would they champion the cause of the poverty-stricken proletariat which Kossuth had seen helpless and threatening? He knew that he could not approach these advanced spirits with the youthful impetuosity of his youthful conviction. He must look elsewhere: listen and learn. And now once again there stirred in him that strange feeling of inexplicable certainty that he had time: time to mature and wait until his hour should strike.

One day in March a buzz of excitement ran through the Pressburg Diet. The deputies pushed their way towards the door and the younger members rushed out of the building to welcome a newcomer with cries of "Eljen!" Kossuth knew at once: Széchényi had arrived.

Széchényi had just returned from England: he was accompanied by Count György Andrássy. Kossuth was startled to see this man, Etelka's nephew, his enemy and opponent, at the great reformer's side. Did this mean the resurrection of an unpleasant memory which he had believed dead or at least buried in the depths of his subconsciousness, the renewal of a private feud? Was he to let himself be hampered in the career that was to bring him recognition? Amid the roar of enthusiasm that greeted Count István Széchényi, Kossuth stood alone trembling with eyes riveted on him, the first man in Hungary.

The Count was exactly like the many caricatures of him that were in circulation. Dressed with a careless elegance, a broad dark stock bulging above the high cut of his check jacket, he made his way among the nobles proudly conscious of their gala uniforms. His face was as always pale, his waved black hair merged without a hint of grey into the whiskers that framed the long big face with its strong aquiline nose. The thin, tight-set lips under the sparse moustache looked incapable of a smile; and yet, although this face was denied the warmth of humour, it was alive with animation. His stiff Anglo-Saxon bearing suggested arrogance, and there was a contemptuous expression in the large dark eyes. But at moments when he thought himself unobserved, there crept into them a look of suffering sadness.

This man who held himself so aloof gave an impression of constant self-contradiction. Thus Kossuth saw Count Széchényi for the first time and the question arose in his mind whether, if Fate so willed it, he would one day be able to pit himself against this man.

The first meeting of Kossuth with Széchényi was no more than a silent fleeting episode: the two men, destined for greatness and antagonism, did not exchange a word. How would it have been possible that the popular magnate should have addressed the unknown lawyer? The echo in Kossuth's soul, his anxious doubting questioning of his own worth and powers, was only the natural expression of his insistent longing to become the "liberator of his country." Like all the breed of liberators and benefactors, born to champion great ideas or to do epoch-making deeds, Kossuth had been given in his cradle that inescapable gift: the belief in his mission. And such men suffer when another seeks to forestall his achievement. To answer the challenge with hatred, mean intrigue or the ignoble effort to clear his path would have been petty. But Kossuth's answer throws a clear light on the nobility of his character. And now begins a long, long period of service as Kossuth undeviatingly followed his ascending star, climbing the long road with bated breath. Fifteen years! The whole first span of manhood! Fifteen industrious and prolific years!

Resolved to get into the limelight at all hazards Kossuth espies the vacant place from which to make a start. Again, as on the occasion of the cholera disturbances, it is a political idea which determines his début in Pressburg. Indignation that the general public should have no inkling of the tenour of these important parliamentary debates prompted the question: What would happen if the country learned of the work the deputies were doing? If the people could be shown the unconciliatory attitude of the Government? It they were made witnesses of this duel between awakening Hungary and the "system"? How tame and halting these strenuous and hard-fought encounters became in the periodical reports made by the deputies to their counties! What was needed was a record of the debates set down while the speeches were still alive, while the ideas still glowed. And so Kossuth surprised the liberal group whose ranks he was allowed to join with a proposition: to found a newspaper for the purpose of supplying the different counties with a report of the sessions. This evoked a lively discussion in the party. The unknown delegate who had at first modestly put forward his suggestion now rose to his feet again and, as if remembering a forgotten jewel, the precious gift of rhetoric, inveighed against the censorship. And, as in Zemplén, the "spell of his voice" and the wealth of his ideas aroused the admiration of the big politicians. His efficiency as cholera commissioner was recalled and even the great Wesselényi, Count Széchényi's close friend and collaborator, gained confidence in this young man. The proposal to purchase a printing works and to entrust Kossuth with the editorship of "Diet reports" was carried unanimously.

A speech—and this success! Will the orator now be content to retire into the background and muzzle his gift of rhetoric in order to serve the cause of freedom as a drudge? Kossuth's renunciation proves his greatness. When the time comes again for him to unsheath the sword of speech how can he tell whether it will not fail him for lack of practice?

The gift of oratory is the real creative power of Kossuth's intellectual composition. He is an orator of genius, and poets are born, not made. But the hour was not favourable for genius: it demanded peace and loyal humdrum work. Will Kossuth succeed in infusing his genius into this unsensational activity?

Thus after the idyllic years the graph of this man's life seems to settle down into a quiet monotony. But here again, as always in his life, an unexpected intervention breaks off the regular curve as dramatically as that which brought the natural course of his affair with Countess Etelka to a scandalous denouement. And once again the interference was the work of a person who seems determined to play the *diabolus ex machina* in his life: György Andrássy thought it necessary to whisper in Wesselényi's ear that this fellow Kossuth was "notorious." And, not content with this, he raked up again the whole intrigue, but omitted the part love had played in it. In diplomatic parlance, he laid mines and, of course, they exploded Kossuth's plans on the very day of their realisation.

Schiller's dramatic genius understood how to present in exemplary fashion the episode in which Gessler is compelled to implore his prisoner Tell to save him by taking over the rudder because he alone can do it. Here again history indulges in the self-same irony: someone else took over the editorship of the parliamentary chronicle, but his heavy style all but killed the paper. And then once more Kossuth was remembered. Balogh, who had meanwhile read sketches in Kossuth's diary of the debates in Diet, convinced his friends that he was "the one man for the job." This time they begged him to undertake the editorship and he consented.

II

The Observer Triumphs

THUS KOSSUTH BECAME AN EDITOR—WITHOUT AN EDITORIAL staff. He undertook a work new to Hungary, with no precedent to guide him: he became a political journalist.

This is a fact which has always been overlooked: but it shows, more strongly than anything else, that Kossuth was a great political tactician. The fifteen years which now follow are not, as were the romantic years, a cæsura: they are rather a period of consciously chosen, carefully planned building-up of a political career.

We know of many instances where a man conscious of his call to political leadership prefers to bide his time rather than to waste himself in premature action. It is just this which differentiates the tactician from the fanatic, the statesman from the demagogue. The period, too, the thirties of the nineteenth century, compels a comparison with the two young politicians, Benjamin Disraeli and Mazzini, who were then entering the political arena in England and in Italy. Both, like Kossuth, were imbued with the conviction that they and they alone were marked out to guide the destinies of their respective countries. But Mazzini dissipates the inexhaustible store of revolutionary substance in a hundred petty enterprises which, carelessly prepared, hurriedly planned and childishly carried out, invariably miss fire. Mazzini was in a constant state of flight from the scenes of his lost actions, hatching fresh plots of bloodshed from abroad, as a result of which bombs burst, assassins' daggers struck down some enemy of the cause and wildly written pamphlets strewed the streets of the towns of Northern Italy. But Mazzini could not wait. Schemes had to be immediately translated into deeds: he had an aim, but never a plan. Temperamentally, in this obsession with the ideal of new conditions which were to be his own creation, Kossuth was intellectually akin to Mazzini—and it was no mere chance that he later, in his first exile, came into proximity with the Italian. But during this period of preparation Kossuth disciplines himself to a prudence of which only a clear-sighted and truly political brain is capable. Similarly Disraeli, now member of the House of Commons since 1837, was awaiting his opportunity in the shadow of the great Pitt, and he waited years. It is important to see the powerful political intellect of Kossuth as close to that of a Disraeli, at least in the way he shaped his life. For it is just this wise renunciation, this avoidance of premature activity and the acceptance, not only of a secondary role, but of a position outside the sphere of high politics which prove indisputably that Kossuth was following his own direction.

The important achievements which filled these fifteen years contributed more towards the final outbreak of March than all the activities of the politicians. Finding no place in the parliamentary arena, he resolved to forge for himself a new political weapon. The editorship of the parliamentary reports was at best a political expedient. The object of the paper was to supply facts; his task was that of a short-hand reporter with permission to edit his short-hand notes. He was appointed because he wrote the best Hungarian: he was selected as a stylist. But only the suspiciousness of the Viennese secret police, the uneasiness of Sedlnicky and his creatures who had had their worries with stylists and poets, with Grillparzer and Bauernfeld, signalled a warning against this risky enterprise. Never yet had there been a news organ chronicling parliamentary transactions. Was it intended to submit the debates to the censorship of the general public? Was an attempt being made to involve the nation in the diplomatic guerilla warfare which the Government was incessantly waging with the fractious nobility? Printer's ink stinks in the nostrils of all police: the stoppage of the printing presses keeps the political atmosphere clearer. But Kossuth already knew a way to defy the prohibition: a lithographed newspaper might fall under the censorship laws, but a written one was free. And he came out with the startling announcement that he would dictate his reports and have them copied by hand.

Once again the ukase meant to hinder became a help. For now the only way to play the editor was as an orator. Enthusiastic younger members immediately volunteered to write to his dictation. When one to-day examines the large white sheets of paper one is lost in admiration of the beauty of the handwriting in which these painstaking young revolutionaries-to-be so devotedly followed their future leader. Among them can already be noted the profiles of ripening men of action: Szemere and Pulszky, comrades of Kossuth in the tempestuous days of March 1848.

His employers in the liberal opposition were delighted at this shift. But no one as yet suspects that Kossuth was consciously elaborating for himself an instrument to ensure the maximum effect of his words, ideas and personality. And now—as can be seen from drawings of the Pressburg Diet—he sits at the window, facing the desk from which the speeches are made, behind the benches of the deputies, but no longer among the crowd of delegates, nor yet among the junior members. He has his own special place apart, a somewhat uncomfortable seat on the window-ledge. This is his observation-post: and in fact he is no more than an observer allowed, as silent witness, to commit to paper what the great leaders of the nation and the representatives of authority say. But anyone observing him cannot fail to remark that his pencil does not dutifully fly across his pad: he devours every word, enjoying the battle of argument with all his senses, like a spectator at a play, and the tension of his expression betrays that he is thinking with the speaker and, in his ever-alert imagination, rambling beyond the words that reach his ears. The observer had become a silent actor in the drama.

As soon as the written reports appear they are disseminated far and wide. In those days no newspaper in the land dared open its columns to political discussion. The political "leader" was unknown and only the subscribers of the *Augsburger Allgemeine Zeitung* learned what was happening in the world. The name of Armand Carrel, the creator of the modern leading article, who had just then launched into attacks of unprecedented temerity against the Government of the citizen king of France, was unknown in Hungary. Lajos Kossuth, denying himself the weapon of speech, created for himself a new one: the newspaper. The book, the printed work, had always since the days of Erasmus been the instrument of the spirit. Now, to keep pace with the hustling nineteenth century, ideas must be propagated by quicker and more adaptable methods. Kossuth was the first to grasp this new power. The "manuscript newspaper," dictated by the observer on the window-ledge, awakened the slumbering villages of the counties. While the reformer Széchényi laid bricks, Kossuth kindled fires: he fought while the nation's leaders talked. And in the famous words of Victor Hugo in his speech on the fighter Voltaire, we may ask: "And what weapon did he use?—A pen!"

For after a very few days, and then with increasing clearness, Kossuth's reports revealed themselves as provocatory leading articles. Admittedly he reported. His memory retained the exact sequence of the speeches, but he knew how to shift accents, to separate the significant from the unimportant, to give prominence to the radicals and to unmask the reactionaries. In the Diet the fight remained as insipid as a drawing-room charade, save for a rare passionate outburst from Wesselényi. But infused with Kossuth's dynamic fury the carefully chosen phrases of the speakers rang like a trumpet-call to insurrection.

More and more resolutely Kossuth threw himself into his task: he was determined to din into his readers the consciousness of their national obligation. The debates dealt with every phase of public life: every agenda was the subject of heated discussion. The representatives of the ruling castes, the State, the Church and the feudal classes, produced spokesmen of conviction. Often the session attained the level of a scientific argument, but then again the mention of some injustice or an incautious remark proffered by some arrogant churchman let loose smouldering dissatisfaction. Kossuth kept silent, the seismograph registering shocks and earthquakes. But afterwards his colourful description breathed a creative spirit into the picture. He knew the phrases the century had coined which would stir his fellow-countrymen: the expression "liberty of conscience" which he first came across in Schiller in his schooldays now found an echo and gained aptness from the present. The nobles in the provinces devoured his paper, passed it from hand to hand and read it aloud at meals. Many sent their hussars to Pressburg to make certain of securing regular copies. The circulation grew until at last there was no option but to have the paper lithographed.

Now Kossuth can wax bolder. Already he makes slight alterations in the text of the speeches; he puts his own words into the mouths of deputies who think as he does; he suppresses the arguments of his opponents. It becomes increasingly obvious that the servant is becoming the master, the observer on the window-ledge triumphs over the orators in the assembly. The debates are transmuted by Kossuth's touch, giving the reader whose eyes have been opened by this gradual education to recognise that only a nation, united and aware of its own strength, is able to fight the battle for freedom.

The battle for freedom! How different is this slogan from that to which Széchényi devotes his tireless energy! Széchényi desires reform, Kossuth independence. Széchényi aims at making his country contented, Kossuth at liberating it. At the same moment the Count's latest writings claim attention. As a free and wealthy magnate he is able to pour out his ideas in these new books, whereas Kossuth must painfully fight his way to the nation as a paid reporter. It is true that Széchényi has travelled, studied the civilisation of Western Europe, he has the right to stand up before a Hungary sunk in medieval slumber and claim the role of a *præceptor Hungariæ*. He too seeks to educate. But his education—what a difference!—takes as its model the gentleman who has passed through Eton or Harrow, Oxford or Cambridge. The complete aristocrat Széchényi is fascinated by the image of an English lord. In all seriousness the Count begins his work of civilising his country after the English pattern: like a restaurateur who places palms and plants in pots on the pavement so as to transform the space into a garden, Széchéyni seeks with externals to rejuvenate and Europeanise his country. He is afraid of the reality so hopelessly behind the times. His new book *Light* promises all manner of innovations: his aim is to establish prosperity, to avert the dangers of floods, to regulate the Danube and the Theiss, to make the rivers navigable, to found industries. His eagerness is unappalled by any amount of work; he studies the writings of specialists, he wrestles with statistics, quarrels with architects about the construction of his pet bridge over the Danube and superciliously ignores the ridicule of his ideas on horse breeding and horse racing. Who could dispute his position as educator of his country?

Already in their first literary attacks Széchényi and Kossuth are worlds apart. Their antagonism is an antagonism of the spirit. And therefore at first blush it seems irreconcilable. Széchéyni converts the nation's economic life, Kossuth its heart. Széchényi's books and Kossuth's reports convulse the world before the revolution: the former decide the niveau of the pre-revolutionary struggle, the latter its élan.

One must be careful how one uses clichés, hastily formulated conceptions. If we call Kossuth's idea liberal, there is a basic difference between his liberalism and Széchényi's. Kossuth as yet knows nothing of economic factors: his object is to serve the emancipation of Hungary. But, despite his brilliant reputation in the provinces, in the eyes of the lords in Pressburg he still bears the stigma of the journalist. There is no evidence that Kossuth made any effort to overcome this undervaluation other than to continue his work. Was it not sufficient that three years' activity had made him the best-known figure in every district of Hungary? He had every reason to be proud of his influence. If the day of insurrection now dawned, would not his readers, that is the whole aristocracy, follow him? He must have been filled with this belief and the bright reflection of his fame spurred him to greater audacity. By now in his reports the speakers in Pressburg all spoke Kossuth's language. They had his pathos, they had his ideas. And scarcely any longer disguised under the make-up of actors not himself, Kossuth appears in person, like an actor performing all the parts at once. Like Shakespeare's Bottom, he wants to play the lion too: he even tries to transfuse Wesselényi's clumsy Transylvanian style with the magic of his own. And in the provinces men repeat the mighty sentences, the pithy slogans, the memorable phrases, and they know Kossuth is the orator who spoke them.

And so his power grew. And then suddenly, as always in his life, a bolt out of the blue toppled him from his pedestal: on the 8th February, 1835, a royal command dissolved the Diet. His job ceased to exist. He was again without livelihood. His lips were sealed. But he had one last opportunity of speaking to his readers and this "Farewell to my readers" called forth all his energies, the passion of his temperament and the force of his conviction. This time he really addressed the people as an agitator.

He admits: "This is the first time that we strive to excite the masses."

The masses? This is the first time this word is heard. This is no longer the talk of a liberal doctrinary: this is the voice of a new figure for which this bourgeois liberal age had forgotten the true name: the demagogue. Since the days of Mirabeau, since the end of the great Revolution, it had been forgotten that there existed below the classes of subjects, ordained by God and made secure by the "System," a conglomerate known as "the masses." Only Metternich was aware of the peril of this monster, this many-headed chimera to which all civilised life falls victim. And now a journalist dares invoke the masses! A word as incredible as the call he makes to it.

He begins: "Our hand trembles as we take up the pen to set down our report of to-day's session. Our heart is filled with courage and anger, and in our present temper the sword would be more fitting in our clenched fist than the quavering pen. We have never yet agitated, never sought to incite the masses and kindle the fires of civil war, and if there is any reproach which the Austrian party can level against us, it is that ever since the beginning of our journalistic career we have steadfastly adopted a Magyar point of view."

What is the meaning of this *captatio benevolentiæ?* At the very beginning of this "report" stands a new, strange, impudent, inflammatory word, unheard since the days of Rákóczi and only timidly whispered when again rumours spoke of risings in Paris, the word: civil war. The loyal Hungarian read it in alarmed astonishment: he did not repeat it, but at the back of his mind it remained alive and grew: for big words live like creatures and, once they are born, cannot be banished from an epoch. Civil war! For thirteen years the idea smouldered in the subconsciousness of the people from the day the word was uttered.

Kossuth asserted that he had never transgressed the limits of legality and yet "this has not prevented the Austrian authorities from harrying our paper incessantly with the most odious persecution. But every time their plan foundered on our own steely purpose and the energy of our doughty representatives. And so they have tried by one magnificent blow to achieve what they have failed to accomplish by intrigue, and to-day was the day on which the hideous storm which has long been gathering on the Vienna horizon burst on our poor country. Loud is the fury of the tempest, but nevertheless our voice shall penetrate the thunder: it is a cry of distress we utter, an anxious cry of desperation, to startle the nation from its sleep of inactivity and to spur it to decisive action. As the screech of the stormy petrel pierces the hollow howling of the wind, so shall our voice, foretelling a mighty tempest such as has never yet been seen, ring out above the tumult of the present storm."

One can recognise in these lines the true pathos of an orator. At this passage the young men to whom he was dictating are said to have sprung to their feet and surrounded Kossuth. Whereupon, fired by their youthful enthusiasm, he found the incendiary phrase—a sentence which introduced a new epoch in the history of south-eastern Europe, the epoch of nationalism: "But one cry forces itself from our throat, a cry which repeats itself as often as we try to utter any other sound: 'Hungary, awake!'" From that day every nationalist movement has imitated Kossuth's awakening cry. A century has passed since this first shout of a new nationalism and still the alarum Kossuth coined re-echoes through the nations. Now for the first time Kossuth declares that his appeal is not made to any particular caste or class: he demands the rising of the whole people. At last he publishes his real aim, reveals his political idea.

He showers angry reproach on Austria: "We have left no

sacred privilege which has not been mauled by the clumsy hand of Austria." And he paints in lurid colours "the black night of slavery which has descended on our country." But already a practical political purpose appears behind the pathos of the demagogue: "We have in superabundance every commodity that Man requires: corn, wine, tobacco, wool, cattle, we have iron too and no lack of money, the nerve of war." And he calculates that the surplus of raw materials, the favourable situation of the Hungarian harbour on the Adriatic, Fiume, and finally the population of fifteen millions make chances very auspicious even in the event of a war against Austria.

The words "rupture with Austria" have been uttered. And what is the reason of this insurrectionary appeal? The king has dissolved the Diet, "and consequently it will occasion no surprise that we have dipped our pen in the red ink of anger." But, even if all have left the house "in silent dignity," "there still remain behind those who have the right and duty to criticise." Proudly Kossuth particularises: "We, the journalists!" It is the journalists' task to present a definite protest in the name of the nation to the faithless king. And carried away by his own temerity, Kossuth gives utterance to the last most dangerous, terrible and significant word: Revolution. "Is not the Austrian government itself taking its stand on the ground of revolution and thereby giving us justification for drawing the sword in defence of our legal right?"

Thus Kossuth, the journalist, lit the torch of insurrection. The land did not immediately catch fire; but the spark was never more extinguished.

III

The Torch of Insurrection

THE WORD REVOLUTION HAD BEEN UTTERED—A WORD WHICH cleared the situation in Hungary in a flash. The word travelled through the chancelleries of Vienna, it disturbed the army of officials and goaded the weary minions of the secret police to fresh activity. Vienna again directed the apparatus of its power against Hungary. For an event which had happened towards the end of the long session had already brought about a change in the policy of Vienna: the Emperor Franz died. The oppressed nationalities of the monarchy gave thanks that this menace had been removed. His successor Ferdinand, weak-minded to the point of imbecility, could not be worse. It was taken for granted that Metternich would rule for him and it was expected that he would replace the brutal obstinacy of the late emperor by a more tolerant system. Now that the emperor was dead the oppressed regions dared to give him his true name; in Milan and throughout the Italian provinces it was openly related that he had persecuted the heroes of the "Risorgimento" with a petty, sadistic, bestial revenge. Silvio Pellico, Frederico Gonfalonieri and those who had ventured upon the first fight for freedom in Austria and risked their lives for the ideal of a united Italy were captured and condemned. Their prison in Moravia was a veritable hell. Their gaoler—it is hardly credible—was directly responsible to the emperor who regulated their daily routine, himself devising tricks to torture them. At his order the young women who were condemned to imprisonment for life were kept waiting years for news of their nearest and dearest. He forbade all reading matter to the poets whom he kept in cages. The "good Emperor Franz" gloated over the daily reports of his servile gaoler. The Spielberg was the toy of his personal revenge. Silvio Pellico was able to describe his imprisonment in an imperishable book; it was the first grave accusation against Austria. The accusation of a poet. Was it any wonder that in Vienna the pen was more dreaded than the bayonet? Insurrection and literature, revolution and intellect were synonymous in the eyes of the "System." Even Grillparzer's attack in Vienna itself advanced in ever bolder verses; from Germany the poems of a young phalanx of liberal and democratic tendencies were heard across the frontier—and now in Hungary Kossuth spoke the word: revolution.

Metternich, now all-powerful, dismissed the Hungarian chancellor, Count Reviczky; Count Fidel Pálffy, his successor, was the same who had engaged as administrator the first great leader of an opposition, Pál Nagy. He was skilful in making inconvenient opponents innocuous. Those whom he might be unable to cope with could be dealt with by the secret police. Metternich now turned a sharper eye on Hungary. Count Széchényi had sent him a dedicatory number of the *Hitel.* Metternich of course recognised that there was need of many reforms in this neglected land; he was not opposed to reforms, for, as he stated: "By reform I understand an amelioration of conditions on the existing basis."

He was concerned with maintaining existing conditions in the face of such dangers as popular exasperation and the insurrection of any national group. The "creeping malady" of revolution was abroad in the provinces, but he, Metternich, was "the old doctor in the hospital of the world." He knew how to nip the disease in the bud before the epidemic broke out. Already in 1819 he had driven out the intellectuals as, in his opinion, there were "no more miserable conspirators than the professors"; in the twenties he had made short work of the Carbonari; and now in 1837 he was still vigorous enough to draw the sting of this Hungarian journalist. For this wise observer of the changes and movements in the life of the State knew that it is not material conditions, but a new spirit which imperils the stability of order. Metternich, the æsthete, the friend of Wilhelm von Humboldt, the best-read and most philosophically trained mind among statesmen, who had been one of the few to recognise the genius of Balzac, directly feared the intellectual. In this year he said to Anastasius Grün: "I make a distinction between thinking, speaking, writing and printing. Thinking? Yes, that is free. Man is born free. Writing like thinking is free. But printing is quite a different matter. There the State must draw the rigid lines which we call censorship." Censorship—to prevent "the daily dose of a pernicious press from corrupting the honest opinions of the middle classes." "Metternich recognised the new power of the press," says Srbik, therefore he persecutes every liberal movement in the press with the greatest energy."

When he read Kossuth's "Farewell to my readers" measures were decided on. The first question for Pálffy, the executive in Hungarian affairs, was whether Kossuth stood alone. Was he not already the captain of a young guard? Were not the younger members of the Diet solid behind him? Metternich scented the secret society which was preparing the revolution in Hungary. His belief was that "all revolutions are the work of secret societies." Gentz called this conviction "Metternich's original falsehood." But the old statesman had tasted the experience of many decades; it had always been youthful societies, whether they called themselves Burschenschaftler or Carbonari, Tugendbündler or, as now, the Reichstagsjugend, who had hewn the breach in the firm structure; and those who held subversive ideas were always ready to hurl the torch of insurrection. The Reichstagsjugend must be watched.

Like other youthful societies they were steeped in romanticism. Bismarck accused the Burschenschaften of "a blend of utopianism and lack of education." It was expedient to take precautions lest these Hungarian hotheads, temperamentally more passionate and infected by Kossuth's pathos, be driven to a real insurrection.

And the danger existed. For already the younger members of the Diet were organising themselves into an independent body. The Diet was dissolved, they held together. What had the Diet achieved? Nothing. Once again it had exhausted itself in complaints and grievances.

Now the deputies went home. Kossuth turned to Pest, hoping to find here a field for work. He was a good weapon; someone would find him useful. A stormy wind blew from Vienna. The reaction was preparing its counterstroke. Now that the leaders of the nation had returned to Pest the National Club once more became the focus of political life. Kossuth was not a member; Széchényi had only invited to membership those who subscribed to his ideas, but Balogh and Wesselényi were so convinced of the importance of the young man that they forced the Count to admit him. Széchényi hesitated, scenting the antagonism of this man who had found a way to reach the people. Was he, Széchényi, to smooth his entrance to the nobility?

Admission to the National Club meant a great deal to Kossuth. Széchényi was forced to yield. The friendship of Wesselényi was too important to risk over such a question and Wesselényi insisted. Ever since he had first met Kossuth he had, to quote his own words, "fallen completely under this man's spell." It was clear that Kossuth had no desire to remain idle. If he had been able to edit a paper for the Diet, why should he not bring out a newspaper in Pest to mirror the political activities in the provinces? His proposal was taken up enthusiastically. The printing press was brought from Pressburg to Pest and set up in the County Hall. Kossuth could now begin.

He skilfully built up an organisation. The brains of the Reichstagsjugend were employed. In each of the sixty-three counties were posted two confidential agents, schooled by Kossuth, familiar with his style and imbued with his ideas. They sent their reports to Pest by express messengers. Haiduks galloped spurring their horses through the land from the hills of Tokay and from the Turkish frontier, from the western outpost of Pressburg and from the distant forests of Transylvania, to deliver the political reports to the chief editor. So greatly had the feeling of the country changed; the majority sided with the opposition; Kossuth was their man.

At the switchboard where these newly developed currents of energy converged sat Kossuth. The brief bald reports of his well-schooled assistants sufficed; Pressburg had familiarised him with almost every political speaker. Now again he recast their words and from the rich material created a fresh, more forcible and more aggressive presentation of the fight within the kingdom. The counties learned that the movement was growing everywhere. Once again in the crucible of his imagination even circumspection was made to glow with a seditious heat.

But it must not be thought that it was Kossuth's fanaticism that set the land in flames. It was rather that now for the first time this bleeding country found a court where it could voice its grievances. The hope that with the death of the Emperor Franz an era of conciliation would dawn was not fulfilled. Already it was beginning to be asked whether the imbecile Emperor Ferdinand were not a greater misfortune for Hungary than his predecessor. The spirit of the Emperor Franz still raged in the offices of the secret police, more shamelessly, more undisguised than ever. Metternich was resolved to stifle this "awakening" before the sleeper had time to rub his eyes. The July revolution of 1830 had brought with it the cruel disillusionment that the order planned for perpetuity could be overthrown. On his orders Count Pálffy proceeded against the Reichstagsjugend. For these sons of the lesser aristocracy were not discriminated from the "subversive middle class" which was in Metternich's eyes the breeding-ground of all dangers. Not, curiously enough, the third estate, the industrial proletariat then growing up in Germany nor yet the peasant serfs of Hungary. The conservatives feared the nobility. The most disturbing symptom for Metternich was the fact that a man of ancient lineage like Count Széchényi was propagating liberal ideas in his writings and by the foundation of the National Club undertaking a methodical re-education of his own class from a feudal to a liberal way of thinking. But Széchényi was a man who must be dealt with indulgently. But his closest allies, Wesselényi and Balogh, were marked out for persecution.

The campaign against the Reichstagsjugend began. Pálffy reflected that Salvotti who had suppressed the Carbonari had made the mistake of giving the popular leaders Pellico and Gonfalonieri the halo of martyrdom. By striking down the anonymous rank and file he could lame the power of the leaders without furthering their popularity. The young romantics had founded a society under the influence of Börne's "Paris Letters" which, like the "Société des droits de l'homme," had for its object the "propagation of the rights of man." The works of Rousseau and Saint-Simon were studied and through Kossuth they heard of Lamennais. A young lawyer, named László Lovassy, began to learn French for the express purpose of translating his writings into Hungarian.

A club of harmless idealists. But every government determined to preserve the integrity of the State in times of great movements must first and foremost beware of ideas, wind eddies which foretell the storm and ring out a warning of the hour of crisis, and perhaps of death. The Society for the Propagation of the Rights of Man really believed that it was serving a new philosophy; Metternich knew better—that it was serving the forces of revolt. These young men might consider themselves as enthusiasts, but for Metternich they were enemies and their ideas a *potentiel de guerre*. It was Pálffy's task to find the tactically right moment to suppress the Reichstagsjugend. There must be no revival of the odious charge that Vienna was persecuting the spirit. Therefore, it would be a good thing if some palpable political excuse for persecution could be discovered. And they soon played into his hand.

Still glowing with excitement over the events in Pressburg and intoxicated with their new ideas, they forgot the self-control which should have decided them to silent patience. Lovassy, for instance, organised a march past the house of Wesselényi, a torchlight procession like those which had honoured the champions of liberty in Marburg, Göttingen and Jena. Wesselényi came out on to the balcony and Lovassy made a speech. He spoke well and the enthusiasm of his listeners carried him away. He said things which surpassed even Kossuth's "Farewell to my readers" in audacity. Wesselényi interrupted him, warning him of Pálffy's spies. But who amongst his audience could be a traitor? Lovassy ended with still greater temerity and provocation.

Who was the spy? No one knew. But the same night Lovassy was arrested. He was charged with inciting to sedition. A number of his associates were arrested with him, among them Szemere and Pulszky who ten years later fought at Kossuth's side.

Kossuth was one of the first to learn of Lovassy's arrest. He hastened to the newspaper office and dictated an article pillorying this outrage of the Government. But he did not publish it. He reflected that his hand-copied paper was only immune from the intervention of the authorities so long as he restricted himself to reporting the political business of the counties. He must wait until they interested themselves in Lovassy's case. And this soon happened. This arrest threw the country into a turmoil. Now Kossuth was able to combine the many voices of protest into one mighty accusation. He no longer hesitated to turn his report into a pamphlet. He risked his own freedom thereby and his friends urged him to moderation, for Pálffy's next attack would be delivered against him. They advised him to await the result of Lovassy's trial which was being prepared without loss of time. But already the Government showed that it was determined to end the hurried procedure with a deliberate deterrent sentence.

Austria was a master in the technique of political trials. The death penalty was an expedient which could only be employed in very exceptional cases. The smell of blood has the peculiarity of lingering for decades. Every form of bloodshed leaves its shadow on the image of royalty. Count Pálffy could depend upon his judges. The case was tried *in camera* and the counsel for the defence was excluded because he refused to swear the illegal oath of silence. The case for the prosecution was hastily put together. In some album or other Lovassy had perpetuated himself as a republican. Treason! He had further committed the crime of harbouring three Polish refugees. He had staged the torchlight procession for Wesselényi, himself "a suspect person." And he had made a seditious speech. Treason, treason, treason! A capable judge dealt with this evidence with a mastery of technicalities; every breath the prisoner drew was clear proof of his guilt. The witnesses for the defence were not admitted, while bribed or official witnesses appeared for the prosecution and the story in which they had been primed beforehand was believed. But was mere proof enough? Was it not necessary to make the accused a scoundrel, a warning to all honest citizens? A hasty search through the records of his past and Lovassy, "indoles perversa omnique legali ordini infensa anima," a knave, a lecher and a rebel, was sentenced to ten years' imprisonment. The sentence was upheld by the higher court. The Government ordered that the ten years should be served in the Spielberg in Moravia.

Kossuth was aghast when he heard the news. He had read *My Prison Experiences*, the cry of Silvio Pellico, the eternal model of all prisoners who bring their complaints before the unseen tribunal of humanity. Before Kossuth's eyes appeared the martyred figures of the strong but broken Federico Gonfalonieri, the delicate Alexander Andryane and the slender Pellico himself. Life in the Spielberg was an inferno, as Dante had pictured it, and the poet had the divine gift of making its horrors real. Lovassy would be the first martyr of the new cause delivered to this infernal prison. Scenes of medieval cruelty, tortures destroying body and soul, rose before Kossuth's eyes. He groaned. It could not be possible that this man in the full flower of his youth was doomed to spend ten years in the darkness of this hell. What was his crime? The passion of a new conviction, the belief in a better world, a religious fervour. It was hideous. What must be done to rescue Lovassy? For Kossuth realised, from the experiences of Silvio Pellico, that Lovassy's life would be destroyed. His fears were justified. When in 1840 an amnesty opened the gates of the Spielberg the young orator and poet was brought home incurably insane.

Once the first martyr of an idea has been created, the idea invariably passes from the realm of the spirit into the militant zone of reality. Now Kossuth wrote with less and less restraint and his tireless reminders succeeded in goading all the counties to a unanimous rejection of the Government's measures. Now the moment was come when, if the Government did not wish to lose the fight after its easily gained preliminary skirmish, it must prohibit this dangerous paper. The prohibition followed. The question now was only whether or not Kossuth would obey. Sooner or later the power of Count Pálffy would overcome the powerless journalist. It is true that the spirit conquered by bayonets and physical force has the tougher life and celebrates its resurrection after years of dumbness. Kossuth too was threatened with the Spielberg. And yet he did not budge.

Heedless of the ban, he went on issuing his paper. He worked now with redoubled energy.

Work and excitement had undermined his health. His passionate spirit dwelt in a body with small powers of resistance and his whole life is, like Goethe's, spaced with serious attacks of illness; physical breakdowns, probably of tubercular origin, are of regular occurrence. And now happened just such an interruption; Kossuth had to profit by the first warm days of May to recuperate in the clear air of the Buda hills. He was now the most popular man in Hungary. Alongside Wesselényi and Széchényi, he was already one of the leaders of the new movement. That was the achievement of an unknown lawyer from Monók after five years' public service. He was feared in Vienna and, since they had endeavoured in vain to hamper his activity, he was marked down for persecution. But the days of convalescence passed in peace. To-morrow he would return in renewed health to his work. Through the open window wafted the blossom-scented fragrance of the trees and meadows. Framed in the wooden square the plain stretched into the distance and deep below, beyond the faintly shimmering ribbon of the Danube, glittered the lights of Pest.

Towards morning Kossuth awoke. It was not yet daylight. In the twilight of the dawn he perceived through the window soldiers, standing stiffly like wax figures with their faces turned towards him. Immediately afterwards the door was burst open and an imperial officer entered and the familiar, hated words, the time-honoured phrase with which Might stretches out the fingers of arrest, rang out: "In the name of the King!"

Kossuth was taken to the old Bastion, the battlements of which adorn the Blocksberg. The Bastion had served the Turks; it had been captured by Prince Eugene at the storming of Buda, since when it housed Hapsburg troops. It was Hungary's Zwing-Uri. Here Kossuth was conducted, a man charged with high treason. A new Gessler in the service of the same Casa Austriaca had seized the person of a new Tell. His gaoler was a Lieutenant Sebes. Times had changed, but the old methods of breaking a "dangerous traitor" survived. Kossuth was refused pen and ink, he was forbidden all reading matter, and no one was allowed to see him. Did they hope thus to lull to sleep the prisoner's thoughts? Zwing-Uri, the Spielberg, the Bastion barracks—these were the *ultima ratio* of Hapsburg might.

The journalist Kossuth was deprived of his pen, his weapon stricken from his hand. Now there was nothing left but meditation.

IV

The Race for the Awakening

THE REBELS HAD BEEN RENDERED SCATHELESS; THE IDEA STILL lived. The chief of police could go on furlough with an easy mind, the chancellor kept watch. But those to whom he gave his confidence scarcely realised that Metternich was beginning to tremble for the empire. It was not those incidents which caused an occasional and passing fever that reminded him that his "system," like all flesh, must one day perish. The weapon of police force was a protection against small revolts. But in the womb of Europe were beginning the pangs which infallibly announce the birth of a new order. Liberalism was the opponent of the conservative idea of government. Sooner or later a new generation would lead the new idea to victory. Not to-day nor yet to-morrow. But might not his minister Kolowrat have been right when he warned him some years back: "The obstinate clinging to what is and this forest of bayonets must one day lead to revolution and to ruin"? A less philosophically minded statesman might have found a way to bolster up his system by a skilful and supple accommodation to the wishes of the only dangerous class, the *bourgeoisie*, and thereby drawn the sting of all revolutionary menace. But this did not occur to Metternich. He hated the middle class, for ever spreading unrest with its striving and ambition to rise above its station. Not even allowing it to participate in the work of government paralysed it. There was one other method of strengthening the status of the Hapsburgs without departing from the position of feudalism. The old and tried principle of *divine et impera* was once again brought out of the store cupboard of political wisdom. Metternich "had his finger on the pulse of Europe"; he felt the awakening of nationalism in several countries. Well, if nationalities were stirring, let them awake simultaneously everywhere. If the peoples of the monarchy awoke Hapsburg would be their master.

The formation of the Reichstagsjugend and Kossuth's cry: "Hungary, awake!" had had a curious effect on Prince Metternich. How circumspect and prudent was the undertaking of Count Széchényi, this magnificent attempt to aid the Hungarian national structure with clever reforms! But in Kossuth's speeches the spirit of rebellion showed itself betimes. Kossuth was crippled; but his appearance gave Metternich the idea of furthering reforms in order to cast out revolution. He actually believed that it was possible to promote the cultural development of nations while at the same time curbing their political development. "He failed to grasp," says Srbik, "that national culture of necessity brings with it the desire for national political freedom. Hitherto a strong shrewd administration had sufficed to satisfy the claims of those classes which were entitled to have pretensions; the nobility of Bohemia and Croatia were, like the Hungarian magnates, gathered round the throne, the feudal families were well represented in the ministries and the army was officered by the descendants of ancient houses. But the aspiring middle class was clamouring for its rights; let them therefore be given the sphere of culture so that they should not interfere in politics.

But was it not already too late? Everywhere nationalism reared its head and a militant spirit was evident in the younger generation. The problems in the provinces were different, but the most difficult again seemed to be in the land which Metternich had always looked upon as "a burden and an embarrassment to the monarchy," Hungary.

V

Martyr. Creative Interval

THE HISTORIAN OF KOSSUTH'S LIFE CANNOT ESCAPE THE FEELING that his arrest and sentence are purposeful links in the grandly conceived plan of this life. This fresh cæsura which interrupts the smooth development of his career severs him for three years from the world. The court, subservient as usual to the will of the Government, sentenced Kossuth to three years' imprisonment, not only as a punishment, but with the definite intention of paralysing this budding instigator. But can prison break a man? Examples were alarming. It was said that Lovassy had lost his mind in the Spielberg that had already destroyed so many lives. But Kossuth was brought to the Buda fortress where he was confined in a bare and narrow room to which the daylight seldom penetrated. The prisoner could cross his cell in four steps. Kossuth's sickly body, early wasted by the fires of exciting fights, suffered in the damp and chilly room; he thirsted for air.

With what careless lack of perception people speak of imprisonment. One must pace with Kossuth this daily to and fro between the barred door and the wall with the oval slit that lets in a feeble light, and back again to the door, always four steps, one, two, three and then the last which brings the body into contact with the damp cold wall that gives the physical realisation of his severance from the outside world; backwards and forwards, three hundred, many hundred times, until it is impossible to go on counting, and still the evening will not come. And the same pacing repeated every day, with the ghastly discovery that it must be the same for seven days until the bells ring out that announce Sunday; and then only a week has passed. Where shall the prisoner turn his eyes already offended by the drabness of the walls? How employ his thoughts which refuse to tire, never allowing the ego a surcease from introspection? How use the senses that long to feel, to drink in life, colour, scents? No one comes near him and now for the first time the prisoner learns completely the great benefit of fellowship with other men. What tragic irony! Kossuth sought the people, and because he was on the point of creating the closest human bond, he was segregated from society and placed in solitude.

When later Kossuth looks back upon the horrors of his three years' imprisonment, he writes: "I had to summon up all the strength of my soul in order to check the extravagances of my imagination in the interminable idleness of solitary confinement. I can understand that prisoners endowed with less strength of soul go mad in these conditions. To save falling a prey to my imagination I took refuge in meditation on practical objects. I calculated the deficiencies in the conditions in our land; I drew from them the lessons of my experiences and knowledge; I weighed each separate question and formed my own opinion. During my imprisonment I was often scared at the thought how far I should lag behind the progressing world. But I did not. In the solitude of my confinement I learned through meditation the lessons that life teaches."

Thus Kossuth himself feels this forced incarceration to be a pause in which his spirit was able to develop its creative powers. In retrospect one can perceive that this creative interval first made possible the full unfolding of his personality. His career was ruined and once again the basis of his existence had been cut from under his feet, but he had gained, what he could never have dreamed of, the glory of a martyr. If he came back, with mind and health unimpaired, the people would flock to him. The returned martyr would be offered the leadership, Kossuth resolved to prepare himself for that day. He wished to be ready for his task. He thought of the figures in history who had voluntarily withdrawn into solitude in order to reach their complete maturity. Wealth had permitted Széchényi years of travel and he had brought home wisdom which had assured him the first place in the land. Little by little Kossuth began to praise the fate that allowed him a rest pause in the battle.

At last permission was granted him to read and write. Now his imprisonment was changed entirely to a period of study. Kossuth had felt himself inferior to Széchényi in all branches of practical knowledge. What did he know about national economy or the practical questions of financial policy? What did he know of art and literature or of that magic island from which Széchényi had brought home his political wisdom, England? Kossuth had taken his bearings from the French, from Rousseau and Lamennais. In order to be a match for a Széchényi he must read Bentham and Adam Smith. He determined to learn English.

Kossuth set about the task of mastering these new subjects

with untiring energy. The days were now all too short. He paced up and down declaiming and practising the more difficult pronunciations. He learnt English alone and from an antiquated grammar, but he learnt it. In these two years he learnt this foreign language so thoroughly that ten years later he was able to carry away the public of Southampton and the House of Commons with his oratory. He read the English national economists. He sent for the latest work of Richard Cobden of whom he had chanced to hear as Cobden had sent it to Széchényi with a cordial dedication.

One should not overlook the importance of these studies for the development of his personality. Now for the first time the idealist turns his attention to practical questions. When he reappears upon the stage of politics he can count on opposing the reformatory impetus of Széchényi with a new well-weighed programme of his own.

But Kossuth never belies, not even now, his natural disposition; his poetic character was not altered by the necessary occupation with material problems. After the work that he imposed upon himself he permits himself hours of relaxation, contemplation and beauty. Once he is able to cope with the English language he begins to read Shakespeare. He keeps to the comedies. *The Tempest* fires his imagination the most. He learns whole passages by heart. In the third year of his imprisonment he is allowed occasional visitors; some of his friends see him and also strangers come to pay him homage. He is only allowed a few minutes of conversation under surveillance, but he is at liberty to make small requests. Invariably he asks for books. One of his regular visitors is a young lady from Pressburg, Therese von Meszlényi; she is the only woman to see him in these three years. He cannot say much to her, but he looks into her eyes and feels the human warmth of her compassion. At night the dream-like memories of his first idyll in Terebes blend with the angelic face of this young lady and the tender love-song of Shakespeare's verse strikes him with a different, personal emotion. Miranda takes on Therese's features and the forgotten trysts with Etelka live in his mind anew: Therese replaces his first love. He recites to himself:

"What is this maid with whom thou wast at play?
Your eldest acquaintance cannot be three hours:
Is she the goddess that hath severed us,
And brought us thus together? . . .

Sir, she is mortal;
But by immortal Providence she's mine."

And so the hideous bleakness of his cell is lit with a new joy of life. His fighting spirit is steeled by the routine of work and Prospero's magic transforms his prison. Kossuth who at first lived in the dread of becoming insane regains his strength and in the elation of his happiness he makes Miranda's exclamation of wonder echo from the white-washed walls:

"O, wonder! How beauteous mankind is! A brave new world! And he replies in Prospero's words: ''Tis new to thee.'"

But, strangely enough, it is this noble work too which guides him back to the great questions of statesmanship. Shakespeare teaches him that there is no dividing line between spiritual and earthly needs, life is whole, and the happy regulation of the external machinery first creates the basis of human happiness. Gonzalo puts into words Kossuth's own dream:

"And were I the king on 't, what would I do?
I' the commonwealth I would by contraries
Execute all things . . .; riches, poverty,
And use of service, none; contract, succession,
Bourn, bound of land, tilth, vineyard, none; . . .
All things in common nature should produce
Without sweat or endeavour: treason, felony,
Sword, pike, knife, gun, or need of any engine,
Would I not have; but nature should bring forth,
Of its own kind, all foison, all abundance,
To feed my innocent people."

Kossuth smiles. This paradise, depicted by the old courtier was not imagined for the present day world, when nature is bullied into yielding her gifts. It is the beginning of the age of machinery; in England industry has transformed economics and all Europe will bow to the new conqueror. At last the Danube basin will have to join itself to the great continental economic system. But out of Gonzalo's vision, the prophecy of a poet made two centuries before, can be heard the longing for the equality and brotherhood of man. *The Tempest* sings what Lamennais preached.

The idyll in the Buda fortress takes on a note of childish pathos: Kossuth accepted the present of two canary birds.

Pulszky describes how even his prison warders were touched by Kossuth's love for his feathered comrades in captivity.

One day—it is now 1840—Therese whispers that she has heard that the Vienna cabinet, reassured by the general stillness of the atmosphere, is intending to declare an amnesty. Kossuth thanks her for all the kindness she has shown him and, boldly translating the English into Hungarian, cites Prospero's words:

"O, a cherubin thou wast, that did preserve me! . . .
Thou didst smile,
Infused with a fortitude from heaven,
When I have deck'd the sea with drops full salt,
Under my burden groaned; which raised in me
An undergoing stomach, to bear up
Against what should ensue."

The amnesty actually followed. Kossuth was released. He did not forget to set his birds at liberty. But, Pulszky tells us, he strewed crumbs on the window-sill so that they should not go hungry. On the day of his release he came back to the fortress to enquire whether the birds had returned, but they had not been seen. And Kossuth remarked: "They were cleverer than I. They did not come back, but I did. But I shall never do so again."

VI

Return to Friend and Foe

THERE WERE URGENT POLITICAL REASONS FOR THE UTTERANCE of the magic word that restored Kossuth to unexpected freedom. His father, László Kossuth, had been untiring in his efforts to enlist the aristocracy for his son's cause and when at last his health broke down he composed a concise and insistent circular letter demanding their support. In this letter which throws a fresh light on his father's character his anger is restrained, his hatred scarcely perceptible. But neither does the censorship of his conscience permit him any gesture of entreaty. He baldly emphasises the fact that his son's paper, despite its manuscript form, was not in any way a private undertaking; he was merely its editor on behalf of and with the approval of the counties. Consequently it was the duty of every county to protest against this unjust sentence and to fight for its revocation. Not a word too much and no appeal to sentiment. Its tone eloquent of the Kossuth pride. The counties prepared a counter-attack against Count Pálffy, the most hated man in Hungary. But the Vienna cabinet would have been as deaf to their grievances as the Emperor Franz had been to the entreaties of the pretty wife of Federico Gonfalonieri, for Metternich's rationalist policy was influenced only by rational, and not sentimental, arguments, had not such a situation arisen as forces every government, even the most autocratic, to listen to the despised populace, that "herd of hysterical women and clamorous children." Once again there was unrest in the Italian provinces. The Quartermaster-General was demanding a material strengthening of the effective forces of the army. Metternich had to summon the Diet to vote the conscription of new classes. There was urgent need of a temporary lull in Hungary. The estates however, through the mouthpiece of Count Lajos Batthyányi, a magnate who had recently joined the opposition, demanded an immediate armistice as a *sine qua non* of any reconciliation. Metternich was clever enough to accept this ultimatum. He even went so far as to allow Pálffy to retire. And so on first of May, 1840 the amnesty was declared and a few days later the prisoners were released.

In the first ebullition of rejoicing at this happy occasion it occurred to no one to consider whether it were reconcilable with the principles of liberalism to send Hungarian troops to suppress the Italian struggle for liberty. But Kossuth, as soon as he learned of the connection, was the first to turn this question over in his mind. It gave him the first inkling of the future conception of a common action by the oppressed nationalities against Austria. Only Kossuth was able to gauge the enormous potency of the book which had fired this recrudescence of the Italian movement: Silvio Pellico's *Prigioni*. The effect of this book was tremendous; Vienna was forced to take notice of the menacing resurrection of the movement they had clubbed to death. Metternich said of Pellico's book that it was "more disastrous than a lost battle."

Kossuth was free. His first thought was for his comrades. How would they return? He learned that Wesselényi had lost his sight in the fortress of Gräfenberg and Lovassy his reason. He alone left prison in full possession of his faculties, tempered, matured and ready for action.

As soon as the news spread that Kossuth had left the fortress people streamed in thousands to the Pest bank of the Danube. He was received with cheers. In the evening the students came with torches to escort him in triumph to the County Hall. How often in the nocturnal hours of his solitude had doubts assailed him whether he had not lost contact with the younger generation. Had he not lost the power to speak to them after four years of silence? And now he was overwhelmed by the jubilation of the masses. The people—the people—had rallied to him. For the first time he was conscious of something he had never experienced, but had always yearned for, the love of his people. This was a day of victory. The will of the people had triumphed. Kossuth's longing was realised; the people was an actuality.

He returned with empty hands, but glorified with the fame of martyrdom. As yet no one knew how his imprisonment had changed him; it was only the patient sufferer that they acclaimed. The liberated martyr now overshadowed the figure of Count Széchényi who had worked in the comfort of his own home while Kossuth suffered for his ideas.

Kossuth was anxious to lose no time in taking up some

activity; to begin again where he had left off. Now that the people *was* ready to listen to him, he wanted to speak to *it*. As always in Kossuth's life, practical reasons were combined with his ideal aims. Just as great writers, for example Dostoevski, have piled work on work under the spur of poverty no less than at the urge of the divine afflatus, so Kossuth saw the necessity to make a living out of his political activities. He, the acclaimed martyr, was once again out of a job, without money, just as he had been eight years before. As ever his only capital was his fame.

Cares multiplied. His old father had died in the second year of his imprisonment. He had used up his last strength fighting for his son's release. In Pest Kossuth was reunited to his mother and unmarried sister. He was now the head of the family; according to Hungarian law he had to make provision for his sister's marriage and to support them both. He possessed nothing. He inherited nothing. He looked in desperation for a means of livelihood. Once again he endured the misery of poverty.

After his father's death friends had taken care of his mother. Wesselényi who had sponsored Kossuth's admission to the National Club was also the first to take charge of his family while he was in prison. His treatment at Gräfenberg had been less severe on account of his impending blindness and so he had been able to write his friend Ferenc Deák to start a collection for Kossuth. The collection realised eighteen thousand gulden. Part of it had already been spent when Kossuth returned home. After the reception in the County Hall, Deák, whose high intelligence already assured him the foremost place in the opposition, led his friend aside and handed him the remainder of the sum, ten thousand gulden, in cash.

Ten thousand gulden! A fortune! Enough to build up a new existence. Deák cordially begged him to accept this present as a token of confidence. It was a great and affecting moment for Kossuth. He accepted it, still undecided to keep it for his own. He eyed the little bag of money as if it were a sacred relic. He weighed it in his palm and hesitated. Did he foresee clairvoyant that this was the first of many times when he would be saved from ruin by the sacrifice of others? Or was he afraid that the acceptance of this well-intentioned charity would tie his hands in his dealings with the opposition group whom he might one day be forced to oppose? Was he reluctant to be under an obligation even to so genuine a character as Ferenc

Deák? Was it political caution or human scepticism that prevented him from accepting this gift? Or was it merely pride?

At all events he refused it. But for his mother's and sister's sake he accepted it as a loan. He meant to invest it shrewdly so that the interest on the capital might assure his mother a carefree old age. But the capital he declined, preferring to leave it in trust to a group of the reform party. However he abandoned this first idea, proposing to his comrades the foundation of an industrial syndicate.

This suggestion was a fresh and startling victory. Just as on his first public appearance in Zemplén he had triumphed as an orator, as after the first edition of his parliamentary reports he surprised everybody by his genius as a journalist, so now he astounded his friends as a national economist. The clever well-read Deák perceived at once the progress Kossuth had made: he wanted to give the purely agrarian Hungary an industry. Long-sightedly he pointed out the political perspective of such an economic undertaking. The land possessed raw materials, ores of all kinds, enough to build up a national industry. But if a powerful industry were added to the agrarian wealth of Hungary, it would become economically independent of Austria and this would be the first guarantee of a political independence. The lyrical orator had become a practical politician.

Among those present sat a magnate who instantly recognised the magnitude of Kossuth's programme, Count Lajos Batthyányi. He immediately declared his readiness to put himself at the head of this industrial syndicate. He also approved the plan to set aside part of the money for the foundation of a technical school. And thus the scheme was set in motion. Happy days followed. This was the beginning of a long series of enterprises destined to fill out the gaps between periods of political activity with economic work. Kossuth had found a new way to give his imagination scope: he was doing creative work and learning the poetry of facts.

His refusal of the collection money made a profound impression on his friends. He was content if the industrial syndicate paid sufficient dividends for the support of his mother and for himself he took not a single heller of this money. Later in England and in America he behaved in exactly the same way. He was determined to find an occupation. But where was he to turn? The Diet was already in session: it was too late to get a mandate as delegate. There was nothing for it but to find work in Pest. His friends advised him to recuperate. He looked pale and worn. He was invited by admirers to a rest cure in the Mátra Mountains and allowed himself to be persuaded. He would need all his strength. Life promised to be difficult.

The evening before his departure he asked Ferenc Deák to go with him to the National Club. To his astonishment Deák hesitated. Kossuth smiled.

"Are you by any chance afraid that Széchényi might not be very pleased to see me?"

"Have you already spoken to Count Széchényi?"

"No. I believe he only returned from Pressburg yesterday."

Deák was silent. Slowly he walked beside his friend to the still white building that housed the National Club. When they reached the door Deák could keep silence no longer. His was an unpleasant duty, for no Hungarian tolerates an affront. What made it worse was that Deák had a great respect for Kossuth.

"Széchényi has had you struck off the list of members."

Kossuth looked at his friend in blank silence. Deák tried to smile apologetically.

"That is the English club rule. You have been in prison. He can have nothing else against you."

Kossuth made no reply. He wanted to cry out that the ideas for which he had paid the penalty were Széchényi's ideas. The only difference was that he was less influential. No, Kossuth held his peace. In moments of the greatest agitation he was dumb. Then his brain worked feverishly, his excitement subsided, inwardly absorbed; to be stored up, an elemental force, and one day discharged in some decisive action.

Slowly Deák walked home with his friend. Kossuth only put one question; he asked whether Wesselényi too had been excluded from the club—Wesselényi who, like himself, had served a sentence of imprisonment.

"No," answered Deák. His broad good-humoured face clouded. His eyes spoke the words his lips were loth to utter. He knew that this hour had turned the two leaders of young Hungary into deadly enemies.

Cautiously Deák attempted to excuse Széchényi's behaviour. He was alive to the pain his communication had caused his friend. They were already standing at his door in the Ungar utca, but Deák would not let him go in. They went together to the "Red Ox." Kossuth's tongue was loosened. He could

PRINCE CLEMENS METTERNICH

From the Municipal Collection, Vienna.

not resist submitting to his friend's sane judgment an outline of his political ideas which he had worked out for himself in prison. Deák recognised at once that Kossuth was already following a different road from Széchényi. Kossuth had ripened, but the first and deepest impulse of his political aims was still: "Away from Austria."

"And how," asked Deák, "do you imagine this can be brought about?"

"It makes no difference how," answered Kossuth. "How can I tell to-day what European revolution or European war will bring about the change. But come it will."

On the third day after his release there was a general meeting of the Pest nobility in the County Hall. Kossuth was anxious to take the opportunity, before leaving for the Mátra, to thank them for their efforts on his behalf.

He spent the night preparing his speech; his first speech for eight years. It must be a confession of his faith; it must show that he had returned to win political leadership. Who stood in his way? Széchényi, only Széchényi! Never before had Kossuth dared to consider the Count who stood at the zenith of his fame as a reformer as his rival. He wielded the weaker weapon; he fought with the pen and now he had to start again, a beggar. And yet, in this hour, Kossuth felt strong enough to drive Széchényi off the field of battle.

Was Széchényi his adversary? Was not his behaviour, after all, to be explained by his exaggerated Anglomania, his ridiculous aping of London club manners, as Deák had suggested? Kossuth meant to force the truth.

Suddenly he had an idea. There was one proof of Széchényi's friendliness. He too had contributed to the eighteen thousand gulden which his comrades had collected. How had he forgotten that? And to set his mind at rest once and for all he fetched out the subscription list which Deák had given him. It was a long list, headed by the richest of his friends. Deák had generously given twelve hundred kronen, Wesselényi a thousand, a Teleki four hundred. So the list went on until it came to the names of the less affluent who had nevertheless contributed their mite. Where was Széchényi's name? Ah, here! Here it was, among those unselfish givers who could ill spare a hundred kronen. Count István Széchényi had parted with a hundred kronen for him and his mother, deprived of her son's support because he had been sentenced by Austria for the ideal of liberty. This man, who had sacrificed a whole year's income for the foundation of the Hungarian Academy, and was now working day and night to realise his pet project, the erection of the first solid bridge between Pest and Buda, had given a hundred kronen!

If a Count Széchényi flung a hundred kronen to the young martyr, a tenth of what Wesselényi and Deák had scraped together, he must have meant to show that he was not concerned for the fate of this Lajos Kossuth. Yes, it was permissible to construe his motive as an admission that Kossuth's return to political life was unwelcome to him. This pittance was intended to show Kossuth Széchényi's contempt, his exclusion from the club to humiliate him and to make it more difficult for him to get back into political life. Kossuth could not think otherwise; and retrospectively we may accept this interpretation. For history gives us the right to perceive in this apparently trivial incident the fortissimo working-up to the great duel between Széchényi and Kossuth which is now impending: yes, truly the germ-cell of the great Hungarian tragedy of '48.

The next day, therefore, Kossuth appeared at the meeting. He was greeted with a spontaneous ovation. Everyone knew that he had come to express his thanks and everyone waited expectantly for the martyr's first speech. Only Deák, sitting beside the almost blind Wesselényi, trembled. He alone knew the promptings of Kossuth's heart and he alone feared that his friend's passionate and uncompromising nature would impel him to avenge his humiliation on Széchényi. If he did that, a conflict would break out, a wound which would never heal. Then the prudent Deák would be placed between the two mortally antagonistic leaders of the Hungarian nation, but it would be beyond even his dispassionate steadfastness of purpose to reconcile them for the cause.

The audience opened their hearts to the fine manly presence of the "martyr," and, spellbound by the infectious power of his speech, guessed nothing of this secret antagonism. All looked upon Széchényi as a friend of the forty-year-old Kossuth, elder and riper by ten years' experience, and so they expected him to add a friendly word of homage to the Count—for Széchényi was now spoken of simply as "the Count." And Kossuth actually did what was expected of him. He thanked Széchényi. But how had his far-seeing political intelligence given a slight, careful and scarcely perceptible nuance to the expected words of thanks! In such a way that they must for all time remain a proof of his prophetic insight. For in this speech he coined for Széchényi the epithet, which to this day glorifies his name; he called him "the greatest Hungarian."

But the construction of the speech shows that Kossuth had only one intention. He began by thanking the counties. "It is close on eight years ago that my country's need caused me to forget my lack of power and decided me, a simple citizen without name or fortune, to tread the thorny path towards a goal. The road was hard; no one had travelled it before me, I was a pioneer; I had little strength and insufficient talents. I possessed nothing save an inflexible will and an iron patience in my still youthful heart. But I held on my way. The powers that be eyed me darkly with threatening glances and I became the enemy of all those who, like night birds, dread the light, and they became the enemies of my cause. I was the object of attacks; of open arbitrariness and secret calumny. But those whose purpose had no need of the protection of darkness, those who, like myself, were accustomed to take every step of their political life in daylight, those who scorned secrecy, became my friends and the friends of my cause."

His audience looked up at him enthusiastically. Only a man certain of his mission could speak with such self-assurance. It was true, whispered his listeners, that Kossuth had been the first to light the torch of insurrection.

Kossuth went on: "And thus, the feeble flame which my weak breath was scarcely able to keep alive, thanks to the encouragement given me by the foremost in the land, became a torch and by its light we were enabled to see how fearful was the darkness that enveloped us. In one important sphere we had already perceived it; it was illumined for us by that brilliant man, than whom I know no labourer for the re-birth of the nation more creative, more successfully assiduous whose work will last, like his, for centuries, so that in the annals of my country I know no greater Hungarian. Every Hungarian will always utter this man's name, the name of Count István Széchényi, with fervent thanks and loud veneration."

He was interrupted by a storm of cheering. This tribute to Széchényi seemed a noble gesture which appeared to guarantee the desire for solidarity between the two men who stood out more and more strongly as leaders of the movement. And already every tongue echoed the phrase which would never die: "Széchényi, the greatest Hungarian."

Only Ferenc Deák noted the exact phrasing and the hidden meaning. He had not failed to observe the lingering hesitation, the conscious emphasis and the suspicion of a smile at the word "one." "Egy nagyfontosságu térszakon"—in *one* important sphere—what lay behind this arabesque of admiration? What did this carefully puzzled out qualification conceal? What gifts did Kossuth allow the Count? He called him "creative," "a successfully assiduous labourer" whose work would "last for centuries. . . ." Instantly Deák perceived the true, the only possible interpretation of this encomium of which the underlying meaning and diplomatic polish had been covered by the cheers. In *one* sphere Count Széchényi might be accounted greater than any Hungarian, so much Kossuth admitted; but this sphere was not the sphere of politics!

If this reading is right—and it is right—then Kossuth had delivered his *coup de maître* as a politician. By differentiating the creator from the politician, he had struck the keynote of a new era. Soon the opposition party would be forced to realise that all Széchényi's constructive work could not replace the new political idea that Kossuth was pursuing. No one would ever speak of "the greatest Hungarian" except with reverence, but very soon the moment would arrive when it would no longer be possible to follow him.

If there is still any doubt of the intention in Kossuth's eulogy the reaction of the man best in a position to feel it must be convincing; that man was Széchényi himself. For he was there. He heard the speech. He leant back in his chair, his thin bloodless lips pressed tight together, the lines furrowed by contempt drawn down more sharply, glancing superciliously at the assembly with a self-conscious look that might barely be interpreted as an acknowledgment. He was curious to hear the first sentences of this tyro, this disconcerting martyr, whom he feared in secret. For Széchényi, for whom Hungary was a problem he had himself invented and that no one but himself could solve, felt the uncanny strength with which this young Kossuth was pushing himself to the front. Now after the opening phrases Kossuth had declared his esteem for Széchényi. What did this mean? Was this thick-skinned peasant from Monók impervious to the blow that he had struck him? Was he so contemptible that he came licking his master's hand like a whipped dog? Széchényi pricked his ears; his over-alert senses took in every flexion of the voice, every nuance in the speaker's gestures, and he noticed the lazy drawling over the words "in one sphere," and the curt, swift, meaning flash of the eyes that accompanied them, the flicker of a smile that passed over the youthful, bearded lips—and it did not escape him that his castigation was being returned with the subtle pinpricks of the weapon which this master of the pen appeared to wield so skilfully: the weapon of wit.

Széchényi rose and walked out with an air of boredom into the anteroom. But his friends waited for the last words of this stirring speech before they followed him. Wesselényi, guided by Deák, asked the Count whether he shared the general enthusiasm for Kossuth's eloquence. The Count smiled, that half Mephistophelian smile that unmasked itself and in his controlled superior voice, replied: "Kossuth spoke like a begging friar."

A begging friar, imploring alms? Such a verdict could only be inspired by hatred. It was the fencer's cry "Touché." Széchényi had understood.

VII

Marriage

HIS HEALTH UNDERMINED BY HIS THREE YEARS IN PRISON AND the excitement of his duel with Széchényi, Kossuth had finally to yield to the insistence of his friends and go to the mountains to recuperate. Contemporaries describe him as sickly and emaciated, aged beyond his eight-and-thirty years. His pale face with hectic spots upon the cheeks, his feverishly glittering eyes impress even laymen as phthisic symptoms and give cause for serious concern. His friends knew that Kossuth had a delicate constitution. It was hoped the mountain air would set him up again. Kossuth travelled alone. He approached the chain of mountains that fringe the northern frontier of Hungary. The Mátra suddenly towered above the plains, gay with the blossom of early summer. The carriage sought a practicable road into the mountains, but soon the traveller had to get out and continue through the dense dark woods on foot. Never since the idyll of Zemplén had he felt a complete release from all ephemeral life. The hills of Buda reminded him of his home, the low ranges of Tokay; the Mátra is wilder, more magnificent. He reached a height of three thousand feet, the air became clearer, he could no longer see house or village and, as in his boyhood when he wandered alone through the woods, he experienced a dream-like sense of isolation from the world. He stayed in a tiny village that made pretence of being a health resort; but even here he kept himself to himself. He lay in the meadows in front of his house basking in the sun and this rest-cure which he prescribed himself slowly gave him back his strength.

One day the post brought him a letter from his devoted Therese von Meszlényi, asking if he were agreeable to her visiting him to nurse him. He had no longer need of nursing, but he bade her come.

Summer was nearly over when they returned. He had asked her to marry him and the wedding was to be celebrated in Pest. But always in his life external unexpected contrarieties upset his plans. His bride was Catholic and he was Protestant. The priest in Pest refused to perform the ceremony. And again Kossuth was the centre of a storm, again through no fault of his. Religious bigots took exception to his marrying a Catholic. The younger generation hotly espoused his cause and many took it as a symbol that their leader was setting the example of bridging over religious differences. The scandal raged in the city; the country was in an uproar. The priest's refusal was condemned as a provocation and some hotheads were only too ready to perceive political motives behind the attitude of the priest. They had no doubt that he was acting on orders from Vienna, as subservient to the tyrannical system as the judges of Pest. Kossuth was urged to go to another county, but refused to give way, as ever determined to force the issue. His pride could not tolerate defeat, his stubbornness admitted no retreat. The Catholic priest pointed out the strict statutes of the Church: Kossuth must adopt the Catholic faith, or else Therese von Meszlényi must obtain a papal licence for a mixed marriage. But Kossuth refused. He demanded to be married, and the people were on his side. And now it becomes apparent that his name already had considerable power behind it: the Church surrendered. The wedding was celebrated and the pair were joined in holy matrimony.

Kossuth was thirty-eight when he married Therese. The peculiar character of this match is already revealed in the way it came about: before his imprisonment Kossuth had only met Therese once in Pest. He carried away no lasting impression of this meeting; for is it conceivable that he should not have written to her from his prison cell or from the solitude of the mountains, if he had thought of her with any feeling of love? No, Kossuth had paid very little attention to the girl. He construed the temerity with which she visited him in his disgrace as proof of her love of liberty and political sympathy; he assumed her attentions, her diligence in supplying him with books, as an expression of pity and womanly nobility. But she loved him. She came to him. Kossuth could not but succumb to such a character as hers. She was like Etelka: she did the wooing, hers was the energy. In the small provincial town of Raab, close to the frontier of Austria and permeated with the spirit of Austria, she had had a hard time of it because of her relations with the "rebel." He was enchanted by her sweet personality; he only hid from himself that her presence meant more to him than that of any other of his comforters. It was not an overwhelming passion, but rather a gentle gradual attraction that drew him to the side of this girl. The story of his marriage is illuminating for his character, for Therese was by no means pretty. But it is a peculiar thing that poetic natures, to whom one falsely attributes a yearning for beauty in the ordinary sense, are often charmed by the image of a woman who is not physically but spiritually attractive.

On all her contemporary portraits Therese von Meszlényi is obviously a lady. A lace cap frames her face, the wide white lace collar of her dark blouse sets it off and concentrates one's attention on the speaking features, so full of character. A high forehead below flat carefully parted hair takes up a third of the face, the long straight Grecian nose more than a third, and above an oval rounded chin is set a wide, but not pretty, mouth, smiling even in repose. The cheeks seem broad, but they give the face a masculine strength and do not suggest the fleshiness of a peasant type. The expression in the high-placed large eyes is one of cleverness, steadfast will and the superiority of knowledge, but they add no beauty to the face. There is no charm, but there is strength. The impression is rather pathetic; she is the perfect example of the woman who feels herself called to be the mate of a great man. Her aspect leads one to suspect, to fear, that she would lure even a cautious and unambitious man to dangerous enterprise.

Doubtless she foresaw that he of all men was destined to a steep ascent before he reached the top, but for the ambitious daughter of a wealthy family the top was synonymous with power. Perhaps her ambitious thoughts stirred the submerged dreams of boyhood, but whether she was the awakener of his ambition, or whether their union was but the meeting of two soaring minds, with her strength of purpose Therese brought him a significant dowry. For marriage is not only the reconciliation of opposites, but also the confirmation of similarities.

This confirmation gave the man the shelter that he sought, the woman the life's purpose that she needed. This marriage withstood the shocks of a long, tempestuous and unsettled life; no tremor shook it, no shadow clouded it. His faithfulness to his wife was touching and even the one lapse we know of in point of fact confirms that for Lajos Kossuth there was no other tie but this. (For anticipating we may say that his relations with Dembinskaja during his exile in Turkey have been explained.)

VIII

"With You—or Against You"

THE GOVERNMENT HELD TO ITS POLICY OF RECONCILIATION. THE leading politicians put their heads together to discuss the draft of a new penal code. Count Széchényi was still occupied with his suspension bridge or else negotiating with the banks about his latest project, the foundation of a Danubian Steamship Company. Throughout Europe in this year 1840, the murmur of pre-revolutionary ideas was hushed. It seemed as if the peoples, once stirred by the spirit of liberty, had sunk back into lethargy, resigned to go on suffering the old yoke of absolutism. Even in foreign politics there was a lull. The European powers had come to an agreement on the difficult problem of Turkey at the London Conference and on the 15th July of this year the London Convention was signed. Once again the "social frame of Europe" had been preserved. Only the few who had prevision and exact knowledge could discern in this apparently healthy organism the symptoms which showed that the disease had only been temporarily relieved, not cured.

Within the structure of the Danubian monarchy the policy of reconciliation with Hungary had only postponed the clash of ripening antagonisms. Metternich alone knew that the order of Europe was enjoying a merely artificial respite. Like himself, the system was in its dotage; like himself, the system despite all medical science must soon be in its grave. A new era was dawning, a new generation was advancing and it availed nothing to disguise the truth. Metternich dreaded revolution as a healthy traveller in a plague area fears the first attack of fever: he expected the revolution which would prelude the extinction of his world. One of the few penetrating observers of the times wrote that year in Frankfurt: "We are living in a dormant revolution; the atmosphere of society is pregnant with negation." When dormant revolution awakes, when the period of incubation is ended and disease manifests itself are dates determined in history by the accident of the moment. It is not the hand that feels the pulse and registers the fever that history holds responsible. The man whose hatred of revolution was the deepest, the man who dreaded it the most, knew best that it was inevitable. In these days Metternich felt the first attack of physical weakness; the old man's health was undermined by fear.

Two events happened which obviously bear the stamp of accident—the kind of accident that History uses as her messenger. Friedrich Wilhelm III died in Prussia and with the new king, Friedrich Wilhelm IV began a new political orientation in this the most important of the German states. "The old Prussia has ceased to exist, the new Prussia has not yet come into being; we are in a period of transition, always a dangerous epoch," said Metternich. And in this dangerous epoch a second accident revived the latent danger: it gave Kossuth back his weapon.

Truly an accident! Kossuth on the lookout for a new occupation found all ears deaf. While he was resting in the Mátra, discontent had been drugged. Széchényi was elaborating his plans of reform. Was it not better to advance with measured strides? Was it not enough "to educate the country?" Was it advisable after the first squall of 1837 had subsided to be torn into the dangers of a hurricane? Kossuth found no inclination for fresh activity and so he had no choice but to wait. But chance intervened. Kossuth was wanted and a place was found for him. A brief meeting, a casual conversation and finally a contract—and the face of history is altered! Already the fuse is lighted; it is now only a question of time before it ignites the powder magazine and then the "dormant revolution" will explode and contemporaries will know that they have been sleeping on the edge of a volcano.

The Váci utca, the pretty shopping street of modern Budapest, was even then the favourite fashionable promenade. Here in the midday hours strolled the ladies and the young dandies, influential politicians, society and those who would fain belong to it. The aristocracy kept to its promenade on the fortress bastion. On one December morning Kossuth was strolling in the Váci utca. It was almost lunch-time and as he turned into the Hatvani utca (the main street which to-day bears Kossuth's name) he was accosted by a strange gentleman. Kossuth did not know Mr. Landerer. He had heard that this Landerer had put his money into a newspaper, but he had never appeared as a politician, he did not belong to the opposition party, but what man who made his living by his pen would avoid a newspaper owner who wished to speak to him? Kossuth was without a job; perhaps Landerer had a use for him.

The conversation was very short. In his thin, lisping voice Landerer explained to him that he had created a new paper which was to be called *Pesti Hirlap;* unfortunately his editor had been taken seriously ill and for days he had been racking his brains how to replace him. Now chance had shown him the very man: him, Kossuth.

Kossuth promptly declared himself ready to accept the offer, provided that Landerer was able to obtain Metternich's permission for him, the prisoner of the Buda fortress, to resume his activities as a journalist. For one thing Landerer must understand: he was not prepared to make any concessions. "My programme is unalterable." Landerer replied: "I know that. Your name is a programme. That is the very reason I chose you." The two men shook hands. Landerer promised to go at once to Vienna to get a decision from the cabinet.

He returned a few days later. Astonishingly enough, he had obtained permission. No objection was raised to Kossuth editing the *Pesti Hirlap*. The first number appeared on the 15th January, 1841.

Kossuth was so delighted at this stroke of luck which offered him at last his big chance that he did not for one instant reflect on the curious way that it had come about; not even when to his amazement Landerer showed him the government's permission. It was not until many years later that it occurred to him that Landerer had acted according to a preconceived plan. Pulszky, later Kossuth's comrade in arms, suspected it. To-day the study of secret documents shows clearly that at the time Landerer was in close relations with the Vienna secret police. Thus by the tragic irony of fate official cunning overreached itself and the man whom it was intended to cripple and control was allowed to wax great—so great that he was able to annihilate his enemies who had given him back his only weapon, the pen.

The country waited excitedly for Kossuth's paper. The cautious publisher was afraid that at the beginning he would not get rid of more than two hundred copies; and in fact when the paper was announced there were only six hundred regular subscribers. But Landerer, a good spy and a still better business man, knew what he had in Kossuth. Even if he were somewhat tamed and his hands vaguely tied by promises, it would not be long before the real Kossuth would begin again to speak with the old infectious accents. Smiling, well satisfied with his choice, and sure of a successful venture Landerer gaily printed the first issue—three thousand copies. But these were not enough! The circulation rose from day to day and quickly reached five thousand, more than that of all the other papers in the country put together. Landerer rubbed his hands and no doubt his joy would have been unalloyed, had he not been harassed by the constant fear that some day an overzealous official might come along and despite assurances forbid the paper.

Even Kossuth was barely keeping to his promises. Certainly he religiously kept off forbidden subjects (the situation in Germany and dynastic questions), but there was amply sufficient material permitted for him to present the picture he wished to show: the true, unvarnished, painfully exact portrayal of the face of actuality. For the first time a journalist in Hungary dared to speak the truth. Officialdom in Vienna when it "insured itself" by prohibiting the ventilation of major political questions forgot that in every age authority is threatened by just this very danger: the utterance of the truth.

At the outset Kossuth cleverly and cautiously disarmed the suspicions of his readers. He concealed the systematic campaign he was initiating, the general attack upon the nation he was preparing. It is an old axiom that daily repetition of the same thing has a transforming and educative effect. The newspaper as a modern means to education had been unknown in Hungary; Kossuth was Hungary's first modern journalist. He stood behind every article; he guided every pen; for he was shrewd enough to make sure of prominent collaborators whose names helped to spread the paper. He let one deal with the question of the National Theatre, another with the problems of taxation; in short in the *Pesti Hirlap* the odious omniscience of a single editor was replaced by the knowledge of experts. But Kossuth reserved the important subjects for himself and when he wrote it meant a sensation. Now at last his supporters who had admired his faith and enthusiasm were able to see that he had mastered actualities. Hitherto there had been but one pioneer who had studied economic theories and sedulously delved in the tiresome tables of statistics: Széchényi. Now Kossuth showed himself in this field too "the greatest Hungarian's" peer.

Very soon the paper began to publish short articles descriptive of the life in the provinces. He conducted his readers through the landscape of his country, depicting the conditions there. With ever increasing clearness there emerged from the pages of the *Pesti Hirlap* a picture of the times, a drab and sinister picture that could not fail to arouse horror and disgust. Everyone knew of the distressful conditions in Hungary, but only when they were presented to the reader in Kossuth's language did they evoke a feeling of shame and anger. Was life like this? Was the country bleeding from such wounds as these? Was it really possible that political prisoners languished in prison for three or four years without even having had a trial? So it was true that half these illegally imprisoned persons were removed by typhoid; that peasants could be flogged at the mere whim of their masters; that the rights of man were trodden under foot. How often had there been rumours of arbitrary juggling in the assessment of taxes; now the paper pilloried this abuse outspokenly, not even concealing the names of the guilty officials. So it was a fact that roads were allowed to fall into disrepair purposely because the lord of one county in his narrow-minded stupidity believed that by cutting off the neighbouring county from the local market he would benefit himself and his friends. These were the conditions in the country! This was the unity of the nation! To what purpose had Széchényi struggled for fifteen years if remote villages and *pusztas* were still sunk in the Middle Ages. Certainly it was meritorious and important to embellish the land by brave schemes and noble buildings, but the fundamental task was to dig up the soil, to sow the seeds of a new basis of life and to uproot the Middle Ages. Salvation must come from below, not from above.

The reader in the most distant village knew that the hour was ripe: a new day was about to dawn. The impoverished nobility had long since approached the enslaved peasantry. All that differentiated them from the serfs was that they were not robots, that they were political members of the nation. They formed the "people" of Verböczy, "the miserable tax-paying plebs." For they had to bear all the burden of taxation, whereas the big landowners, the magnates, paid no taxes. Széchényi for reasons of political economy had made a stand against this immunity of the aristocracy. But Kossuth judged only from a humane standpoint. He was tireless in running down every medieval abuse. He who had read Lamennais could no longer bear the thought that men should still be punished by flogging in his country, that Hungary should lack orphanages and hospitals. In staring headlines—as we should say to-day—he published the news that in the course of the winter numbers of people had perished from cold and hunger in the streets of the capital and he added the challenge: "Such phenomena are not the result of transitory causes. The main reason of the evil lies deeper. The nation must awake to the consciousness of what is meant by the common good! It must absorb into its heart's blood the conviction that everything which impedes the full development of creative forces breeds misery and want and causes damage to all alike." And he points out that "the education of the working classes, that essential fundamental condition of national prosperity, has been excessively neglected."

The education of the working classes! How modern, how audacious that slogan sounded in the year 1841! Was it not sufficient to give the upper strata the manners of English society? Was it really necessary to begin with the lowest classes? But how was this possible, seeing that these serf and peasant classes were held in slavery, living outside the nation? And here, never forgotten and saved for this moment, was proclaimed Kossuth's most powerful conviction: his faith in the brotherhood of Man. It is the bible reader, the disciple of Lamennais, the believing Protestant facing facts with the clear sight of the seeker after truth. He was no Danton. He was—and this can never be sufficiently emphasised—no demagogue. He had no need to court the favour of those who were nothing to-day in order to use their help to raise himself to power. His position was assured, and every day the love of his readers made it more secure. If he raised his voice for the poor and the oppressed, he did so in order to lift them out of their animal existence up to humanity in the original Christian meaning of the word. Everything he did and planned, his achievements and his mistakes, was all part of a single purpose: to make Hungary a people.

The step from dismemberment to union, from castes to brotherhood, the making of a people out of a nation is historically decisive. It is not the casual benefactor, the reformer, but the creator of a new way of living, the prophet of a new meaning of life, that earns the love of his people. In one of his leading articles Kossuth wrote: "Hitherto a constitutional difference has been made between the nation and the people. Because these two terms are not synonymous, because even to-day the mighty bond of common rights and interests is still only a pious wish, we are what we are. We thought, poor fools, that unity made possible the peaceful process of transformation;

for the Hungarian aristocracy is strong enough in numbers for it to be able to reconcile its interests, in very many things, with those of the classes outside the aristocracy. And we believed that we might consider this meeting on common ground a bond of union in the melting process." For to him Hungary was in the melting pot. He hoped that the befogging mysticism of the Middle Ages would at last give way to perspicacity. "For the age of usurped reputations is over. Common sense is master. Common sense and science which knows no privileges and whose doors, like those of the star-strewn temple of divine love, are open to every mortal alike." In this belief in the divinity of Man he made his appeal to the privileged nobility to give up their selfishness and narrow-mindedness, to put themselves at the head of the nation and to wave the banner of equality of rights and constitutional progress. To them he addresses his proudly threatening summons: "With you and by you, if you are ready; without you, and even against you, if need be!"

Thus Kossuth opens the battle with a campaign at home. He had kept his promises; Vienna had no grounds for disquietude. For before he could march against the enemy without, he must first annihilate his adversaries within. He must educate and build up, rouse the lukewarm and form a battle front.

The echo of his appeal was stupefying; the magnates against whom his attack was launched felt the blow. But now there fell into their ranks the man who had first stood up against them, now undisguisedly Kossuth's opponent: Count István Széchényi.

IX

The Adversary

"ADVERSARIUS INFESTIOR QUAM HOSTIS." KOSSUTH KNEW HIS Livy. It was not the enemy in Vienna, but the adversary at home who barred his way. The *Pesti Hirlap* had won the hearts of the people. Kossuth had made himself the first man in the nation. Now was the moment for his adversary to come out into the open. Count Széchényi took the offensive.

Had not Kossuth always known it? The very first time he saw the Count in Pressburg he had an inkling that this man would try to keep him back. On his release from prison Széchényi had hardly troubled to conceal the hostility of his smile behind the mask of indifference. Now he lifted his visor. Since the memorable day when Kossuth had made his speech of thanks and Széchényi had walked out, the two men had not met. On the appearance of his paper Kossuth had expected some sign of life from his opponent. Would he be able to forgive his rival's growing popularity? Would he look on in silence whilst even the most respected and oldest members of the Reform Party, even Wesselényi and Batthyányi, more and more openly inclined to Kossuth, and actually became his most ardent collaborators? Széchényi could not help but think that here was a new grouping in the young movement, perhaps a split, the formation of an independent new party—and that its leader would be Kossuth.

Now Széchényi must show his hand. Now or never; for to-morrow it would be too late. He who had been the first to show his polemic talents in literary feuds again took up his pen. He wrote "The People of the East," a diatribe against Kossuth.

Thus Kossuth's most influential opponent sat in his castle, or in the club rooms of the *Nemzeti Kaszino*, a soured and lonely man, having no pleasure in his fame, because his glory waned while Kossuth's name was on every tongue. Indeed, Kossuth's shadow had fallen upon the Count. Birth had set him on a pinnacle above his fellows; he remained aloof from choice. He was ready to devote his energies to educate his country, but for those who lived in it, the people, his lip curled in an unuttered *odi profanum vulgus*.

If we look back and trace the curve which the hero worship of Széchényi has drawn in the book of history, we see clearly in this year 1840 a sudden drop which coincides with Kossuth's martyrdom, and only rises almost to the temperature of love long after his death. To-day, almost a century later, this posthumous affection of his people for the "greatest Hungarian" has found a remarkable renaissance.

Széchényi was lonely. He was hurt by the injustice with which his self-sacrifice had been rewarded. He reflected on all that he had done for Hungary. He had given her new life, intellectual activity, economic regeneration. And in addition the gift of beauty. His careful planning of improvements to the twin city Buda-Pest. His tireless energy had founded a drama league which was to bring to life a National Theatre; had planned the regulation of the Theiss and the widening of the Iron Gate, opening an unsuspected horizon to Danubian river traffic. Széchényi earned his people's gratitude, but he did not win their love. In silence the Count suffered this noticeable estrangement. Nothing betrayed the grief it caused him. As the great poet Arany said: "We never knew what was hidden in this heart of him whose garment was the snow of equanimity and the ice of disdain."

The *Pesti Hirlap* carried everything before it. The journalist Kossuth was already the most influential man in Hungary. Even the waverers and the indifferent were convinced by the way he grasped the nettle, pilloried abuses and painted the picture of reformed conditions. Then once again Széchényi returned to the attack, no longer insidiously, but openly.

Széchényi's attack against the *Pesti Hirlap* was a sudden denial of the very things that he himself had preached. He welcomed the government's policy of reconciliation and ranged himself alongside the system he had opposed and its master, Metternich. He proclaimed the dawn of a new era. He accused Kossuth of being a politician influenced by sentiment and not by common sense, of stirring up passions and tending towards unrest; of mistaking the clamour of the masses for the voice of public opinion; of idolising popularity, and chasing after the plaudits of the mob.

Not even Kossuth's own articles had stirred up passions as

Széchényi's pamphlet did. Nothing strengthened Kossuth's popularity more than this attack of Szénchényi's. For plain logic and an instinctive sense of justice told the reader that the Count was choosing different standards for himself and for Kossuth. And the younger generation which Széchényi spoke of with contempt ranged themselves closer behind Kossuth. But even men like Wesselényi and Batthyányi now openly went over to Kossuth. For Széchényi was wrong. Kossuth was not a politician influenced by sentiment. His three years' imprisonment had changed him from an idealist into a realist. If he stirred up passions, he did so in order to gather impetus for his political aims; for the Vienna government, however cleverly it might camouflage its real policy by a show of conciliation, could only be broken by direct assault. As a practical politician he knew that he needed the masses. He was one of the first modern leaders who realised clearly that without the masses behind him he was powerless. And so we have the historical paradox: that the realist politician has to woo the masses like a demagogue, whereas the rational politician, Széchényi, in his ignorance of the laws of mass psychology, tries to pursue an unrealist policy.

The consequence of this quarrel with Kossuth is of historical importance: the Count flees from Demos back into the arms of the court; he finds support in Metternich.

This complicated the situation more than ever. In disgusted amazement the liberals rally round Kossuth. Is the Count a renegade? Has he gone over to Vienna? His behaviour was incomprehensible.

The truth was that Széchényi feared a revolution. This phobia grew steadily into an ever-present obsession. But the idea of revolution is not presented to his epoch by any frivolous adventurer. When an epidemic breaks out, the victims of the disease know that it is prevalent as well as the doctors. No one can hide this knowledge. The victims of Hapsburg absolutism in all the provinces under their rule knew that the day of reckoning was at hand. And Prince Metternich, "the most experienced doctor in the great world-hospital," had known since 1840 that his world was moribund like himself. "The revolution must come," said observers in Vienna and Berlin.

Kossuth's star was at its zenith. He was now the hope of Hungary. The future of his country depended on him alone. He was no demagogue, courting popular favour. But he was the people's darling. Yet, as always happened in Kossuth's life, in the moment of assured success an accident, perhaps a misunderstanding, knocked the weapon from his hand.

What actually happened is wrapt in mystery, but we know that one day Kossuth, after four years' work as editor-in-chief of the *Pesti Hirlap*, asked the owner of the paper, Landerer, for a rise of salary. This seems justified, in view of the enormous increase in the circulation, and it is hard to imagine that Landerer would on this account have dismissed the man to whom he owed the success of his paper. However, this much is certain: that he gave Kossuth the choice of resigning his position or withdrawing his request, and moreover in a most high-handed manner. How are we to explain this incomprehensible behaviour on the part of a business man, as Landerer was, except by presuming the influence of political reasons? There is no doubt that Landerer was a tool of the secret police. Their cunningly hatched plan to cripple Kossuth had miscarried. His popularity had increased; he was the acknowledged leader of a possible revolution. His weapon was the pen? Very well, then, it must be struck from his hand.

Kossuth was dismissed. Once again toppled from his pinnacle, once again without employment, once again robbed of certain victory at the last moment. But he was no more the petty lawyer who had to leave Terebes because of an exaggerated affair. He was no more the Diet reporter who could be thrown into prison for his youthful impetuosity. He had become—Lajos Kossuth. Now Kossuth was sure of himself. If he were repulsed, he felt strong enough to take up the cudgels. But the time was not yet ripe. There was still hard work to be done before the hour came. The true revolutionary must know how to wait. But that was no excuse for inactivity. Kossuth had no evidence that Landerer was in the service of the enemy. He only guessed it. But Kossuth felt himself so big that he could afford to look his real enemy in the face. He could measure swords with Metternich.

X

When Greek meets Greek

SINCE METTERNICH'S OCCUPATION OF THE PALACE IN THE Ballhausplatz in Vienna, the doors of the Prince's study had opened to admit all the great men of the time, hereditary princes, generals and ministers, ambassadors from every country in the world, and also the foremost spirits of the age, except those in whom his police spies scented liberalism. To be received here was accounted an honour. In another epoch princes and cardinals pilgrimaged to the home of Erasmus; Goethe's house in Weimar, and later the Villa Wahnfried in Bayreuth, was similarly the Mecca of all ambitious dreams. The man who was received here was ennobled; he was assured of his place in history. Prince Metternich, the unassailable and, it might well be thought, the indispensable master-servant of his sovereign, only honoured with an audience such persons as he wished to reward for services rendered or those from whom he wanted something important. Anyone who visited Metternich had to pay for the privilege: not to him, of course, but to the state he served as chancellor. Even unknown gentlemen from Austria's provinces, colonels from remote frontier stations were suddenly admitted to the chancellor's study, pushed, as it were, before the footlights of international politics, like supers entrusted with an announcement vital to the plot. Hardly any of these visitors left the baroque palace as he came: he had first been enrolled in the invisible guard of creatures working for Metternich; if, on the other hand, he had shown himself intransigent, he carried with him the mark of Cain, ever afterwards to be the object of police surveillance.

In these *tête-à-têtes*, these private conversations, decisions were often reached where official conferences and lengthy correspondence would have failed. Metternich purposely cultivated this "system of interviews"; a psychologist *par excellence*, he wanted to look his opponent in the face, read his thoughts, estimate his strength and to spy out the weak joint in his armour.

He set out to charm, to dazzle, and to bemuse his visitors. His purpose was to bribe each one according to his foible. That is why a contemporary who saw through Metternich called him "the Circe of Despotism."

It is certain that Metternich's private interview with Kossuth might have scotched the Hungarian rebellion. Here for a brief moment the history of the nation and with it the history of the world hung in the balance. Metternich received Kossuth in 1844, four years before the catastrophe—and he let him go, the man who had come as an enemy, with hatred in his heart.

The story of this meeting is only briefly touched on in the available sources. But it is the dramatic climax, the turning-point in the development of the struggle between Austria and Hungary. Both parties have given their account of this interview; they have set down their impressions of each other, but they have not lifted the veil upon the subject of their discussion. We can only make a guess at what transpired at this historic meeting.

"Lajos Kossuth, tired of the ill-paid exploitation of his energies by the *Pesti Hirlap*, applied to the government for permission to publish a new paper and tried to further his request by a personal application to the chancellor" (Srbik). This is all the historians tell us regarding Kossuth's reasons for seeking an interview with Metternich. The date substantiates this explanation. Kossuth had quarrelled with Landerer over the question of his salary and the government in Buda had refused him permission to publish a paper of his own. But was this a reason for going to Metternich? What was Kossuth in the eyes of imperial Vienna at the time when he sought an audience with the chancellor? Merely a journalist. A member of that hated profession which was the object of Metternich's most ruthless persecution. "A journalist is a man who has missed his vocation," Metternich was fond of saying. Was Kossuth, the most notorious journalist in Pest, to be granted an audience by the deadly enemy of a free press? A journalist moreover without employment? Four years ago, after his release from prison, his friends had had to get up a collection for him to keep him from starvation. Where was the money? In what senseless enterprises had he squandered it? While Széchényi who was bitten with the same bug of liberalism had been trying to modernise Hungary, in close touch with Vienna and the court—what had this Kossuth done? Agitated, stirred up trouble, polemised. Impossible to entrust him with a newspaper. Had they not just got rid of him, with Landerer's help? Still more impossible to grant him audience in the Ballhausplatz, to give him the distinction, accorded only to the elect, of being allowed to enter the study of the chancellor. That was the opinion of Vienna, and also of Metternich's adviser, the Hungarian chancellor Count Apponyi. And yet this out-of-work journalist was received by Metternich.

It is a moot point whether tactical considerations decided Metternich to grant Kossuth an immediate audience. Certainly his maxim: "Meet your opponent" had always justified itself. Now, in the year 1844 this fellow Kossuth had already written enough for this shrewd observer to recognise the lion by his claws. He was curious to see this Kossuth, to hear what he had to say. And his main object naturally was to pull his teeth. And so the Prince gave immediate orders for Kossuth to be admitted. There can be no doubt that Metternich was consciously aware that this interview would be of historical importance.

Kossuth must have been equally alive to this when he decided to face Metternich, to knock a second time at the closed doors of Austrian arrogance. This was to be the crowning satisfaction of his pride; that he, the village lawyer of Monók, whose political career had been cut short in 1823, should now, after twenty years, be received by the guide of Austria's destinies almost as an equal, at least as an opponent.

His application for permission to publish a newspaper was only an excuse. Certainly his application would be granted, that Kossuth believed, and his political efficacy would be assured. He did not underestimate the importance of this object. But more important still was the chance of standing face to face with Metternich, the mortal enemy of Hungary.

But could he have believed that Metternich would grant him this privilege without a *quid pro quo?* Was it not a fortunate accident for Metternich, unless it was a triumph of the machinations of his secret police, that this dangerous tongue was silenced? Surely Kossuth must have asked himself the question, what would Metternich demand of him in return for his complaisance. For in Austria every favour had to be paid for. No one knew that better than Kossuth; no one had been more violent than he in pillorying this "system of bribery" to which even the most honest had succumbed. Was it possible that he thought Metternich would grant him a favour without asking anything in return? Or was it his sole object to learn from Metternich's own lips how much he was worth to him? Enough, he asked for this audience; and when, contrary to the expectation of himself and of his friends, it was granted with astonishingly little delay, he did not retreat. He drove up to the Ballhausplatz —Hungary's most dangerous and seditious agitator, to see the power behind the "system."

He must have been astounded when he stepped into the chancellor's study. There sat Metternich—he did not rise—leaning back in his chair, and beckoning him to approach with a tired and shaking hand. This was a senile, broken man. And the old man smiled; without condescension, without arrogance. He smiled ingratiatingly, with a suspicion of cordiality, a smile which instantly bridged the mighty gulf between them.

Kossuth was greatly taken aback. The despot was an invalid weakling. The unfeeling tyrant was an amiable old gentleman. He had expected to see a Mazarin in modern dress. And Metternich was no less surprised to find the revolutionary he was awaiting a man with the dreamy eyes and melancholy expression of a poet.

It is indubitable that Metternich knew his opponents, his enemies in the Hungarian camp particularly. He knew Kossuth best of all—at any rate he thought he did. He had noticed that he had undergone a certain transformation, that he had become more inclined to moderation and prudence. Despite all his bluster, signs were not wanting that this demagogue might gradually become fit to take his part in the work of government. Only recently in his farewell article to the readers of the *Pesti Hirlap* he had even proclaimed his loyalty. "The time is past," he wrote, "when our enemies can slander us by questioning our allegiance to our princes (!) and our government (!); when they were still capable of casting aspersions on our loyalty(!!) and suspecting our aims and motives; we are beyond all that, their calumnies have neither beaten, nor abashed us."

The man who had come to ask his permission to bring out a new paper was the man who had written this. Would it be clever to grant it him? Metternich was not sure. He meant to make his decision dependent on this interview. His plan—for a diplomatic fox of his calibre has his strategic plan ready for such a critical occasion—was simple: there were only two ways of rendering his opponent harmless: to overpower him, or to bribe him. There were precedents for both. He had tried bribery with Gonfalonieri and failed. He must have been reminded of the Italian's proud rejection of his temptation, as he read the proud conclusion of Kossuth's swan song as editor of the *Pesti Hirlap*. "One thing I claim," he had written, "and that is a clean conscience and the consciousness that I have never been influenced by base interests, that my conviction has never been venal, and that neither the frowns of the mighty nor the violent passions of my fellows have swayed my purpose."

Kossuth not venal? Kossuth—the Gonfalonieri of Hungary? The experienced sceptic smiled. He was curious to find out. Luck had often been on his side in these unequal duels where the one had behind him the exchequer and the whole apparatus of state, while the other stood there with empty pockets. Even Kossuth, despite this pathetic manifesto, must be malleable. Or why else was he there?

The interview was a long one. It ceased to be an audience; it became a conference. Metternich, past-master in every psychological difficulty, exercised all his charm and infinite amiability to smooth over the awkwardness of the first few minutes. He was clever enough to begin the conversation with a few general remarks on Hungary, a non-committal expression of admiration which flatters every patriot. He praised the country, he praised the new city of Pest (which he could scarcely have seen), he carefully avoided any mention of Count Széchényi; he even spoke of the "spirit of reform" in a more friendly tone than might have been expected; and only then, after this affable *captatio benevolentiæ*, did he let fall the words "conservation of the *status quo*," followed immediately by the antithesis "revolution." The preliminaries were over.

Now it was Kossuth's turn to speak. In terms identical with his confession in his farewell article which the Prince had laid aside a little while before, he protested that he had no idea of being a "revolutionary"; he again laid stress upon his "loyalty."

At this time, and even later, until the beginning of the March revolution of 1848, Kossuth took it for granted that Hungary could not, and ought not to, break away from her royal house, the Hapsburgs. All he wanted was a "free Hungary": free of the tutelage of Austria, free of the illegal interference of the Vienna central government in the rights of Hungary that were guaranteed her by her ancient constitution. In his view, Austria had no interest in the social, economical, and inner political problems affecting the situation of a separate, independent state which, in his opinion, Hungary was.

He explained this to the Prince, dispassionately, in clear, if picturesque, language, in his excellent German. This lecture, in spite of its restraint, was a threatening revelation of a serious and worthy opponent of his political conceptions. If Kossuth meant—and he honestly did mean—to be "loyal," by his adherence to the House of Hapsburg, well and good; but he still showed himself to be a revolutionary, more fanatical, and more dangerous, than Metternich had previously suspected. For what Kossuth wanted was not reforms which were becoming alarming in their accumulation; not regroupings which might eventually upset the balance of inner political power. What he wanted was: a complete social upheaval; an upsetting of the rigidly fostered order of society; a loosening of class restrictions; and as a consequence the liberation of that part of the proletariat actually living in a state of serfdom. This was anarchy; the destruction of the "system." This was revolution. The "peaceful revolution" perhaps, carried through without resort to arms, of which Metternich had so often spoken.

Kossuth had not minced his words. He spoke frankly, as he always did, and fearlessly. And Metternich, listening to him, enjoyed, what all the world could not but enjoy, in Zemplén or in Pest, as later in London or in Washington: the magic of that melodious voice, the richness of his picturesquely ornate language, the infectious utterance of the heart which gripped by the very honesty of its conviction. The old man began to like his adversary. He recognised his cleverness, his wit, his honesty, his greatness. And so, instead of resorting to the panacea of bribery, he sought to win him over by convincing him.

To the amazement of the courtiers waiting in the ante-room, this audience which had been fixed for half an hour lasted several hours. Metternich struggled to convince this visionary that, in the last instance, there were but two ways of thought: the conservative and the disruptive; and that his system was the best imaginable way of governing the vast conglomeration of states of which he was the head. But Kossuth only smiled. Here was the opposition of two fundamental attitudes, two philosophies of life, two types of mind: the classical and the romantic. It was no wonder that they did not understand each other. When Metternich called the political principle of liberty "disruptive," Kossuth smiled; and Metternich smiled when Kossuth dismissed the principles of order as antiquated. Metternich despised enthusiasm, he worshipped cleverness: as a statesman he was a mathematician, as a tactician a diplomat. Kossuth threw his whole soul into the fight; he hated moderation and the sovereignty of reason. "No pathos!" was Metternich's watchword. "I pride myself," he once said, "on never having mistaken romantic fiction for history." Compare this with Kossuth's: "Whosoever condemns enthusiasm, tears up Man's patent of nobility. The man who calculates without enthusiasm may be anything, but never a great man."

Metternich thought: "This young man, proud, ambitious, fanatical, a sentimentalist, is honest. His world is the exact opposite of mine. An anti-rational world. He hates moderation, he rebels against discipline. He does not know what judgment means. He is a fanatic. Therefore he is wrong. And I will put him in the wrong. A pity I have to fight him. He is very likeable."

Kossuth said to himself: "This old gentleman, proud, still ambitious, keen-witted, temperate, a rationalist, without any trace of fanaticism, is of course honest. He is 'eighteenth century.' He belongs to the dying epoch that I have to fight. He despises emotion, he knows nothing of the soul of the individual, much less of the soul of the nation. Certainly he has learned philosophy, but unfortunately it is the philosophy of the rationalists that he loves. He has read Machiavelli and Voltaire; I, Rousseau and Lamennais. There are no bridges between us. He is a calculator—therefore he is wrong. A pity I have to annihilate him. He is much more likeable than I imagined."

They could not understand each other. The conversion that Metternich was at so much pains to bring about miscarried. Now the more simple remedy must be applied.

The opinions of the historians disagree as to whether Metternich made a direct attempt to bribe Kossuth, or whether he only "cautiously proposed," as Srbik puts it, "that he should of his own free conviction support the intentions and actions of the government, and without in any way placing himself under a moral obligation, should himself fix the compensation for his expenditure of time and work." Even this euphemism makes it clear what his proposition was: that Kossuth should tie his hands and, for so doing, he could indemnify himself to whatever amount he chose. And thus, after several hours' discussion, the point was reached which should have been the actual subject of this conversation. Metternich tempted Kossuth, as he had tempted Gonfalonieri and a hundred others.

Kossuth's Protestant nature got the upper hand. Was he,

the descendant of the martyr of Eperjes, to let himself be bought? He who had himself been acclaimed a martyr? Now, after these hours of dignified argument as man to man, he was up against the Jesuitical cunning of the Prince who would stop at nothing to bring him to his knees. But he did not yield. He pointed out politely that he had not come to ask for a present or an appointment; his only request was that the chancellor, now that he had met him and learned his strongly loyal views, would revoke the unfair decision of the censorship and grant him permission to bring out his paper.

Metternich made one last effort to obtain at least some promises from his opponent. If Kossuth were not prepared to write for the government, for such compensation as he thought reasonable, he might at least engage himself "not to refer to certain delicate subjects," presumably all those which, if vented, might give a handle to the opposition.

Kossuth rose to take his leave. But the powerful impression which he had made on Metternich decided the Prince to hold out some hope of the licence he was asking for. He wished, as he expressed it, "to leave ajar the entrance to the government party."

Kossuth bowed. He thanked the chancellor with emotion, for the interview had agitated him considerably. But he went. Poor as he had come; without employment, without prospects; but as a man of honour, the son of his father, a true Protestant. His pride had predetermined the result of this audience. It was a defeat. But history has often willed defeats in order to force victory.

XI

Disarmed

KOSSUTH'S VISIT TO METTERNICH HAD BEEN UNSUCCESSFUL. HE wrote from Vienna to his friend Deák giving him an account of the interview. Deák consoled him by saying that the chancellor had committed the greatest political mistake of his life. "Accustomed as he is to meeting only sycophants or venal opponents, a character like yours must have made him think that he was dreaming." Prince Metternich sent another message to Kossuth by an adjutant to say that, although he was unable to grant the permission for his paper, he was ready to give him salaried employment, now or at any time, in Vienna. Kossuth replied ironically. But now he was again condemned to inactivity. Once more the weapon had been struck from his hand. What was he to do?

He retired to Tinnye where he had bought himself a small farm out of his savings as editor of the *Pesti Hirlap*. He was a disappointed man. He felt the need of rest. The excitements had exhausted him, physically and mentally. He was a wreck—he repeated to himself in his nights of wakefulness—a wreck, although the country manifested its loyalty to him, although the subscribers to the *Pesti Hirlap* vied with one another in haste to cancel their subscriptions after Kossuth left the paper, although the audience at the Ballhausplatz should have taught him the high respect the chancellor had for him as an enemy.

But his resignation lasted no longer than the attack of physical weakness; it was an ailment which the invigorating village air soon cured. Once again he was surrounded by idyllic beauty, and he brought out his flute to complete the bucolic atmosphere. In Tinnye he spent his days in his own family circle, and his old mother lived with them in the simple farmhouse. It was like old times in Monók. Kossuth looked after his small estate himself. Now that he was a landowner in a small way and rode over his own fields, not as at Terebes a dependent of the Countess, but a landed aristocrat, he was determined more than ever to show that he acted according to his principles. There was a great stir in the village: the serfs and peasants whispered to each other that Kossuth had addressed them as if they were his equals, that he politely raised his hat when he passed them, that he questioned them about their difficulties and offered them advice. This was unheard of in this country where the labourers that worked the fields had for centuries been treated as slaves. The peasantry in Tinnye, close to Pest, formed an enclave of devotion round Kossuth long before his name reached the ears of the people who did not know how to read.

His stay in Tinnye began with all the promise of another creative interlude. But soon the summons of his enormous following penetrated his village solitude. He wrote to his blind friend Wesselényi in Transylvania that he intended to retire from politics altogether; he found himself a failure, disarmed. Deák vainly tried to comfort him by pointing out that his honesty had succumbed to the wiles of the Vienna government, and he was the first to say openly that Landerer was a paid agent of the Vienna secret police. Kossuth was only conscious of his failure. And he was very grieved at his inability to see through people, a weakness which accompanied him all his life.

But what is the despair of a man whom others look to for help? A Cincinnatus will always leave his plough when he is needed. Kossuth's friends were determined to get him back. The counties sent to him the best fighters of the new party who acknowledged Kossuth as their leader. This was the first occasion that delegates of the people sought out Kossuth—as was to happen so often later. "Tinnye became the Mecca of the opposition," writes a contemporary.

The love of the people, first experienced in the hour of despair, steeled his hesitancy. The change from depression to a desire for action always happened with Kossuth in an instant. He wanted to make himself felt. But how? Without a paper?

But with the same ease with which he had given up his profession as a lawyer, when he had to, he now finally cut himself adrift from journalism. He did not edit a paper again until the March revolution. And now, freed from the daily political detail of journalistic routine, he set energetically about the work of realising his economic plans. In swift succession he founded new enterprises, carefully elaborated schemes, just as Count Széchényi had done before him. But Kossuth's schemes were more modern; they were based on the principle of a regrouping of social classes. He had studied Friedrich List; he knew that the nation could only be freed from the tutelage of Austria and made independent, if it were not dependent on finding markets for its agricultural products and forced to import industrial products. Added the fact that Austria had erected a tariff wall within the empire and compelled Hungary to take manufactured goods burdened with enormous duties. Independence from Austria! Kossuth never showed that he understood by this anything but economic independence.

In quick succession he founded a tariff protection union, an industrial union. He planned the erection of factories, the building of a polytechnic, the laying of a railroad from Vukovar to Fiume in order to assure direct access to the Mediterranean harbours for Hungary. He no longer spoke of an eventual rupture with Austria; he was diplomatic enough to keep silent on that point. But after his interview with Metternich there is no doubt that he only urged on the industrialisation of his country because he foresaw the possibility of a complete rupture.

His undertakings began to flourish. But here again Kossuth operated differently from Széchényi. Széchényi had meanwhile (1845) been made a councillor of state by Metternich's favour and appointed head of a commission to prepare the necessary and difficult work of river regulation and road building in Hungary. Széchényi was so clever in his negotiations that the Vienna government put at his disposal enormous sums for expenditure in Hungary. The Count's success incited Kossuth to do no less. But his work had the result of bringing the people closer together. An industrial union is a man's affair. And yet it at once acquired a social importance. The wives of the members of the board, under the ægis of the beautiful Countess Batthyányi, instituted a private club as an offshoot of the union; they held weekly meetings, they got up charity bazaars; and "Industrial Balls" became the biggest social event. When the "Honi" Society was formed—a society for the protection of the goods manufactured by the young national industry—the fashion was revolutionised. The women pledged their word to wear only "Honi" materials and to use none but "Honi" manufactured articles in their households. This first ebullition of "housewife patriotism" was Kossuth's work.

But the peaceful constructive activity of the disarmed "revolutionary" was doomed to failure. It was endangered because it necessarily must lead to a political change. But it foundered also on nothing less than Kossuth's own enthusiasm which blinded him to facts.

Whereas Széchényi's undertakings flourished, because they were cleverly built up on capitalistic principles and properly managed, the most important of the companies founded by Kossuth, his Trading Company, went bankrupt. And why? Were its aims less real, had it less promise as a profit-making concern? No. But Kossuth had put in as manager a loyal partisan, named Szabó, and one fine day his protégé decamped—taking with him the original capital of 84,000 gulden. The collapse of the company was a dreadful blow to Kossuth. Again a failure because he was so poor a judge of human nature that he had placed his confidence in the wrong man. He heard the derisive laughter of the men in Vienna who had declared themselves ready to "Europeanise" Hungary, under the presidency of the Special Commissioner for the Development of Hungary, His Excellency, Count Széchényi.

But the Hungarian is ever ready to honour human greatness for its own sake, and not to judge according to success. Already a new group was coming into being among the liberals of the aristocracy, the "Opposition Club," their aim being to separate for good from the reform party which truckled to Vienna, Széchényi's steadily decreasing following. Now even Wesselényi openly joined this left opposition, and no lesser man than the highly respected Count Lajos Batthyányi undertook the presidency. The club considered its most important practical task to be the assuring of a seat in the new Diet at the forthcoming elections in 1847 for the man who had long been its leader. Now at last Kossuth must be put in his right place. At last he must be independent of all the vagaries of life, free of the tutelage of any Landerer and anxiety for his daily bread. It could not be a difficult thing to get this man elected.

1847. Hungary, like the German provinces, was openly demanding a constitution. Had not Metternich in his strange prophecy in 1840 said: "Now everything will quiet down, but in 1847 everything will go to the devil?" In Hungary liberalism was threatening revolt. One step further, and Hungary too would demand a democratic constitution, a responsible, independent cabinet, taken from the parliamentary majority. Kossuth demanded that "the free soil of Hungary should be inhabited by free men," and he said plainly enough, that he intended to usher in the "age of self-government." Was he caricaturing Széchényi's anglomania?

But still more dangerous was Kossuth's announcement: "We wish to make the people of our country into a Hungarian nation. Therefore we must keep our eyes fixed on social reforms." What? This too? Not only was this revolutionary being misled by liberal ideas to constitutionalism, but here was that most destructive of all theories, socialism. Indeed Kossuth ventured on a clear acception of Proudhon.

It must be said to-day that Kossuth's interpretation of socialism was much more akin to the early socialist doctrine than to the later socialism of Karl Marx; the ideal of nationalism is more lively than the economic theory. But to Széchényi and to Metternich this was a proof that Kossuth belonged to the group of dangerous agitators who threatened the permanency of the Hapsburg monarchy. But whereas Metternich saw the menace growing in all countries simultaneously, and was loth to fasten the responsibility on individuals, Széchényi saw in Kossuth alone the dangerous instigator, the culprit, the "perturbator." And so, as Széchényi considered the regeneration of Hungary as his personal concern, he took Kossuth's threatening words as aimed at him. For a time he managed to control his anger, but one day he suddenly left Pest, retired to his castle and shut himself up there for three days. No one was allowed to enter his room. He hardly touched the food the servants left outside the door. The candles burnt in his study far into the night and dawn found him sitting pale with undiminished energy at his desk. At the end of the three days he returned to Pest and sent to the printers a pamphlet with the innocent title "Political Programme Fragments."

When the pamphlet appeared there was an uproar in Pest. Széchényi had provoked his adversary in "The People of the East" now he turned and rent him. Rage, indignation, disgust are not sufficient explanation for this cataract of hate. This diatribe verges on insanity. The pamphlet was passed from hand to hand. People stood in groups in the streets of Pest to read it. Kossuth was urged to make a statement. But before he could take up his pen, the opposition papers had already answered for him. The next day it was known that the pamphlet had missed fire. Hate had dug the grave of Széchényi's fame. Kossuth replied disdainfully: "The Count is suffering from bilious fever. He has called me an agitator and threatened me with prison. And this Christian bilious attack breaks out in 1847.

I have the misfortune to know His Excellency very exactly, and I also know His Excellency's position well enough. I have not read his pamphlet, but I can imagine what points it is made up of. The first is: self-praise; melancholy variations on the theme: thankless, stupid, blind people, why do you not dance with bandaged eyes while I pipe the tune?—The second is a confused rigmarole, a manifesto of confidence in the government of which he is himself a member; the rest is scorn, accusation, dirt and denunciation against me." And Kossuth concludes: "His Excellency is very ill and I am very sorry for him."

XII

Third Metamorphosis

KOSSUTH WANTED TO BRING ABOUT HIS REFORMS PEACEFULLY, his election to the Diet would give him the possibility of realising his aims. But in his most intimate circle of friends it was known that it was also a question of bread and butter. Once again, for the fourth time in his life, his fifty-sixth year found him without means of subsistence. The bankruptcy of his Trading Company owing to the defalcations of Szabó had made him a beggar. He was forced to sell his property in Tinnye. He removed to Pest. Once more a spell of inactivity, a search for a profession to give him work and livelihood. Once again his friends collected for him so as to tide over the time till the elections. Thus the election day would decide Kossuth's future. It decided the fate of Hungary.

Kossuth's chances of election were not by any means favourable. In spite of his enormous popularity the more level-headed among the voters asked themselves whether a seat in the Diet was the right place for their famous and beloved leader. Some were unable to reconcile themselves to the thought that Kossuth was by profession a journalist, others held him responsible for the failure of the Trading Company, especially as the Industrial Union also had now virtually ceased to exist. A deputy, they thought, should be above all things an experienced practician. However, some counties were so penetrated with the new spirit that Kossuth's election there was certain. But Kossuth wanted to receive the mandate in Pest itself. Pest had become the central point of Hungary. Here it must be decided whether his doctrines were approved, his personality acknowledged. His friends warned him. But Kossuth remained inflexible. He refused to budge. It was here that he was set on receiving the first endorsement of the nation, here where he had suffered martyrdom for his ideas. This was typical of Kossuth's pride. Just as once he had thrown up the law and faced uncertainty because his pride would not let him remain in Zemplén, so now he was ready to risk everything and face uncertainty again in the event of his non-election.

And this was on the cards. For Pest was now under the social domination of Buda. The government did not omit to make the most of its connections with the aristocracy of Pest. The news of Kossuth's candidature had had an electrifying effect in the government offices of Buda. No stone was left unturned to prevent his election. The townsfolk, the middle class, were of course liberal in their views; they had reason to expect that his election would strengthen their hopes of a constitution. But the citizens of Pest were mostly Germans and their national sympathies put them under an obligation to support the policy of Vienna. And in the first place they had no vote. In order to paralyse the government's agitation, Count Batthyányi put himself at the head of an organised propaganda campaign for Kossuth. Batthyányi was one of the most popular figures of his time. He was handsome and a favourite with the ladies; he was a dandy like Széchényi; but (in contrast to the dour, reserved Count) Batthyányi was a good mixer; more a Hungarian Don Juan than a Hungarian lord. Everyone in Hungary knew that his good looks had made him a *persona grata* with the Archduchess Sophie, that ambitious, influential woman who had almost become empress, had not Metternich fulfilled the wish of the Emperor Franz and had the imbecile Ferdinand crowned emperor, and it was rumoured that Count Batthyányi had scorned the love of this great lady.

Kossuth's opponents never rested. He was vilified as a gaol-bird, and the old calumny that Count György Andrássy had once circulated was revived. Kossuth was too proud to contradict these rumours by bringing documentary proof of his trial and acquittal in Zemplén. He wanted to be elected on his programme, by virtue of his ideas.

And so the election day, the 19th October, approached. From all districts of the large county of Pest the voters streamed into the city. A contemporary reports: "Led by the liberal magnates on orientally accoutred horses, some in their splendid national costume, others in smart peasant dress, the endless stream of Kossuth's partisans poured into the city, to the waving of the national flag, the sound of the Rákóczi March, singing patriotic songs, and shouting the name of their chosen candidate with continuous cries of 'Éljen': and as they marched they chanted in loud and solemn chorus their election cry:

Who has a God, who has a state,
Choose Kossuth for your candidate.

While the little band of the opposition seemed to apologise for its tame procession and hardly dared to hum their counter-cry:

> He has no God, he has no state,
> He's just a windbag who can prate."

The decisive election battle followed the next day. It lasted from the morning till late evening. In the entrance to the County Hall where all the voters met a large table was set up and on it an urn into which the voting papers were dropped. Kossuth was elected by 2948 votes to 1314. That is, with a huge majority.

When Count Széchényi learned that Kossuth had been nominated his anger knew no bounds. If Kossuth were elected? What mischief would he stir up? Like every magnate, the Count was a member of the Upper chamber of the Diet; but he waived his claims to a permanent seat, in order to gain a seat in the Lower chamber as the elected deputy for a county. There he meant to cross swords with Kossuth where his dangerous influence would expand. But he was disappointed. He was not returned. But Széchényi was not deterred by his defeat at Odenburg. His hate was greater than his pride. And so he let himself be nominated again in a bye-election in the county of Weiselburg and was elected.

The news of Kossuth's victory was hailed in Pest with indescribable rejoicing. The voters besieged Kossuth's house. Then Count Batthyányi appeared on horseback, carrying the national flag, at the head of a cavalcade of nobles. They formed the head of the procession. When it reached Kossuth's house, Batthyányi gave a signal to a lad walking beside his horse, and suddenly, above the noise of drums and trumpets, arose the notes of the *tárogató*. Kossuth, now deputy for Pest, came out. Batthyányi embraced him. The crowd cheered. This was the first great triumph of Kossuth's life. He was acclaimed by the people whom his words had unified: by the whole Hungarian nation.

This was a day of rejoicing. At the age of forty-five he achieved his third metamorphosis: lawyer, journalist, and now politician. It had been a long and roundabout road. But he had reached his goal. He was in his right place at last.

He and the revolution—they had grown up together. They had both tirelessly awakened the sleeping nation to self-consciousness, and now they were sure of their following, if, to-day or to-morrow, the hour should call the nation to revolt. Kossuth felt himself armed. He had never ceased longing for this day, ever since he had heard Kövy's warning and the gipsy woman's prophecy in the forest. He and the nation: it was his Protestant belief that fate had entrusted him with the mission of welding the dismembered nation into one brotherhood, one people. And as he let himself be carried by the cheering crowd out to the meadows by the Danube, he withdrew from the merry-making, and turned his eyes towards the hills. Batthyányi put his arm round his friend's shoulder. He put no question to him, but as if in answer to his unspoken query Kossuth whispered: "Now I know that the people love me. This is the happiest day of my life."

PART THREE

INSURRECTION

I

Europe Ablaze

MANY PEOPLE LOOKED FORWARD TO KOSSUTH'S MAIDEN SPEECH with the excitement of enthusiastic first-nighters before the appearance of a famous actor in a new role; others, with a smile of sceptical superiority anticipated the opportunity of watching the public performance of this tub-thumping journalist, considering him a dangerous, but amusing adventurer.

The first question in the opening debate was whether now at last the privileged aristocracy should be subjected to taxation, as Széchényi had demanded in his *Hitel* more than twenty years before. Was the pet dream of the enlightened liberals to be realised and the serfs given real freedom? The debate went on interminably; for the landowners, in so far as they were not altogether against the motion, demanded compensation and this was difficult to estimate. At last it was Kossuth's turn to speak. The man who began, pale and trembling, in a hardly audible voice, seemed like a savant, mastering his material with a sovereign certainty and presenting it with compelling logic, a doctrinaire in love with his theory because it expressed the truth. The first parliamentary speech of deputy Kossuth was an academic lecture. He enumerated the points in favour of compensation, and he urged the nobles not to let slip this psychological moment. The speech showed in the first sentences that Kossuth was equal to the situation. He held his rhetoric and temperament under control, and made a sober appeal to common sense. As Kossuth himself once said: "The naked presentation of facts is the most convincing form of rhetoric."

And the result showed that conviction carries the day when a speaker knows how to convince. On the 6th December, 1847, the motion was carried by thirty-seven votes to thirteen that the landowner must accept payment of compensation from the peasant in lieu of service, if and when he offered it. This exonerated the peasant. A breach had been made in the ancient constitution; the medieval caste spirit had been defeated by the spirit of Lamennais. Kossuth had succeeded in making the most important stride towards making the nation a people.

This was the breath of a new epoch. Kossuth was not the stormy petrel Metternich had feared. Now step followed step. It was to be the task of this Diet, the first diet of which Kossuth was a member, to accomplish things neglected for centuries. Kossuth demanded, as the first necessity for Hungary, help for her industry. He called for trade relations with England, for only direct trade with England could end the absurd situation where Hungary, which imported cotton for twenty-four million gulden annually, was compelled to pay 120 gulden per hundred-weight more than if she had imported direct from England. Kossuth's practical common sense won all along the line. He had used the creative interval of his imprisonment to good purpose. Even his readers were astounded at his grasp of national economy, no less than at the assurance with which he propounded his views.

But there are moments when anger is too strong for the assumption of control. The question of the taxation of the aristocracy was still the subject of heated debate. Kossuth had too long stood in the battlefront against these privileges. Now it was necessary, to force a decision, that he should show his claws. "The beggarly privilege of immunity from taxation can no longer be upheld. This privilege is opposed to divine justice, to the Christian spirit of civilisation, it is opposed to the interests of millions of the people, it is opposed to the very conditions of existence of the country. It is a rotten branch and as such it must be sawn off, cut away without mercy." He was possessed with Protestant anger. The nobility were unjust towards the people; they were relapsing into slavery. The whole country had been sacrificed for the sake of a beggarly privilege. Kossuth shook his fists, his voice rose, it regained that sonorous music, the magic that always carried away the masses at the climax of his speeches. He became a priest, offering prayers to heaven. "O my country, my poor, abandoned country, how long shall your decay endure!" Wild excitement roused the assembly to its feet. A tornado of applause rocked the house.

Kossuth had established his reputation as an orator. Then the "Transylvanian question" in the year 1848 was the occasion of a great enunciation of principle which historians have declared his greatest speech before the revolution. The effect of this speech was unique in the annals of the Pressburg Diet. He was the first of a long list of deputies whose names were down to speak; but when he had finished, no one else dared to mount the rostrum, and even the opposition voted for Kossuth's motion, the first proposal of a change in the political situation. Transylvania, the province which formed the buffer between Hungary and the east and south-east, was inhabited principally by Magyars, a few hundred thousand Saxons who had settled there very early on, founded their friendly towns and enjoyed far-reaching privileges, and by numerous Wallachs who spoke Roumanian. But from the earliest times, owing to its Magyar majority, it had always been closely attached to its Hungarian motherland. Kossuth demanded that an end be put to the retrograde dismemberment of Transylvania, "the continued withholding of the child from its mother's arms." Unrest was rife in the area of the Danube. The language question had greatly excited the countries inhabited by Slavs, notably Croatia. Now Hungary aimed at materially strengthening her position through Transylvania. There was unrest in the south-eastern lands of the Hapsburg monarchy, as in every other country of Europe. Metternich was right in his gloominess about the future.

His success as an orator nourished Kossuth's pride. Now at last, after a struggle of twenty years, he had worked his way up to being the leader of the opposition party—and the opposition was practically the whole nation. Kossuth's chief supporters were the conservatively minded Batthyányi and the shrewd and prudent Ferenc Deák; but Kossuth overshadowed them. He begot the ideas, he found the energy for the attack, he set the pace, he led.

The hour called for action. Once again the Vienna government tried to conciliate. King Ferdinand addressed a weak-kneed edict to his Hungarian people in the language of a nervous father who is conscious of his injustice, but refuses to admit it. Metternich alone heard the screeching of the stormy petrel. He knew that Europe would soon be ablaze. He knew too that Hungary, the "annexe of Central Europe," had not become restive without good reason. The spring wind blowing in the valley of the Danube foretold the bursting of the storm.

On the 29th February of this year, 1848, Baron Rothschild appeared in the State Chancellery with all the signs of intense agitation and urgently demanded an audience with Prince Metternich. The prince was just about to leave for an audience at the palace, but naturally the "secret victor of the battle of Waterloo" was admitted. Rothschild came with the news that revolution had broken out in Paris and that Louis Philippe, the citizen king, had abdicated. Metternich reeled. He clutched his desk, and could find no words but: "Eh bien, mon cher, tout est fini!"

On the first of March Széchényi too learnt the news of the February revolution in Paris. He noted in his diary: "Now the fat will soon be in the fire. *Mundus se expediet.*"

Europe was ablaze.

II

The Tocsin Sounds

ALREADY ON THE 2ND MARCH, IMMEDIATELY ON THE RECEPTION of the exciting news from France, the young Hungarian leaders met in conference. How the times had changed! A few weeks earlier the liberals would have met at Széchényi's house; for even at that date it was still believed that Hungary could be served by reforms—and, however much Széchényi had alienated himself from the opposition by his alliance with Metternich, he was still the man of the reform party. But now the conference was held at Kossuth's. In the most exciting hour of history, but a short while before the approaching avalanche reached Hungary, Kossuth, a recently elected member of the Diet, was already the axis of the party. For he was destined to be the man of revolution. There was not a man but knew this; even Széchényi, his adversary for the past ten years; and he too turned up at Kossuth's in the hour that called for a decision.

In these few days Kossuth had not only outwardly assumed the role of leader; he was not only a strong disciplinarian within the liberal party among which there were easy-going and jealous elements who would have liked to bring about his fall; he had at the same time completely understood the part he had to play. And without any precedent; for he was to give history the pattern of the national leader. His own transforming genius compelled his following. But a leader needs friends; loyal intimates, the little nucleus who have his trust and in whom he is able to place full confidence. Kossuth chose in addition to the few who had accompanied his beginnings with their friendship two men: Pulszky, to whom he later owed so much, and another, a young man, almost a stranger and yet trusted by him from the first moment. The choice of this apostle, twenty years younger than himself, remains one of the rarely beautiful mysteries of history which will never be probed. Do we not know the tender affection of Goethe for Fritz von Stein, the son of the woman he adored? Like her, the Countess Etelka

Andrássy had once been to Kossuth "a sister and a wife"—and it was her son Julius Andrássy who at once attached himself to Kossuth, with the devotion of enthusiastic youth.

He, too, was present at the conference of the 2nd March. Count Széchényi noted in his diary on that day that Kossuth "made his splendid declaration." Then afterwards Széchényi attempted to hold Kossuth back from his next step: "I use all my eloquence . . . my words have no effect . . . I yield rather than pour oil on to the fire." His protests were of no avail. The following day, the 3rd March, Kossuth made his great speech. It was the call to revolution.

For revolution meant: the change from absolutism to liberalism. As the absolute monarch refused voluntarily to surrender so much of his powers that the realisation of the new ideas might be made possible, revolt against this stubbornness had only one name: revolution. There was no question of begging for this or that concession. Things had gone too far. This was the final crisis. The only man who saw this was Kossuth.

For everywhere in Europe the fire of the "new spirit" was alight. Kossuth had waited a quarter of a century for this revolt against oppression. Must he not think of the February revolution as his revolution? The revolution in which his ideas had triumphed?

(But it was only years later that Kossuth, then in exile, discovered that Prince Napoleon, who at the time was considered a true revolutionary and a man of the people, was really nothing more than a vain usurper, hankering after fame and power.) In those days the people of France seemed to be the advance guard for all peoples in the fight for freedom. And so two weeks later, on the 17th March, a band of young Hungarians who had made their way to Paris presented themselves to the man who for them incorporated the idea of this revolution: Lamartine. To them Lamartine said: "If you bring the good wishes of your country to the new-born liberty of ours, then we reciprocate them. . . . Return to your fair home and tell them there that she has as many friends in France as there are citizens of France." These words, spoken at such a moment by such a man, could not fail to produce an effect on the grave decisions which the Hungarian people had to carry out. And at the same time it so happened that the father of Christianity himself openly professed the new ideas; Pope Pius IX declared himself for liberalism, and blessed the Italian volunteers who were taking the field against the oppressor. The oppressor was Austria. And then, in this same month of March, the people in the German provinces adopted this programme. It was not a struggle for reforms, but for the new spirit. Young Europe decided for Kossuth—and against Széchényi.

On the morning of the 3rd March, Kossuth entered the assembly, fully believing in his mission and convinced that the decisive hour had come. He was simply and plainly dressed in a black suit and wore a broad-brimmed black hat. But he had altered his appearance by shaving his chin and cheeks, but leaving a bushy fringe of beard. This beard which was soon given the name of "Kossuth beard" became the fashion. The men who believed in him adopted it as an outward symbol of their allegiance.

Kossuth mounted the rostrum and began to speak, a parliamentarian replying to a previous speaker. The debate was on the subject of banking conditions. But in his analysis of these conditions the speaker was forced to digress into a presentation of the internal situation in Hungary. Suddenly his voice rose to its full magnificence, for he wished to sum up in one sentence the immediate task before them: "Let us suit our policy to the greatness of the hour." Once again he asseverates his loyalty to the House of Hapsburg—for the insurrection of 1848 is not yet directed against the dynasty; even in Milan no one believed in a secession, only in an autonomy under a Hapsburg prince. "Let us draw strength from our civic duty for a resolution corresponding to such extraordinary circumstances. . . . Even unnatural political systems may last long; for there is a long way between the patience of peoples and despair. But political systems which have lasted a long time may have lost strength; their long life makes them ripe for death. But death is not a thing that one may share or stay. I know that for an old system, as for an old man, it is hard to separate from life. I know that it is hard to see the things which a long life has built up, crumble piece by piece. But where the foundations are not truly laid, collapse is the inevitable fatality. But the people is everlasting and we wish the fatherland of this people to be everlasting!" And the revolutionary, who had languished three years in prison because of the Hapsburg, added in this moment when he felt power within his grasp: "And we wish that the glory of the dynasty that rules over us be everlasting. . . . But only a dynasty relying on the liberty of its peoples will excite enthusiasm; for heart-felt loyalty is only possible to the free man. . . . A pestilential wind reaches us from the charnel-house of the Vienna cabinet. . . . The gallows and the bayonet are ill-contrived means to cement goodwill. Who can reflect without a shudder that sacrifices should be imposed upon the people, without spiritual and material compensation?" His accusation concluded with the demand for a government responsible to the Diet.

Indescribable enthusiasm followed this speech. The country was ablaze. Even to Vienna, and to all the cities of the Austrian provinces, the echo of this challenge was carried. In this hour Kossuth knew that he had triumphed. The 3rd March established him as leader.

The fight began. The House of Hapsburg was not defenceless. It had troops everywhere. And it had them well distributed. In Italy there were Hungarian regiments under the command of Radetzky; a German general commanded the Hungarian garrisons. It was not to be hoped, at least not yet, that the Hungarian officers would ever be disloyal to the Hapsburgs. But things had not yet reached this pass. The assertion of loyalty to the dynasty allowed no one to believe in serious complications.

But Hapsburg had yet other weapons. The old principle *divide et impera* must be once more victorious. The emperor's advisers well knew that a national insurrection could be paralysed by the insurrection of other nationalities. Hungary was a state of minorities; the Magyars made up less than half the population of their country. Nationalism had not only been awakened in Italy, but also in Croatia, in the areas inhabited by the Serbs, and the attitude of the strong German element in Transylvania was at least doubtful. Vienna did not yet despair. Vienna sought allies and found them.

Once again fortune seemed to favour the system. Pope Pius IX had blessed the rebel troops? Well, the Pope showed himself to be a weakling. But the revolution in Italy spread rapidly, kindling the whole peninsula. Radetzky marched in. Force seemed the last hope. But the real powder magazine was Hungary. And therefore Metternich determined to drive out the devil by Beelzebub. Panslavism had also recently advanced on the chess-board of politics new, nationally inspired figures. Metternich found a new face, a useful tool, in the officer Jellasich, the most capable brain in Croatia. If Kossuth incited Hungary to open revolution, he should be dealt the death blow by Croatia.

Metternich's choice was a happy one. Jellasich came of an old baronial Croat family; the family had always been in Austrian service, his father had even been a lieutenant-fieldmarshal. Baron Franz Jellasich had distinguished himself in fights with Bosnian marauding troops. A wild youth had given him the reputation of a "Croat Casanova." This was the man chosen to fan the distressing "Croatian question" which had so long excited the Hungarian Diet into a Croatian rebellion.

Kossuth and his adherents had acknowledged the wishes of Croatia for a certain measure of self-government, but opposed their veto on any attempt at secession from the kingdom. For Kossuth was a nationalist. The inviolability of the frontiers of the kingdom of St. Stephen was sacred to him. But Jellasich too was a nationalist. The whole troubled area of the Danube kept discovering new nationalisms, like the Hydra. Could they be suppressed or killed by contempt?

It was too late. The seed of nationalism had begun to grow. This was a national revolution, exactly as the French revolution of 1789 from Mirabeau to Danton had been.

As yet no one in Hungary had any suspicion of the danger that was looming. Vienna worked in secret. That had always been the strength of the system. Days of quiet followed Kossuth's proclamation of the 3rd March. It was decided to present the demand for the constitution with all reverence and respect to the king. In Pressburg everyone was confident of an early success. But it was otherwise in Pest. In Pest the headquarters of all presumptive revolutionaries, malcontents and fanatics, journalists and students, was the Café Pilvax. Another Palais Royal. A contemporary thus describes it: "Doors and windows were kept open so that the huge crowds in the street could listen to the thunderings of the heroes of March. Outside gathered soldiers, Magyars and Croats, with feathers in their hats, women with ribbons in their hair, round-faced tradesmen with jet black hair, Jews, long-bearded Wallach priests, dirty gipsies, students, workmen in their blouses." Among those who sprang on to the tables and from time to time shot off their revolutionary speeches for the benefit of the crowd, was a slim young man with fiery dark eyes, flowing hair and a small moustache above a shy mouth. But when he spoke the fire passed to his voice and resonant verses rang across the square. This young man of twenty-five was Sándor Petöfi, the poet, and the crowd who read his poems daily in the papers flocked to overhear him in the Café Pilvax. He leapt down from his table in the Café Pilvax, like Camille Desmoulins in the Café of the Palais Royal—and he was in the midst of the revolution.

Kossuth worked systematically. But neither was Széchényi inactive. He still believed that he could avert the revolution, if he were entrusted with full powers. Széchényi as chancellor of Hungary, Széchényi in full control, this seemed acceptable in Vienna. The Count makes this entry in his diary on the 4th March: "Good ideas usually come too late. If I were now equipped with full powers. My conditions: ten thousand gulden down, five thousand every month. Fixed expenses, the costs of meetings, e.g. heating, lighting, stationery. Grand Cross of the Order of St. Stephen. Hand written authority as drawn up by me, containing full powers and guarantee. Can nominate whom I please—all must obey me." Széchényi thought of everything. "Opposition and other clubs will be dissolved." The lonely man who had fallen between two stools was ready to make a last attempt to smash the Kossuth party. On the 5th March he notes: "Splendid weather. At Metternich's house; he talks only to me. The princess: 'Bonjour, citoyen.' I: 'Merci, délicieuse sans-culotte.' "

They were still able to joke in Vienna. Metternich proposed, on the 7th March, to the cabinets of the three Great Powers that they should form a united front against France in order to isolate the new republic. Meanwhile the democrats in Vienna were working feverishly to get Hungary to join them in a revolution for the 13th March. Baron Doblhof and the poet Bauernfeld sent the Magyars powder and shot. On the 8th March Széchényi becomes alarmed: "I wash my hands. I have made an honest offer." Yes, he had, but the government did not trust him even now. Széchényi was advised to return to Pressburg. On the 12th he writes: "I am agitating energetically against Kossuth's tendency. I am utterly tired and exhausted. God is great, whatever happens. First in Vienna, and then here I appear as deceived or as deceiver, or everywhere as one who had ruined everything." And on the 13th: "The revolution has actually broken out in Vienna. It is incalculable what is happening now. Three hundred young people shout: Down with the government, down with all magnates."

On this 13th March the people of Vienna had really risen in

THE BATTHYÁNYI—KOSSUTH CABINET IN THE DIET

The Archduke Palatine is addressing the assembly. Behind him, to the left, are Batthyányi and Kossuth.

From the Portrait Collection of the National Library, Vienna.

revolt. The booksellers began by handing the government a petition for the abolition of the censorship. The people massed. Archduke Albrecht, commanding the Vienna garrison, gave the order to fire. The people took up arms and erected barricades. There was bloodshed. Officers hurried to the palace and demanded audience. The principal demands of the people were: freedom of the press, arming of the citizens of Vienna as a national guard, and—the dismissal of Metternich. The emperor surrendered. Metternich had to go.

The previous evening everyone in the government buildings knew that the next day would bring the revolution. Metternich's opponents, above all his old adversary Kolowrat, were jubilant. What did they care that the whole system was falling to pieces? Now suddenly on the eve of the catastrophe no words were bad enough for Metternich. The magic of his name faded before the old man had left the Ballhausplatz. The same thing happened as when a king takes an unconscionable time dying; the whole court turned away from him, so as to be betimes in hailing his successor. Metternich alone refused to believe the threatening omens which announced the Ides of March. In his own drawing-room that evening Princess Félicie Eszterházy asked him with touching *naiveté:* "Is it true that you are leaving to-morrow? We have been told to buy candles to illuminate to-morrow, because you are being dismissed." But the old prince merely smiled; he left the drawing-room and went into his study. There he noted: "Dreams vanish, truth remains. This will only be clear to the very last of our successors." These were the last words he wrote as statesman.

The next day found the people already in the streets. Orators bellowed at the crowds, but it was not until one of them began translating into German Kossuth's speech of the 3rd March that the revolutionary fever seized the mob. And so Kossuth's appeal to the Magyar people became the baptismal speech of the revolution in Vienna. Now the people went mad. Cries of "Down with Metternich" filled the air. The mob surged towards the Chancellery; they tore down the imperial eagles from the public buildings; Metternich's garden on the Bastei was overrun with people and trampled under foot. Many of them were common people, but among them there were also ladies who were lifted over the railings by their liveried servants. The majority were fashionably dressed.

At one o'clock in the afternoon the chancellor realised the

gravity of the revolt. He succeeded in reaching the palace which was protected by troops. At two o'clock firing was heard. It was now evident that the "system of order" was incapable of guaranteeing order. The mob was attacking the palace itself. Gas escaped from the street lamps and caught fire. The centre and the suburbs of the city were in an uproar. An officer of the city militia, the wine-merchant Scherzer, brought the emperor the demand for Metternich's dismissal. He was followed by a deputation from the faculty of medicine. Metternich tried to have Prince Windischgrätz, one of the most determined generals, invested with extraordinary powers. But it was too late. The Archduke Ludwig urged Metternich to resign. The next day the danger reached its height. The chancellor still refused. He based his refusal on his oath to the Emperor Franz on his deathbed that he would never abandon his son. Then the Emperor Ferdinand, who had been silent throughout, rose and said: "I am the sovereign and it is for me to decide. Tell the people that I agree to everything." Metternich received permission personally to announce his retirement. At nine that evening he went out into the hall where the deputations were waiting with the Archduke at his side. With immense dignity he announced that he was laying down his office, because he was assured that his resignation would be to Austria's advantage. But then he added the significant words: "When monarchies vanish, it is because they surrender themselves."

The news of Metternich's departure filled the city with wild jubilation. Windows were illuminated, flags waved. Now the students posted themselves as guard over Metternich's villa. The chancellor felt exhausted. He retired to bed. Dr. Jäger felt his pulse; but again the smile of wisdom spread over the old man's wan face: "You would do better, my dear doctor, to feel the pulse of Austria."

This was the end of a statesmanly domination. A world order fell in ruins; the ideas of the classical political doctrine yielded to the new Romantic theory. Metternich went, Hapsburg toppled, a new power stretched out its hand for mastery: the people.

III

The Voyage of the Argonaut

ON THE 14TH MARCH IT WAS KOSSUTH WHO ANNOUNCED IN the Diet in Pressburg the news of the events in Vienna. He was deeply moved; excitement had taken the colour from his face and his usually powerful voice sounded hoarse and unsteady as he alluded to the fall of Metternich. Then he pulled himself together and raising his voice continued: "It will now be our splendid task to steer the movement wisely. We must be intent on keeping the reins in our own hands, for only so can we advance constitutionally. But if they are wrested from our grasp, then God alone knows what may ensue." He therefore recommended the sending of a deputation to the king to hand him the demands of the nation; it seemed to him essential to have the laws they had determined on sanctioned before rumours of the events in Vienna spread and the people be carried away to an undisciplined revolt. These demands contained all the points which the precursors of the revolution had fought for: an independent responsible ministry; the abolition of the censorship; the transference of the Diet to Pest; equality before the law; the removal of all foreign troops and their replacement by Hungarian soldiers sworn to allegiance to the constitution; the formation of a national guard; the release of all political prisoners; educational liberty; trial by jury; the dissolution of the court chancellery; the union of Transylvania with Hungary.

The pride of the Magyar was stirred: he wanted self-government. But not at any moment was there a thought of defection from the dynasty. The word republic in Hungary had an evil sound. Chodwitz explains the Magyars' dislike of a republican form of government by the oriental character of the race: "The cold, sober, abstract form of government is diametrically opposed to their fiery, passionate temper." Even Kossuth thought of the crown with a constraining childish awe. Even if the present wearer of the crown of St. Stephen was an imbecile, no one in

Hungary ever contemplated overthrowing the monarchy. But in Vienna, at the court itself, there was a party of Ferdinand's enemies; its moving spirit was the Archduchess Sophie who bore Metternich a grudge for having carried through the succession of the invalid Ferdinand in the face of all opposition, thereby preventing her from becoming empress. Now she had the chance to be revenged upon the man she hated; she had vigorously helped to bring about his fall.

But Kossuth had no thought of acting against the Hapsburgs. The disorders in Vienna were to be utilised to carry through the long-planned laws. Before the delegation for Vienna was appointed, a group of students appeared at Kossuth's house. A black-haired youth with glowing eyes had listened to Kossuth's speech; now he buttonholed him and cried excitedly: "If you will make a speech, in two hours you can incite a public meeting to proclaim a republic." Kossuth turned to the lad and answered in a voice of thunder: "I have half a mind to call a public meeting which in two hours will see you hanging from a lamp post."

Kossuth was no republican. No Magyar had reason to love the Hapsburgs; but destiny had linked Hungary with the House of Hapsburg. In their hour of direst need she had contemptuously rejected Napoleon's appeal: now when the sun of freedom was beginning to shine, she had no desire to act otherwise. It was decided to send Kossuth at the head of a deputation to Vienna. A number of young men belonging to the Reichstagsjugend volunteered to join it.

That evening a torchlight procession with the students at its head paraded the streets of Pressburg cheering the "Liberator of Hungary." Kossuth appeared on the balcony at the side of Count Batthyányi, the venerable magnate who had been the first to join the young leader, and obeying a sudden impulse embraced him to the delight of the enthusiastic crowd. And at this moment Kossuth pointed with a grand gesture to his friend and his voice rang out above the sea of heads below: "Here stands your first responsible prime minister!" He was answered by a yell. Thus, swayed by the overpowering feeling of the moment, Kossuth was carried away by his own ecstasy to play into another's hands.

The jubilation in Pressburg was unbounded. Now even the Germans who invariably maintained a rigid distance from their Magyar neighbours joined in the ovation, for was this not the festival of brotherhood? Only one man stood aloof, pale, like the villain in the play, irresolute: Széchényi. On the night of the 14th March he noted in his diary: "I perceive already that Hungary stands on the threshold of complete dissolution. Poor Prince Metternich! The system of the Emperor Franz which of necessity led to absurdity has brought about your downfall." He commiserates the prince and again in Széchényi's melancholy there is a mysterious clear-sightedness: on this day no one as yet suspected that the dismissed statesman would be driven out with whips and scorpions. . . .

The 15th March dawned, a glorious spring day. The Ides of March! A fateful day in history! Kossuth smiled happily as he strolled that morning on the soft banks of the gently rippling Danube, waiting for the signal of departure for the "Voyage of the Argonaut." Friends gathered round him: swift messengers brought the latest news from Pest. The whole country was working for him. He could confidently mingle with the throng that at last went aboard the steamer. The actual head of the deputation was the archduke-palatine Stefan, an upright man who had espoused the cause of Hungary, although he was a scion of the Hapsburgs. The deputation consisted of thirteen members of the upper and fifty-nine of the lower house; it was accompanied by a host of dignitaries, prelates and deputies, and finally a swarm of Reichstagsjugend, two hundred strong, crowded on to the deck. They had to be there, the heralds of a new era who were themselves the spring-time of the nation.

The ship started on its voyage; its name *Béla* in gold letters glittering in the sun, the Hungarian tricolour, red, white and green, proudly fluttering at the masthead. The barque of youth. On that day even the most venerable seemed like a boy in disguise. The Serbian Patriarch Rajasich was on board, for this spring-tide of the nations would at last guarantee the Serbs in the Banat freedom of language and religion. Next to Batthyányi whom Kossuth had offered the Patriarchate of the New Hungary was the militant poet Baron Eötvös. A face of a byegone age, the perfect aristocrat, but with splendid youthful eyes: Prince Pál Eszterházy. It was he who had had the courage to utter the revolutionary words: "Rather a constitutional hell than an absolutist paradise!" There were people at the Vienna court who prophesied that the prince would soon get what he hoped for: hell and the constitution. And among those on the deck also Count Széchényi. When Batthyányi had begged him to accompany the deputation he had accepted without demur. Why had Batthyányi invited him? Did the "Patriarch of the New Hungary" wish to have beside him the man who was the enemy of the liberator—Kossuth's enemy?

Vienna flocked in crowds to the meadows by the Danube to receive the Hungarians. Salutes were fired, all the streets were gay with flags; the horses were taken out of Archduke Stefan's carriage and it was dragged by the enthusiastic crowd as far as the gates of the imperial palace. But the centre of interest was Kossuth. "He was showered with flowers, pretty women waved their kerchiefs at every window, the entry was a triumphal procession,"—so Pulszky describes the welcome. "The people, still in the first days of tasting the uplifting sensation of having political rights, felt themselves encouraged by the arrival of this deputation of the Hungarian nation which had so long fought for justice and liberty. The two neighbour nations gave a brotherly demonstration that they belonged to each other."

Kossuth was the hero of the hour. The next day he met Prince Eszterházy in the street and they embraced. Széchényi who witnessed the scene made the note: "If Kossuth demands it, the people will pull down the palace itself."

The people of Vienna loved Kossuth. And this love which welled up to him from the mysterious depths of a people's heart embraced the whole Hungarian nation whose delegate he was. After centuries of despotism the two peoples breathed the first morning of their freedom and embraced in fraternal understanding. Kossuth realised with emotion how easy it is for peoples and how hard for governments to understand each other. But still he saw with perfect clarity that nothing really had been won as yet. With grave and quivering voice he warned the citizens of Vienna: "Do not let yourselves be too carried away by your joy and do not believe that you have already attained everything which is necessary to make a people free. It is true that absolutism is broken, but the instruments of that tyranny have by no means been removed. The arrogant bureaucracy still battens on the blood of the people, the aristocratic landowner still grows rich on the toil of his subjects, the sovereignty of the people is still faced with the danger of a threatening, uncivilised soldiery, and this soldiery is ever ready to obey the orders of its officers, the command of the emperor whatever that command may be. Citizens of Vienna! Be on your guard and do not trust too far the promises of a dynasty!"

On that day the echo of his warning soon died away. For all signs indicated victory and every vernal breath of that March day seemed filled with liberty. The gag of censorship, the policeman's truncheon had banished the word liberty since the days of the Vienna Congress, and now the streets of the imperial city once more echoed with the cry of freedom. The Viennese were like an army of prisoners that had been unexpectedly released and were still dizzy with their first joy. The fight against the court entrenchments had still to go on as before. It was only on the night of the 15th March that the Viennese received the emperor's promise to summon a meeting of the deputies from all parts of the empire. This promise and the forced retirement of Metternich so roused their enthusiasm that when the emperor drove out of the palace they unharnessed the horses and drew his carriage. But the wary democrats missed the decisive words "people" and "constitution" in the imperial declaration. Now popular feeling veered and indignation broke through again. The people, led by the property owning classes, pressed forward again to force new concessions. At the head of the movement stood the student legion who were armed; the most respected professors of the university gladly assumed the command in this fresh attack. Later an attempt was made to fix the responsibility on a few individuals, such as Fischhof and Goldner, who belonged to the Jewish intelligentsia, but the names of Jenull, the Rector Magnificus of the University, and of the foremost scientists of the faculty of medicine, such as Lerch, and finally of the Commander of the Civic Guard, the wine merchant Scherzer, show that this popular movement was really a movement of the German bourgeoisie.

Prince Windischgrätz again advised the threatened emperor to open fire on the demonstrators, but the emperor kept repeating: "I refuse to let them shoot." On the evening of the 14th March an extraordinary council was held at which the seventeen-year-old Archduke Franz Josef was present. The Emperor Ferdinand showed himself resolved at last to grant the constitution. The empress, who was popularly spoken of as "the reigning empress," tried to persuade her feeble-minded husband to abdicate. Metternich was recalled once more to the palace and it was he who made her promise not to take this overhasty step. Ferdinand remained—and as the court clique delivered their last attack against the proclamation of the constitution, the imbecile monarch whose sole anxiety was that there should be no bloodshed rose and spoke the deciding word: "The constitution shall be granted. Am I emperor or am I not?"

So up to the arrival of the Hungarians the revolution had been plain sailing. Now, two days later, the Hungarians, still dizzy from their welcome, had to fight a hard battle for their freedom at the court of this same emperor. The archduke palatine was received alone. Ferdinand replied to his address in Hungarian, but without committing himself in any way. Then the whole deputation was ceremonially given audience. The solemnity of the moment was calculated to weaken the easily impressed Magyars, but the demands were drawn up in black on white, and indeed they had the day before in Vienna been framed in still more categorical language. The Pressburg Diet had laid down twelve points. The emperor remained stubborn. He was surrounded by the same advisers, the late government, all—except Metternich. The emperor was like a child repeating a lesson. The deputation was sobered and excited. Kossuth was the only one who realised in this instant that the Hapsburgs were exhausted: strength and the future were in the people. He knew that he could do with this people what he wanted. He felt that the fate of the emperor lay in his hand. If he gave the command for the final assault upon the palace, the student guard and the national guard, followed by the masses, would force their way into the imperial palace and make an end of the Hapsburg rule. But he rejected the thought; the strictness of his religious conviction stifled the unfolding vision.

The deputation waited restlessly. Prince Eszterházy and now too Count Széchnéyi had declared themselves ready to use their personal connections at court. The prince asked for an audience with the Archduchess Sophie, the ambitious schemer and arch-enemy of Metternich, whose dream it was to secure the throne for her son, the young Archduke Franz Josef. In this momentous hour she kept him waiting; but Eszterházy declared bluntly that this was no time for court etiquette, for "nothing less than the throne of the Hapsburgs was at stake."

The deputation waited. Still no answer. Meanwhile the real masters in the government met the leaders of the deputation. No longer high and mighty, they begged the Hungarians for their advice and help. They even offered the more level-headed leaders, Batthyányi and Eötvös, places in the central government. A word to the emperor would suffice to seat Batthyányi in the place vacated by the State Chancellor Prince Metternich. Batthyányi was tempted, but he refused; he wanted to serve Hungary, the new Hungary.

That evening Archduke Stefan again insisted upon seeing the emperor and declared that if the main demands of the Magyars were not granted he would resign immediately. His resignation, as the court well knew, meant anarchy in Hungary. And now at last the archdukes and duchesses who had been playing at government during these days without a chancellor presented the rescript to the emperor for his signature.

"My dear cousin, Your Serene Highness Archduke and Palatine! Learning from the humble address which I have received at Your Highness' hands in the name of the estates of my kingdom of Hungary the desires of my loyal Hungarian people, I do not hesitate to declare, in obedience to the sole promptings of my fatherly heart, that I will make it my care to fulfil all those wishes on which the welfare and the constitutional development of my beloved Hungary depend." Thus begins the emperor's manifesto of the 17th March, 1848. He concludes: "I am disposed while maintaining intact the unity of the crown and union with the monarchy, to gratify the desire of my loyal subjects for the formation of a responsible ministry in a sense conforming to the laws of our country."

This was victory. For three centuries Hungary had fought for the recognition of its rights. For three centuries it had suffered unspeakable oppression under the despotic rule of the House of Hapsburg. Now constitutional liberty was guaranteed. The deputation could feel itself already to be "the first Hungarian representative ministry." Early on the morning of the 17th the return journey began. It was quickly decided that Batthyányi accept the position of prime minister. Kossuth had prophesied aright.

The departing Hungarians left behind the Viennese in a state of lively enthusiasm. But on that day a curious scene was enacted which attracted little notice. A Hungarian by the name of Ecsegi, an engineer in the service of Count Keglevitch, marched through the suburbs of the city carrying the emperor's picture and shouting "Eljen!" The crowd which had followed him for hours, shouting with him, finally demanded that he make a speech, for every Magyar was a born orator. Thereupon Ecsegi climbed on to the roof of a cab and said: "Viennese! You rejoice because you are getting a constitution and because Metternich has been kicked out. But all that is not enough. I tell you that if you leave in office so much as one coal-carrier among those who have been your rulers, then the reaction will slip in again through the door of the stove and it will rob you of your constitution and take its revenge on you."

In this unexpected warning of a non-politician gleams the suspicion of the future. An engineer, a man in the street, who knows how to follow the laws of logic, awakes from ecstasy to cold sober thought, and that means, to pessimism. No one takes him seriously, his words are straightway forgotten—and only much later does Pulszky remember having heard of this demonstration, then when events have justified his prophecy. At midday that day, intoxicated with victory, the Argonauts arrived back in Pressburg.

IV

The Day of the Poet

IT IS NOT THE 3RD MARCH, THE DAY OF BAPTISM OF THE revolution, and not the 17th March, the day of triumph of the Argonauts, but the 15th that the Hungarians made their national holiday. For it was on that day that the revolution broke out in Pest and Buda, the twin capital of the kingdom. Here alone in Pest was there a bourgeoisie, that middle class which in Western Europe had long since carried the flag of intellectual culture and was now ready to take over the reins of power from the hands of a discarded feudalism. The Café Pilvax had been the haunt of the pre-revolutionary militants. Now it became a historical centre. For at its tables sat Irinyi who had framed the twelve points which formed the programme of the Argonauts, Jókai, the great novelist to whose epic stories we owe the realistic presentation of the period, and lastly the genius of Hungarian poetry: Sándor Petöfi.

Petöfi is at once the most fascinating and the most touching figure of the new Hungary. The early portraits of the poet—the finest is that by Barabás—express with startling clearness the premature extinction of his flickering star. Like a comet the life of Hungary's greatest poet blazes and dies and it is no mere accident that he has been compared to Byron. He had Lord Byron's charm; like him, he shaped his language to unheard melodies; like him, he hurled himself into a war of liberty and threw away his life, clearly foreseeing his end. This son of a village innkeeper, born on New Year's Eve 1823, ran away from home at the age of sixteen to join a troupe of actors. But he was not destined for a career upon the boards; he refused to sing in popular farces. He had no wish to play the buffoon, he felt himself a tragedian. Self-assured, imperious, like all true geniuses, he could not tolerate another having more success than he. "One day I shall kill this fellow," he said of an actor who was more popular than he was. The fiery outbursts of an ambitious temperament won him enemies everywhere. His friend Jókai has recorded how the critics mercilessly pulled to pieces the first poems of this boy of twenty-one.

But more dangerous than the pundits with admonitory forefinger to the young poet are the well-meaning friends who recognise him and try to introduce him into the *salons* of the aristocracy. A noble, Petrichevich, attempts to be the Mentor of the Hungarian Byron. With a sure aversion to everything that is not genuine Petöfi contemptuously rejects his well-intentioned admirer's patronage. For he is a poet whose roots are in the broad plains of the Danube landscape. His song is of the Hungarian Puszta and for the people of the Puszta. And yet this impetuous poet finds a weekly paper which, together with Jókai, he can fill with his verses. The metropolis needs this native minstrel of the people who, like his prototype François Villon, shocks the comfortable citizens with his wild drinking songs.

At the same time this vigorous son of the Hungarian soil is saturated with the poetry of Western cultures which, surprisingly enough, he reads in their original languages. Like Kossuth he loves Shakespeare; his imitations are exemplary. And so this boy of five and twenty becomes famous in Pest; all the newspapers compete for verses and pay him—a miracle unparalleled in the social history of lyric poets!—high remuneration. His reputation spreads beyond the frontiers of his country, he is spoken of in the *salons* of Paris and Heinrich Heine writes to a Hungarian friend: "First and foremost: give my love to Petöfi."

The poetic spirit of Euphorion finds complete life in the gentle melodies of his lyrics. But soon the resolve to take his part in the rebirth of the new Hungary breaks through his work; more and more clearly, more and more challengingly, until the great apotheosis of his patriotic poems. About 1847, guessing the approach of the day of freedom, he decides for a political career. Petöfi, like Lord Byron, begins his Icarus flight.

The disproportion between his ambition and reality is grotesque. The young man comes forward as Diet candidate in his home county, and is so ridiculed that he is forced to flee from the town for fear of personal violence. But his failure does not discourage the poet. The true inflammatory force burns within him and when at last the events of March bring freedom it blazes forth in great and lasting speech. Jókai, Petöfi and their circle of young poets in the Café Pilvax learned of the world-shaking events on the 14th March. They met on the morning of the 15th. None of them had slept, each one had hatched his plan, each one knew that this day must be decisive. But Petöfi carried in his pocket the fruits of a sleepless night, the manuscript of his immortal revolutionary poem: "Arise, Magyar!" Already a small gaping crowd was gathered round the café; the streets began to fill; the newspapers had roused the citizens with their Vienna news. Now the first duty of a citizen was no longer calm, but action. The mob loudly demanded that something at last should happen. Negotiations with Vienna? They had been going on too long. The capital must show that at last it was taking over the role of leadership within the country in a befitting manner. The excitement increased and the expectancy. Expectancy of what? Of the alarum, the signal. And the signal came. Suddenly out of the smoke-grimed rooms of the Café Pilvax swarmed the little band of youth, with Petöfi at their head. They led the mob over to the square in front of the National Museum and there, on the steps of this pathetic building, the poet addressed the crowd. He spoke haltingly, without the magic of Kossuth's voice; but the fame of the poet and the fire of his words inspired his hearers with enthusiasm. Jókai broke the spell. Following a sudden impulse, the band of poets set off for the printing works of Landerer—Landerer who had betrayed Kossuth. Petöfi and his friends forced their way in, the poet sprang upon a table and here for the first time he hurled his poem at the astonished compositors. Landerer wrung his hands; but the young men made him print the national song there on the spot. The compositors obeyed and a few hours later they were able to distribute Petöfi's poem in thousands of copies on the streets.

Its effect was terrific. The freedom of the press had at last celebrated its triumph. Petöfi's audacity had effected what painful negotiations in Vienna had still failed to achieve. The enthusiastic mob marched on. They wanted their storming of the Bastille. For what is a day of revolution if no prisoners are set free? There was an unfortunate individual, named Tánssics, who had been imprisoned in the Buda fortress for a year for having championed liberty of speech. A mob a thousand strong fetched the old man from his dungeon. He was not unlike the Saint Mark of Albrecht Dürer, with the magnificent head of an apostle. The Pest revolution had its liberated martyr. The procession next marched to the National Theatre where Jókai had to show himself and the famous stage beauty, Rosa

Laborfalvy, kissed the poet. The crowd cheered. With this kiss the actress won the poet who was many years her junior for life: she became his wife.

The spoils of this day were rich. The freedom of the press, the opening of the prison, and finally the formation of the first National Guard which the City Commandant, Count Zichy, taken unawares, helplessly authorised. This was the poet's day. Petöfi had achieved his boldest ambition: he had been the first to realise the revolution. He had even surpassed the man whom all considered the "father of the revolution": Kossuth.

But the glittering action of the youthful Euphorion, born of poetry and culminating in brilliant fireworks, had no impetus of its own. The days that followed began to show sobered, anxious faces. What was going to happen next? Who was leading and whither? The citizens looked to Pressburg. They waited for Kossuth. And Kossuth came to them.

V

Victory and Anxiety

NO SOVEREIGN COULD HAVE RECEIVED A GREATER OVATION THAN the first Hungarian ministry on its return from Vienna to Pressburg. The leaders stood in the bows of the *Béla*, behind them the cheering band of Argonauts. Salutes were fired. The young National Guard paraded, the whole population flocked to the river to receive their leaders as victors. Count Batthyányi was the first to step ashore. He was followed by Kossuth, overcome by suppressed excitement. This was the moment for which he had suffered martyrdom, of which he had dreamt as a boy. He fell upon his knees and spread his arms as if in blessing over the crowd; he bared his head and said: "Welcome, beloved country! God bless our fatherland! We have returned to serve thee alone, after all our struggles in which the inspired youth of our cities have borne their part. But this victory is not to be ascribed to any single person or any single party. It has been won by all of us, for we have all striven for it. We bring to our country the greatest blessings: Independence and Greatness!"

The day ended in jubilation. The rejoicings in Pest and the triumphal celebrations in Pressburg could not fail to make everyone conscious that the New Hungary had become a fact. Even Kossuth who had been filled with misgivings in Vienna because the old clique still sat undisturbed in their offices at court could no longer help believing that the burden of three hundred years had irrevocably been lifted from Hungary. Hungary was free! It was true that the king had not accepted the twelve points drawn up by Irinyi, but the royal decree had notwithstanding given the pledge of freedom. "From to-day on Hungary shall be governed from Buda, and no more from Vienna." In this crucial sentence was the guarantee of a happy future. Count Batthyányi had been appointed by the king as the first responsible prime minister of Hungary. After this victory no pessimist could fear the future.

So thought the people. They bowed in respect before Count

Batthyányi, they united in love for Kossuth. The historian says: "Kossuth's popularity throughout the country was miraculous." And now, too, the sole and last opponent added his voice to the rejoicing of the nation, this nation which through Kossuth had become a people. Even Széchényi admitted: "Bolder and more courageous spirits, with whom higher invisible forces seem to have been allied, have placed the future of our country on a new basis which our ant-like labours would perhaps never, or only after generations, have been able to bring about."

The prime minister was busy forming his cabinet. This was easy: the leaders were known and ready. It was only possible to put in a good word for one or another of the many meritorious pioneers of the revolution. And so Kossuth interceded for the young Szemere, one of his favourite adherents, who had been among the band of Reichstagsjugend at the time when Kossuth was fighting with the pen. Szemere seemed loyal, and Kossuth wanted to have this fearless and resolute, if somewhat radical, ally at his side. Batthyányi naturally heeded Kossuth's recommendation; and thus Kossuth created in the person of Szemere—a future enemy; once again his generosity gave the army of his opponents a new auxiliary. It was given to Kossuth to love people, but not to see through them.

The cabinet seemed practically fixed; the Palatine had already submitted it to the king in Vienna and obtained his approval. Kossuth had asked for himself the most important post after that of prime minister, the Ministry of the Interior. It was evident that he should have been given it. Archduke Stefan proposed it to the king and in view of the enormous popularity the liberator enjoyed no one dared to deny him his wish. How nobly he had behaved in renouncing the prime ministership in favour of Batthyányi! Kossuth could set his mind at rest and go to Pest where the people were clamouring for him.

The liberation of the people had had a very curious result. The newly liberated looked askance upon the new rights of their neighbours. Was freedom meant for all alike? Already on the 19th March, two days after the victory, the superior German merchant classes suddenly discovered that this new freedom would also be enjoyed by their most dreaded competitors: the Jews. The Jews still lodged in the narrow square of the Buda hill and in a few streets in the centre of Pest. Were they now to mingle with the rest as free and fully privileged fellow-citizens? Their sons, enthusiastically carried away by the wave of nationalism, already had the audacity to offer themselves for the National Guard, now in process of formation. But this was not how the townsfolk interpreted freedom. They had not read Lamennais and learnt the spirit of humanity and brotherhood. It was for them Kossuth had thought, it was for them Kossuth had striven.

In the night of the 20th March small parties of citizens made a surprise attack on the sleeping Jews in the Jewish quarters of the city. Such scenes had not been witnessed since the days of the cholera insurrection when the Jews were burnt together with their masters. Some Jewish National Guards in uniform were standing sentry in front of a Protestant church. They were greeted with cries of: "Down with the Jews!" This was already on the 17th. On the 19th a huge mob assembled in front of the town hall where a Jew happened to be posted sentry. The guard drew his weapon in self-defence; someone attacked him and was wounded. A riot ensued. The most violent scenes were enacted in the streets where the Jews lived. New slogans were placarded demanding the disarming of the Jews and their removal from the National Guard. At four in the afternoon began a regular Jew-baiting drive; the newly emancipated townsfolk decided to take matters into their own hands. The city council was tainted with pro-Jewish sympathies. "The gruesome phantom of a riot which had nothing in common with the revolution stalked through the streets. The mob seethed into the Kiraly utca, the main thoroughfare of the Jewish quarter. The poor Jews fled—they were mostly old people—with the mob howling at their heels. The crowd rushed savagely from place to place, continually attacking any passer-by who looked as if he might be a Jew."

But Kossuth's spirit also dwelt in Pest. The Reichstagsjugend was worthy of its master. They put themselves at the head of the National Guard and routed the Jew-baiting mob. Finally soldiers were called out, all the squares had to be occupied by troops, whole battalions camped in the city. At last the riot was suppressed. But it flared up afresh in the provincial towns.

It was obvious at once to the dispassionate observer that this attack against the nationally enthusiastic Jewish population was originated by the recently defeated reactionaries and was instigated by Vienna. "These were the first heroic deeds of the reaction. It began with the Jews and meant to finish with the Magyars. For the Jews were, like the Magyars, democrats, but they began as always with the weaker part" (Chownitz).

Kossuth in Pest recognised with grave concern these unmistakable omens of fresh struggles. The suspicion dawned on him that Vienna was secretly preparing an attack. Was it possible that his words of warning addressed but four days ago to the Viennese had been prophetic? Full of misgivings he returned to Pressburg.

And now for the first time it became evident that the victory had been too easy. One of the most shocking moments of Kossuth's life—never yet described or understood in all its tragic import—was his reception on his return of the completed cabinet list from his friend Batthyányi. Did it include any new names? No. Kossuth himself had begged Deák, the calm and prudent thinker, to accept a portfolio and Szemere was his man. Baron Eötvös, the poet, had of course to be found a place in this "ministry of brains," and Prince Eszterházy, the champion of a "democratic hell," might be counted as a partisan of the new government despite his feudal origins. These were men who valued Kossuth. Kossuth had made Batthyányi prime minister—what did Batthyányi do for Kossuth in return?

Would he be given the Ministry of Foreign Affairs? Would he be entrusted with responsible powers to carry on negotiations with Vienna and work for a closer contact with the France of Lamartine and Guizot? Would he at last be allowed to send his ambassadors to the land of true democracy, England, and to give testimony to Hungary's fight for freedom in the White House, before the democracy of the New World? There where the spirit of George Washington dwelt eternally alive? But it was not Kossuth, but Prince Eszterházy who received the Ministry of Foreign Affairs and already he was assuming his old diplomatic mien, letting fall no hint of the immediate tasks which Kossuth would have carried through. Was then the Ministry of the Interior to be his sphere? To control the police, to regulate the reconstruction of the administration and—this more particularly—to create laws governing the press which would at last make a fact the freedom of the press? But Batthyányi was content to give this post to Szemere. He was not mistaken in his man: the draft press law which Szemere submitted a few days later was so reactionary that fresh disturbances broke out in Pest and the destruction of the bill was demanded—successfully. (Szemere's press law was compared with that of the citizen king Louis Philippe and was solemnly burned in front of the town hall of Pest with outraged curses.)

Was Kossuth to be Minister of War? To build up the army, to urge on with iron energy the organisation of a Hungarian military force purged of the pro-Austrian officers, and arm the country still menaced by the intrigues of reaction? But the Ministry of War was given to an old General, Meszáros, who only with difficulty adapted himself to this new role which must at first have appeared very strange to an old imperial officer. What niche was then to be found for Kossuth? The poet Baron Eötvös was a splendid placard for Culture and Education. (And this sensitive poet was the first to flee during the autumnal tempests of this year, before even a shot was fired.) Deák was indicated for Justice and as Minister of Commerce Klauzál was in his proper place. What remained for Kossuth?

Kossuth bit his lips as he perused the list. He came upon the one name that he had least expected to read there: Count Széchényi. Here he was again, his old antagonist, the tireless jealous companion of his career. Had he not retired into the shade, the privy councillor, excellency by the favour of Metternich, now that his high protector had fallen? Metternich had been forced to flee, a hunted quarry; his steaming horses were drawing his carriage across Bohemia and Germany; no one would harbour him, he was hated everywhere; and everywhere the fugitive was recognised. With difficulty the gouty old man reached North Germany, and there too he was spied out and hounded on, despised and rejected, until he found a ship to take him to the hospitable shores of England. Metternich in exile—and Széchényi raised by the same wave which had annihilated his protector? Batthyányi had invented a Ministry for Public Works and Agriculture in order to include him in his cabinet—and Széchényi had accepted. His admiration for Kossuth had burnt out like a fire of straw. Fear of Kossuth had forced him into this ministry of his former political opponents and ranged him among the revolutionaries.

Fear of Kossuth? But what remained for the martyr of the cause, the father of the March revolution? Batthyányi had only one gap in his list and as he could not pass Kossuth over—the man in the street would never have stood for a ministry without Kossuth—he begged him to fill the gap. Kossuth was offered the Ministry of Finance!

Kossuth was silent. But he accepted the portfolio.

What did it matter what office was given to Kossuth? Whatever his province, he would lead. So thought the people. But Kossuth saw it differently. He perceived that the list had been drawn up with a cunning skill so that he should be paralysed. Paralysed by an office which must of necessity make him unpopular; paralysed by the presence of Széchényi who would not cease to cramp him with the arrogance of his inveterate antagonism; paralysed by his colleagues who were clever enough, but not strong enough, to exploit the initial victory.

This is the most painful episode in the struggle between the House of Hapsburg and Hungary. But it is also—and this must be fully emphasised—the most fateful. The first cabinet had to prove to the people that Hungary was able to govern itself and that after fifteen years of struggle Kossuth was going to lead it to the serious realisation of his ideas.

Who had prompted Batthyányi to such a combination of the reaction with the new spirit? Kossuth found his suspicions confirmed: the old rulers still sat in the chancelleries of Vienna and in the palace, active and ambitious, watched the Archduchess Sophie, mother of the young Franz Josef, whom the witty Viennese had long since named "the archduchess Camarilla." She saw to it that the rights sanctioned on the 17th March were soon nullified. This was the first political triumph of Vienna within a few days of their most ignominious defeat; it was meant that Kossuth as a minister should be exposed as well as crippled; for it was clear that the task of putting order into the muddled finances of Hungary would be his undoing. It was to this plot that Count Batthyányi had lent himself. At this juncture no one could have done the Hapsburg a greater service and Batthyányi, perhaps in exaggerated fear of a further aggravation of the conflict through Kossuth, had done this service. A year later the House of Hapsburg requited it—by executing him!

The composition of this cabinet must have made it evident to Kossuth's clear-sightedness that the valuable time for real constructive work would pass in inactivity. And so it was. In the few days which remained before the dissolution of the Diet nothing happened, and even later when the signs of coming storm were unmistakable nothing happened either. The ministry had paralysed itself. Kossuth knew that as Finance Minister he would have to work against the whole cabinet in order to assure the first victory by permanent success.

At first Kossuth was anxious to avoid any unnecessary conflict. Vienna had yielded and must be trusted in return. But soon the Vienna camarilla dispelled the confidence of awakening Hungary itself. At that time no one could have known that the emperor and king Ferdinand was, on the 17th March when he complied with the wishes of Hungary, preparing a counter-attack. The court had let Metternich go without a word, but Metternich's spirit and example still dictated its behaviour and thereby that of the feeble-minded emperor. The principle of *divide et impera* that had stood the test of centuries was once again to save the Hapsburgs. Had not the Croats revolted at the same time as the Hungarians? Was not this awakening an epidemic among all the nationalities along the Danube? The king of Hungary had rewarded the leader of the "Awakening Croats" with his approbation and a diamond scarfpin, whereas, in the opinion of the court, Hungary was guilty of insurrection. Against Hungary more effective gifts than diamond pins must be employed.

On that same 17th March the emperor sent a personal letter to Baron Jellasich, the most energetic leader of the Slav movement. Jellasich had been an Austrian officer, a simple colonel of a frontier regiment with no prospects of making a career from his remote garrison. Panslavism brought him into prominence; Jellasich began to travel about Croatia agitating against Hungary, which had for centuries ruled Croatia as part of its territory under the administration of a "ban." Thus the emperor of Austria protected Colonel Jellasich whom, as king of Hungary, he should have persecuted as a rebel! In this letter written with his own hand the emperor promised to appoint Jellasich Ban of Croatia, although the appointment belonged to Hungary—formerly to the kings of Hungary and now to its responsible ministry. But very soon it was realised with alarm in Hungary that Croatia was ripe for a revolt against them. On the 25th March a national meeting was held in Agram at which the "Illyrians" resolved to send a petition to the king asking for independence from Hungary. Jellasich was proclaimed Ban of Croatia.

This was the first counter-stroke of the court against Hungary. The journalist Chownitz had been right: it began with the Jews and was continued with the Magyars. The reaction was taking the offensive against democracy.

However the indescribable excitement at the events in Hungarian Croatia did not lead to the results desired by Vienna: instead of threatening Croatia in an outburst of anger, the new Hungary decided on a just and worthy attitude. A new generation had grown up; in this spring-time of the nations let the Slav Croats too enjoy their freedom. If they wished to use the Croat language, well and good; Hungarian should only be employed in their common legislation. The answer given the Croats is a moving document of the new spirit: "Croats! Beloved brothers! After three centuries of oppression we stand at last upon the threshold of independence and freedom. The things that we have fought for, we have won for your no less than for our own welfare. The device under which we have fought is not our nationality, but the sacred name of liberty."

This manifesto was published in Agram in Croatian and Hungarian. At the same time Kossuth delivered a speech on the 28th March in which he expressed his conviction that "the steps taken by the Hungarian Diet had been received with grateful enthusiasm in Croatia." But this was a mistake. Jellasich went on agitating. And now in the Hungarian province of Croatia begins the first dangerous counter-stroke against the New Hungary.

No one as yet suspected that the events in Croatia were the result of a well-laid plan. Like all idealists when they enter the political arena, Kossuth was on the horns of a dilemma. The Illyrian movement might be tolerated as a thesis, but as a political activity it must be paralysed. Kossuth still believed in the illuminating force of an idea; freedom must have an ennobling effect and must range the Croat brother alongside the Hungarian champions of liberty in the struggle yet to come. But in Vienna the tactics of internal conflict were better understood. To-day we know that the exploitation of the Illyrian movement for the purposes of reaction was premeditated. The policy of Vienna was actuated by hatred of democracy and fear of Kossuth's Hungary—even though the most dangerous agitator's hands were tied by the moderate ministers of Batthyányi's cabinet. That policy was to use one nationalist movement to scotch the other.

In the confusion at the Vienna court following the expulsion of Metternich the archduchess Camarilla kept her composure. She, the wife of Franz Karl, the brother of the emperor, deliberately aimed at compromising Ferdinand's régime by further troubles and forcing the obstinate imbecile to abdicate. Not her husband whom she dominated like a minor, but her son, the handsome young Franz Josef, was to be emperor. Her allies were the arch-abbot Rauscher, the prominent churchman who later exercised the greatest influence as archbishop of Vienna; Prince Windischgrätz, the commandant of Prague; Count

Stadion, the governor of Galicia; and the secret and most important ally of this camarilla was the Ban of Croatia. The hated nationalism was to be made the invisible auxiliary of absolutism.

Suddenly the new Hungarian government was startled from its apparent lethargy by the news that the emperor had simply revoked his warrant of the 17th March. Twelve days later, on the 29th March, the king declared himself no longer bound by his royal word. Consternation in Pressburg. Even the most circumspect and pro-Hapsburg member of the cabinet, Prince Eszterházy, had not thought this possible; nor had Batthyányi reckoned with this. Once again the tempest was let loose in the Pressburg Diet. The Archduke-Palatine declared his readiness to proceed at once to Vienna and to threaten resignation. Was the game then to begin all over again? Kossuth looked angrily at Batthyányi. So this was what they had made of their victory; wasted fourteen valuable days; a cabinet of tired men vigilant to see that no step was taken towards reorganisation; and already the old despotism was showing again its ugly face. Batthyányi had wished to cripple Kossuth? Now he showed that, whatever his office might be, he still remained the impulsive, animating force of the government.

He sprang to his feet and all the aggravation of the past days coloured his voice: "I say that this rescript is an outrageous mockery. Who is playing this wanton game with our country? The all-pervading spirit is that of the hated bureaucracy of Vienna; in their eyes the Hungarian independent ministry in Buda is no more than an insignificant post office. Little they care for the future of the imperial house of Austria, little they care for the blood of citizens which may now flow in rivers. They come out into the open to palter with the sacredness of a royal promise." And at the end of his great speech Kossuth demands that those guilty of this treachery to Hungary be arraigned.

That evening when the steamer brought the news to Pest, the mob demonstrated against the castle with cries of: "To arms!" The central committee in Pest threatened open revolution. Petöfi delivered a fiery speech against Vienna. It seemed now as if the moment had come once more to unleash all the forces of the people and to strike the decisive blow. Only one thing was lacking before the red flag of revolt could be unfurled: Kossuth must give the signal. But Kossuth held his hand. In this hour he proved his statesmanship. Had he been the insurgent, the demagogue, the gambler with destiny, he would now have taken the offensive with the excited masses, cleared out the feckless cabinet and seized dictatorial power himself. Chaos still reigned in Vienna, the succession states were still in ferment, the Vienna populace could easily be brought back into the streets, and before any general from the provinces could bring up his troops the Hapsburgs would be driven out and the might of the ruling house broken for good and all. But Kossuth stood loyal. But he demanded that the king keep to his word.

The decision of that day, the 30th March, is of historical importance. Kossuth had the power in his hand to carry through, alone and with certainty, a second revolution. He did not use it. If now the Hapsburg fail to keep his word, if now blood be shed, if now the country be hurled into the adventure of a war: Kossuth must be acquitted of any blame.

But once again the storm clouds lifted. The Palatine returned from Vienna: the king had reaffirmed the competence of the cabinet, and had signed this ratification with his own hand. So it was peace after all! Kossuth was glad that he had resisted the temptation. In another speech he said, alluding to these recent days of crisis: "Strange are the ways of Providence: I, a plain citizen, was for some hours in the position to decide the fate of the Austrian throne. And even now, if I were to say: we do not want the king's answer—the blood of my countrymen would flow at my bidding. But there is no more execrable crime than to gamble with the life's blood of one's fellows and a nation's peace."

Kossuth wanted order, strength and peace. His Protestant spirit had made him a rebel so long as the dignity of Man was endangered. Reconstruction must begin in a free country. Kossuth concluded with a final conciliatory word for the imperial house: "The king must not believe that his might is in any way impaired by the changes in the system or the concessions which he has made. His power is enhanced and now will be fulfilled the prophecy that the second founder of the House of Hapsburg will be that ruler who gives his peoples a constitution."

Simultaneously the old, blind Wesselényi addressed the excited townsfolk of the new capital in similar strain: "If the chains of tyranny are to be broken, then the people must be worthy of their freedom. Now there is but one duty: obedience. For anarchy is a bridge across which the absolutism that has been driven out always returns."

Fresh jubilation swept the country. Thanksgiving services were held everywhere. Monók, Kossuth's native village, decided to erect a statue to the liberator. On the 11th April the thunder of cannon announced the arrival of the king in Pressburg. His Majesty solemnly entered the palace where the final meeting of the Diet was being held. The nobility in gala dress, the high dignitaries of the church surrounded the sovereign pair. Batthyányi stood beside the archduke-palatine, immediately behind the king. Speaking in Hungarian, Ferdinand once more reaffirmed his promise, which guaranteed peace and freedom.

The following day the Hungarian cabinet moved to Pest.

VI

Confusion Worse Confounded

KOSSUTH HAD SHOWN THAT, EVEN WHEN SIDETRACKED AS MINISTER of Finance, he could still keep his grip upon the political leadership. Now he meant to demonstrate that he could cope with the special demands of his difficult office. He was fortunate in finding in Franz Duschek, a former Austrian official, an authority on matters of finance; he gave him his unreserved confidence and Duschek was ready to serve Kossuth with the same devotion as he had once served Metternich.

Heedless of the effects of this new and difficult work upon his health, Kossuth gave himself no rest. The Minister of Finance alone worked while the others slumbered. Having demanded in his pre-revolutionary programme the abolition of statute labour and the freedom of the peasantry, he had now to come to an agreement with the landed nobility. Where was money to be found? Hitherto the Court Treasury in Vienna had independently disposed of the revenues from Hungary. Not only the revenues from taxation, but also every kind of inland duty was drained into the great vat of the Viennese treasury; the gold and silver from the Hungarian mines was delivered directly to the Vienna mint and Hungary was thus robbed of her natural riches. As far back as 1835 Kossuth had pilloried these arbitrary methods of the financial administration. Now the power was in his hands. He acted with dictatorial thoroughness. A waggon load of gold and silver which was on its way from Kremnitz to Vienna was stopped by his orders and sent back to the mint at Kremnitz. For obscure reasons the Hungarian krone had fallen and was sinking steadily. Kossuth inquired into the cause; he made the Vienna National Bank send immediately over a million gulden in specie to the Bank of Buda. The Vienna treasury tried secretly to have the enormous revenue from the duty on tobacco transferred to Vienna, but Kossuth was vigilant; he had the money brought back. Gradually the financial position of the kingdom ameliorated.

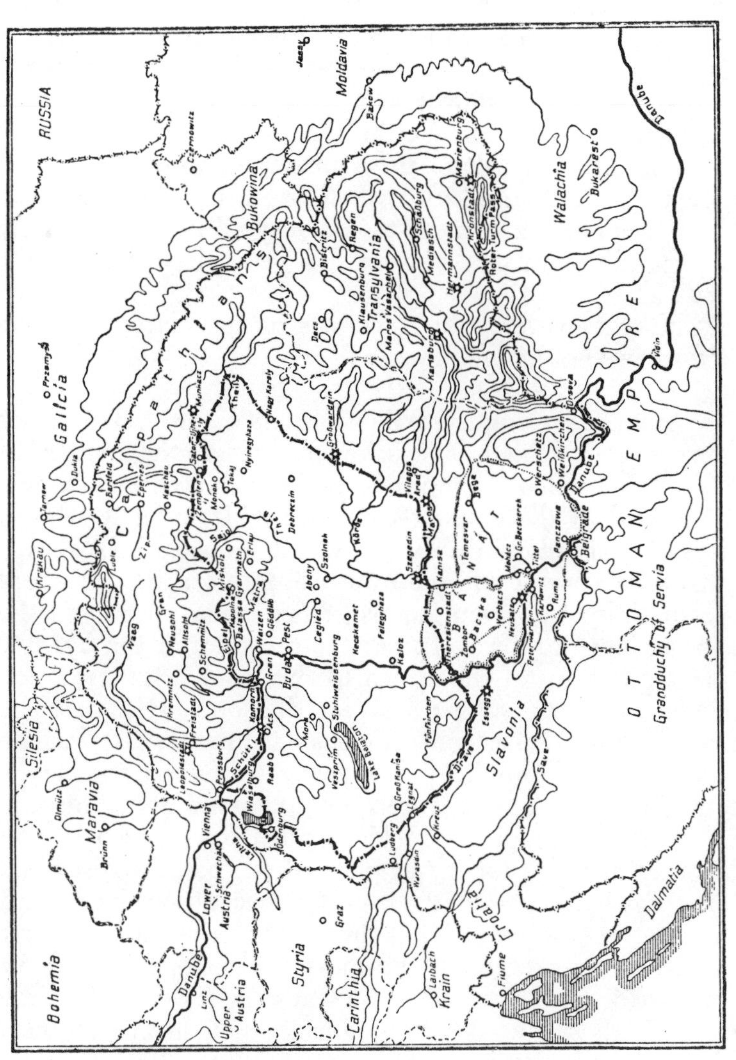

Hungary's frontiers from 1815 till Peace Treaty of Trianon
" " after " " " "
Austrian frontiers in 1848

He next turned his attention to mining problems, for rightly administered the mines gave the country its guarantee of financial independence. His aim was to make Hungary financially autonomous. The mint should coin Hungarian money, the National Bank should issue Hungarian notes. In a few weeks, on the 24th May, thanks to Kossuth's extraordinary energy the imperial governor authorised the issue of Hungarian bank-notes. They became known as "Kossuth notes"—and soon these Kossuth notes were to be the symbol of prosperity and of decline in the life struggle of the Hungarian nation. . . .

Duschek was so enthusiastic over Kossuth's brilliant financial operations that he exclaimed to Pulszky: "If we can only govern the country in this way for five years, it will become a paradise."

But Pulszky's answer was: "You talk of five years. We can be glad if we are not hanged in one."

Sinister rumours continued to flow in from Vienna. It was not without reason that historians have nicknamed the mother of Franz Josef Camarilla. The proud and clever archduchess was indeed the soul of the counter-movement. It was she who in these days of trial upheld the dignity of the House of Hapsburg; it can thank her that it still held the sceptre until the threshold of our own times. Contemptuous of her timid entourage she kept unswervingly to her purpose: the salvation of the dynasty and the safeguarding of the crown for her son. But her pride was greater than her mother's love. She once said that she would rather sacrifice her son's life than see the dynasty cringe before a mob of impudent students. While Batthyányi's cabinet was sleeping on its laurels, she gathered about her the strong men of the empire. Field-Marshal Radetzky was still with the army in Italy; for it was planned to quell the disturbed areas of Italy before resubjugating the succession lands and Hungary by force of arms. Till then let the revolution be left in the belief in its power, let the masses learn disappointment and then, when their patience was exhausted, it would be time to incite the purposely awakened nationalisms against each other. The Ban Jellasich was in high favour with the archduchess. He was given a free hand.

On the 10th May Jellasich began the campaign against Hungary. He revealed himself now openly as a Panslav and gave the address of welcome to the Slav Congress which met in Prague. Inspired by the influence of Bakunin and other prominent Slav leaders, the idea of Panslavism here first gained political force and from this day never faded. In every country nationalities were fighting for their existence. Kossuth had welded together democracy and nationalism for Hungary. Now the Slav peoples were following in his trail. On Whitsunday there was an open riot in Prague. Once again the students, the barometer of all revolutionary epochs, bore the brunt. Windischgrätz hastened back to Prague at the head of the army. He occupied the heights above the town and threatened to bombard it. But his threats had no effect. Shooting began. A stray bullet struck Princess Windischgrätz as she watched the fighting from a window of the Hradschin. Her bereaved husband had to carry on with his duty. That evening he gave the signal for the bombardment to begin. The artillery opened fire and immediately one part of the town burst into flames. Now the surrender of the town was only a question of hours. Even the bravest cannot but give in when big guns fire upon a defenceless city. Prince Windischgrätz was quickly able to suppress the rising; but he could not stifle Czech nationalism.

And now it becomes apparent how dangerous it is to play with the idea of nationalism in the countries of South-Eastern Europe. Now suddenly every little minority awakens and, heedless of geography, aspires to a reorientation according to nationalist principles. The eternal powder magazine of Europe begins to smoke. Hungary is rocked in every corner of her kingdom, for she numbers the most minorities. The Serbs living in Hungary, having their own church, the Greek Orthodox, now remember the national ties that bind them to the inhabitants of the principate of Serbia still under the supremacy of Turkey. They send a deputation to Pest in order to profit by the March liberation for their belated national consciousness. Kossuth receives them. And this reception gains a historical importance; for from this day dates the hatred between Magyar and Serb who had for so long lived in harmony as neighbours. As short a while ago as March, the Serbian nationalist leaders had declared their steadfast unity with their native Hungary. But the influence of the Croat movement kindled nationalist aspirations. The deputation presented itself to the new government. In the spirit of his democratic conviction Kossuth promised the Serbs complete equality. The deputation thanked the minister. But now something very curious happened—the deputation came back a second time. What did they want? Kossuth thought that they were there to express their thanks on behalf of the liberated peoples. But they began to talk politics and suddenly their spokesman, Stratimirovitsch, asked the minister whether it were compatible with the new idea if the Hungarian Serbs attempted to unite with the Serbs in Turkey with a view to the creation of a great South Slav empire. Kossuth was thunder-struck. The idea was high treason. Never would Kossuth tolerate an infringement of the unity of the kingdom of St. Stephen. He frowned and flung his questioner his answer: "In that event let the sword decide between us."

Simultaneously the Saxon and Roumanian minorities in Transylvania awoke. German nationalists sent envoys from Breslau, Leipzig and other towns to give their Transylvanian brothers the promise of their support. Likewise the Wallachs discovered, thanks to the propaganda of a Roumanian professor Barniatu, that they were the oldest inhabitants of the ancient Roman province of Dacia and as such were inferior to nobody. Thus fresh troubles within the frontier threatened Hungary and this land, loyal to the crown, was being secretly goaded by the agents of the camarilla and abandoned to the dismemberment of nationalities.

The new government was no match for the intriguers of the Vienna court. Batthyányi appeared not to notice all these troubles. He relied upon the king's promise. But when Jellasich became more and more openly provocative, Batthyányi went to Vienna and appealed to Ferdinand with the result that the general in command in Slavonia, Baron Hrabovsky, was appointed royal commissioner and instructed to charge Jellasich with high treason. Batthyányi was satisfied and on this day, the 14th May, he privately celebrated his triumph over Kossuth, the victory of a pro-Hapsburg policy over the impatient innovator.

Kossuth was ill. The strain of overwork had been too much for him. He had once again to recuperate in the Buda hills. He still carried on his work as Minister of Finance, but he was weary of daily raising his voice in warning in the cabinet. He alone mistrusted the honesty of Vienna. But Batthyányi's success in the matter of Jellasich seemed to justify his policy. On the night of the 15th May, Kossuth paced restlessly about the rooms of his modest cottage worrying. He was coughing and hid from his beloved wife the fact that he was coughing blood. He believed that he had not long to live. What had he achieved? He was a minister—but his hands were tied; he stood alone in a ministry that in the course of a few weeks had been at pains to retrace the road that his twenty years of toilsome labour had opened for them.

The next morning he was surprised by news which rent the dark clouds like a ray of light. Once again the Vienna populace had taken to the barricades against the reaction. Soon after reports came in that the military had occupied the city. By way of answer the National Guard and the Legion marched against the palace. The situation of the government grew worse from hour to hour. All the students were armed. The Minister of War, Count Latour, had sent all available troops to the Italian provinces to help Radetzky to establish order. In the long run this measure proved a wise one, for it saved the monarchy. But for the time being Vienna was denuded of troops. The emperor was forced to give way all along the line. At 2 a.m. on the morning of the 16th May he proclaimed a second constitution, promising to summon the Diet to ratify it. The joy in Vienna was unbounded.

The camarilla was playing for time. Radetzky once victorious in Italy, the army would be at hand to overrun the obstreperous mob and to purge Hungary of the heroes of March. Jellasich was given renewed encouragement by secret messages. The nationalism of the Croats was still the surest weapon against nationalist Hungary. The Archduchess Sophie had profitably studied the history of the French Revolution; she had no intention of waiting until these democrats openly declared themselves republicans. The strong and loyal army lay in the south. So why not go south where there was safety? The indulgent emperor Ferdinand was easily convinced that the peril of the streets might grow greater any day. What might not happen to-morrow?

Vienna learned on the morning of the 18th May that the emperor had fled. The news plunged the populace into consternation. Vienna was an imperial city. How could it live without its emperor?

Now corporations and unions, students, artisans and intellectuals, vied with each other in petitions begging the emperor to return. But the court stood firm. The emperor declared himself deeply distressed at the events of the 15th May and expressed his sad conviction that "an anarchist faction was determined to rob him of his freedom." Popular feeling veered. The gravely menaced democracy gathered its forces for a counter-stroke. On the 26th May barricades were erected in Vienna, and Pillersdorf, who was carrying on the business of the government, was compelled to give new promises and make new concessions in the emperor's name.

These events had an immediate effect on Hungary where the reaction was showing its horns more and more openly. On the 10th May Lederer, the commandant of Buda, gave orders to fire on the townsfolk because the excited masses demanded the arming of the National Guard which the general had refused. Terrible scenes ensued; the people indignant at the "brutal soldiery" clamoured for Lederer's dismissal. The poet Petöfi again put himself at the head of the mob. Lederer fled and the appointment of Hrabovsky as commander-in-chief, subordinate to the Hungarian ministry, reassured the people. The flight of the emperor made the subterranean intrigues of the camarilla clear even to the well-disposed and loyal ministers. But what happened? The cabinet sent Prince Eszterházy to Innsbruck to reassure the court as to the plans of the ministry. Actually nothing happened; inactive, dilatory, the cabinet waited with incredible lethargy for the development of events. Already alarming news was coming in from the frontier districts and Croatia. Acts of violence were reported in the Orthodox Serb areas, the Wallach were growing restless, and Jellasich was inciting the whole of Croatia to open insurrection. He seized the town of Varasdin and took possession of the public funds—and this in peace-time.

Kossuth came down from his retreat and, pale and wan, appeared at the meetings of the cabinet, exhorting his colleagues in the feeble voice of a sick man to act. He was listened to with complacent smiles. He had to be satisfied with giving Hungary the possibility, by reorganising her finances, of being able to declare her independence, if that should be necessary. But he knew that there was only one effective weapon, if Hungary was to emerge victoriously from these troubles: a Magyar army. Her sons were still serving in foreign regiments, fighting under Radetzky on Italian soil or with Windischgrätz in Prague, and only Hrabovsky's Drave command might perhaps hold up Jellasich. But Hrabovsky made no move. Jellasich was pressing forward and Buda was garrisoned, on the old Hapsburg principle, with foreign regiments, Austrian and Italian. On Whitsunday there were fresh disturbances; the Italians began a fracas with the National Guard and there was wild shooting

THE EMPEROR FRANZ JOSEF IN THE YEAR 1848

From the Portrait Collection of the National Library, Vienna.

in the streets. And still the cabinet preserved its apathy, looking to the king, to Innsbruck.

It was now time for the camarilla to advance the king on the chess-board of internal politics. Draft letters were presented to the emperor which he copied and signed with his own hand. They were intended less for the addressees than for the general public. In June these letters fell like autumn leaves borne on the wind from Innsbruck. The emperor's letter to the archduke-palatine: his promise very soon to visit his loyal Hungary. A letter to the Ban of Croatia, summoning Jellasich to Innsbruck. A letter to the governor of Transylvania, investing the archduke-palatine with full powers as "alter ego" of the king. And now on the 17th June another letter to the archduke-palatine in which General Hrabovsky was ordered to relieve Jellasich of his office.

In spite of this the insurgent troops advanced. Fighting occurred at Szeged; the Serbs pressed on. But the cabinet had full confidence in the letter-policy and ridiculed Kossuth's warnings. The news arrived that Jellasich had been taken from Innsbruck in irons to the fortress of Kufstein. That meant the end of the Croatian rising. But at the same time the Croatian regiment stationed in Agram expelled their Hungarian officers. How were these two things to be reconciled? At last, on the 26th June, the government learned that the deposed traitor Jellasich had been—received in audience in Innsbruck; "not as Ban," to quote the court circular, "only as Baron." This shameless sophistication could not fail to alarm even the most trusting.

Now Kossuth could contain himself no longer. He said to his friends: "If this poor nation does not end by helping itself, its ministers are hardly likely to help it." The outlook was more threatening. The Agram newspaper was not afraid to publish openly that the Archduchess Sophie had greeted the Ban Jellasich with the words: "My heart is with you." And her heart, as everybody knew, was the heart of Hapsburg policy. The enemy of Hungary was the friend of the ruling archduchess.

Now some decisive step must be taken. "We are standing on the edge of the abyss!" cried Kossuth. If the government abandoned the country to its fate, he would resign. His warnings fell upon deaf ears. As a minister Kossuth had accomplished a vast deal within his province, but as a politician, as Batthyányi had foreseen and hoped for, he was paralysed. There was nothing for it but to return to the opposition. Back to his personal freedom and then forwards to a fresh assault. On the 29th June Kossuth resigned.

To the people his resignation was synonymous with the end of freedom. Now everything was lost. Even Batthyányi saw that a government without Kossuth would be a government without the people at its back. On the night of the 30th Kossuth's friends and Batthyányi himself begged him to retain his office. The count admitted that his policy was wrong. He promised to break with Széchényi; he agreed to accept all Kossuth's demands and to propose to the new parliament which was on the eve of opening the creation of a Hungarian army. Kossuth withdrew his resignation.

But his personal victory over Batthyányi did not give him back his peace of mind. Even if he remained minister, instead of resuming his old leadership of the determined opposition, he had still to find a way of restoring his former contact with the people. He had too long been bottled up in his sick room in the Buda hills and in his office at the ministry. Now once again he took up his old effective weapon, the pen. In a passionate article on the 2nd July he made a vehement appeal to the king to trust the loyalty of his Hungarian subjects and warned him against the new friendship with the Slavs. "The Panslav element offers no future to the house of Austria. If it is victorious, its victory will benefit a foreigner."

Never had an Austrian statesman prophesied so clearly the fate of the House of Hapsburg. Perhaps at this hour Metternich would have heeded Kossuth's warning. But the Archduchess Sophie, who had involved Jellasich in her intrigues, little suspected that to save the dynasty for the moment she was preparing the ruin of the dynasty in the future. Sooner or later, as Kossuth had prophesied, Panslavism must break up the mosaic of nationalities that formed the Danubian monarchy.

VII

The Day of Weakness

AT THE HOUR OF OPENING THE DIET WAS BLACK WITH PEOPLE. Punctually Kossuth arrived. He was deathly pale, hollow-eyed from illness, worn with pain. Two deputies had to support him as he walked unsteadily to the speaker's rostrum. He was unable to begin and had to recover himself by leaning on the desk. A hundred voices called to him to sit. In a dull voice Kossuth answered: "Yes, later, if I have to, and if you permit me." Then again a pause. Surely this man would not be capable of speaking for longer than ten minutes. He began with an indistinct and scarcely audible preamble. But once he had commenced to speak, unsuspected strength infused his tortured body, triumphant melody crept into his feeble voice. And he spoke for several hours, a fanatic, master of incomprehensible clarity.

"Gentlemen, our country is in danger!'" For the first time the situation was given its true name; a minister of the government made plain admission of its gravity. In this time of anxiety Kossuth was the only one who had the courage to tell the unvarnished truth. He stated that Croatia had already gone over to open insurrection. But once more he urged the choosing of conciliatory methods. "Be just towards Croatia and do not suppress the revolt by force of arms, but with the sacred name of justice!" He shrank from bloodshed. He who had forced Batthyányi's consent to the formation of a Hungarian army wished to avoid the appeal to arms. Was it not possible to make the Croat people see that they too, as part of Hungary, would enjoy all the rights of a free nation? Kossuth pointed out that the new constitution had gained for the Croats, no less than for themselves, their national independence. "When a people takes up arms to gain more liberties, it plays a hazardous game, but I can understand it. But when a people says: I cannot tolerate your freedom, I do not want what you offer me, but I prefer to bow under the old yoke of absolutism—that is something which I cannot understand." Kossuth saw through

Jellasich's game; he knew that the Ban of Croatia was driving the country into the arms of the reaction. The cabinet's efforts to reach a peaceful agreement with the rebel Serbs had found no echo. War was imminent. In this hour of need Kossuth called upon his country to defend itself. With blazing face and mighty voice he thundered: "The readiness of the nation to defend our fatherland has far exceeded my hopes. God has let me live to see this day: the Magyar's soul is stirred and I no longer doubt the future of the nation."

At last Kossuth came to the vital question, Hungary's attitude to Austria. "Has the emperor in Innsbruck reprimanded the Ban? No. The Vienna cabinet has thought fit to point out to the ministry of the Hungarian king, in the name of the Austrian emperor, that it will abandon its neutrality towards us unless we conclude peace with the Croats at any price. This means that the Austrian emperor declares war upon the Hungarian king; that is, upon himself." This dialectical formula suddenly illuminated the whole danger of the situation: by the March constitution Hungary, after centuries of struggle with the House of Hapsburg, had won her independence. According to the pragmatic sanction, the king was again king of Hungary and only by personal union also sovereign in Austria. The emperor's threat meant that the emperor—or rather the ruling court—was encroaching on the rights of the king of Hungary. What would be the outcome? The tendency of the court, even if it were nowhere openly expressed, must be to incorporate Hungary with Austria. Hungary's counter-aim must be to prevent this and to sever the kingdom from the empire.

Under the veiled threat which Kossuth uttered, quivering with excitement, the thoughtful could guess what he had left unsaid for fear of giving the signal for disloyalty too soon. On the 16th March he had not abused his power; he refused to do so now. But as sentinel over the liberty of Hungary he warned the court against their dangerous plotting. "Vienna may well be grieved that it can no longer rule us. It is all very well to respect a grief, but one nation will not subjugate another for the sake of it. But, loyal as we are, it is not to be expected of us that we compass our own ruin. Vienna wants to take out of our hands again the Ministry of War and of Finance. Our answer is: Come and fetch them!"

A storm of cheering greeted Kossuth's speech. His proposal to send a message of greeting to the new Germany and to bring about "an alliance between Hungary and free Germany" was likewise received with acclamation. But the Archduke Johann, who, as imperial administrator in the emperor's absence, had opened the German National Assembly in Frankfurt refused to receive the Hungarian embassy, while the Germans questioned the legitimation of the envoys of an independent Hungary. Lasalle was right: these men in Frankfurt too lacked the strength to be the pioneers of freedom. How splendid was this idea of Kossuth's to unite those genuine democracies, Germany and Hungary! But such union is less swiftly accomplished than that of reaction with reaction, police state with police state, absolutism with absolutism; and history teaches that these unions are the stronger. For he that believes in might, rules better than he that is the victim of an idea and only relies on might as a last resource, and then in deepest contradiction to his principles.

In this hour of need Kossuth had at last risked an appeal to might. Kossuth at last demanded the creation of a Hungarian army. "Because the peril threatens to become a great one." So he excuses his departure from his pacific principles. The industrious worker had the complete programme in his pocket; he had prepared the finance plan for an army of two hundred thousand men. One final appeal—and the assembly storm round the speaker's desk. Friends and strangers fling their arms about him. With the classic cry: "*Megadjuk*" ("We will give it them") the Diet carries Kossuth's demand. "And now," we read, "a vast silence fell upon the assembly. Hardly a breath was audible. Kossuth whose failing strength seemed only to be kept up by his strength of spirit, crossed his hands over his aching chest and bowing to the house with tear-dimmed eyes, said: "You have all risen to your feet as one man. I bow before the greatness of this nation!" Men wept. A wave of emotion swept the house. Now Batthyányi too was on his feet embracing Kossuth. This momentous hour had bridged all differences. Besides which Kossuth, the outsider of the cabinet, had by this resolution saved the government.

The army was created.

After this triumph Kossuth's health broke down. Once more the quiet of the hills received him. And once more the self-torture of the lonely hours destroyed his rest. What drama was enacted in his soul? The fanatical struggle to remain true to his ideals and the duty to protect Hungary rent him between opposite resolves. If only on the other side, in Vienna and in Innsbruck, the same lofty thoughts had determined policy!

But the revolt in Croatia and in the other frontier districts continued dangerously. Was war inevitable?

A few days later Kossuth went out for a drive. He met the first newly formed volunteer corps, the hussars of Colonel Lopresti, with their tall shakos ornamented with cocks' feathers, their red waistcoats, wide white sleeves, green breeches and streaming red cloaks. A thrill of joy ran through him, only to be succeeded by the fever of care. What could he do to avert war?

It may be that Kossuth's vacillation in these days of crisis was due more to his state of mental conflict than to his physical debility. Only thus is his indecision comprehensible. For several days he absented himself from the meetings of the cabinet; but then one of the most important decisions compelled his presence. Austria demanded that the Hungarian contingent should be sent to Italy where Radetzky was still fighting unsuccessfully in the insurgent provinces. There can be no doubt that Kossuth, the creator of the future Hungarian army, had intended the units which had been already formed solely for the defence of their own country, and not for the suppression of the Italian nation in Lombardy and Venetia. But an amazing thing happened. Kossuth recommended the sending of the troops. For the first time his speech fell flat and the small but weighty opposition booed his decision.

No attempt has ever been made to excuse this day of weakness in Kossuth's career, nor yet to find an explanation for it. If the dilemma which of necessity besets the idealist when he makes an incursion into practical politics is not sufficient explanation, then it may well be that Kossuth, already scenting the smell of blood and powder, clung desperately to loyalty, even if by so doing he were false to his ideas. The pragmatic sanction, he must have said, enjoins Hungary's aid when Austria is in danger. To fight nationalism for the sake of loyalty! He must have salved his conscience with a sophism which, formulated epigrammatically, denoted: "Whoever is against the Croat insurrection, must also be against the Italian." In vain the speakers of the opposition interrupted that by denuding Hungary of her embryo army they were inviting Jellasich to walk into Budapest. Kossuth stuck obstinately to his way of thinking which seemed to him the narrow path between the abysses of extremes. The majority was with him. But—curious spectacle—the conflict in his own breast was unconsciously reflected in his behaviour. The orator stammered, the dialectician contradicted himself. Suddenly Kossuth demanded moral assurances. In return for Hungary's loyal obedience he expected the emperor Ferdinand to pledge himself to give the Italian provinces their constitutional freedom! He looked to the successor of the tyrant Franz I for understanding for the sons and brothers of the prisoners of the Spielberg! The opposition sneered. To expect a constitution at this moment when those in Innsbruck were doing their best to destroy the constitution of the 17th March? Kossuth felt that his *via media* led into a blind alley.

The following day clearly revealed the weakness of his position. Batthyányi forced Kossuth to declare that he had only expressed his personal opinion and had not spoken as minister. And now the assembly realised that even within the cabinet Kossuth was fighting a hopeless battle. The opposition grew. Batthyányi, Deák and Széchnéyi had to defend their standpoint, but they could not prevent it being decried as an Austrian standpoint. Finally the motion for the despatch of troops was carried, but with Kossuth's amendment that the constitution must be promised to the hitherto enslaved Italians.

While this was going on Jellasich advanced and his superior, General Hrabovsky, took no steps to hinder him. Once more Hungary appealed with an address to the king, begging him to act against the Ban "who was foolhardily contemptuous of the king's summons to obedience." The king's answer was that he soon afterwards appointed Hrabovsky commandant of Pest, thereby ordering him to leave the insurgent area and opening the way to Jellasich.

The Hapsburgs were clever political strategists; this had assured the continuance of their rule through centuries. But it also led to their collapse. The nineteenth century brought nationalism into being as a new political reality. The most elaborate system can only temporarily divert the youthful energies of this idea; it cannot weaken them. The continent still seemed imbued with the spirit of liberalism, but already in Prussia appeared the figure of Bismarck, in Italy Mazzini and Cavour, creating slowly but surely national unity. In the Danube area the formation of national states could not be brought about without disorders, for here nationalities and territories overlap. Kossuth was right when he won national independence for the kingdom of St. Stephen; on this one day he had been willing for the sake of political tactics to forget his prophetically envisaged goal. His tactics were mistaken. He was to learn this in a terrible lesson.

VIII

Too Late!

A FEW DAYS LATER, ON THE 12TH AUGUST, RADETZKY ENTERED Milan as victor. Now the camarilla could drop the mask. Their object had been achieved: Hungary had been held in check until the insurrection in the southern provinces had been quelled. Count Latour was justified; he had risked denuding Vienna of troops, but now the victorious army under the great field-marshal was free to return to the disaffected towns and areas. The victory not only assured the Hapsburgs mastery in northern Italy; it demonstrated to the imperial court and all loyal subjects of the Hapsburgs that the army could be depended on. For in Radetzky's army Hungarian hussars had fought side by side with troops from the Croatian frontier, Polish lancers with Tirolese riflemen, Czech infantry with German grenadiers. Every soldier with Radetzky knew that he was fighting to defend the House of Hapsburg.

Those who had eyes to see in Pest had no illusions as to the meaning of Radetzky's victory. "Beware of the Italian army!" warned the papers. "The reaction will now restore the monarchy with the sword!" Indeed the picture altered in a flash. The emperor put off receiving the Hungarian deputation—one of the many which visited him in Innsbruck—until the moment when he was getting into his coach to return to Vienna. He was most ungracious. Batthyányi was waiting for him in Vienna. The prime minister's policy of conciliation must surely at last lead to a successful issue. Now was the moment for the king to keep his promise to come to Budapest. Already in June, Széchényi had besought the king: "I am moving heaven and earth to get the king to Buda," he notes in his diary. The court, and principally the Archduchess Sophie, had made loose promises. But now after Radetzky's victory his appearance in the heart of Hungary would have sufficed to relieve all tension. This would have been the triumph of Batthyányi's policy and the abandonment of the foolhardy plans which Batthyányi and Széchényi alike suspected behind Kossuth's insistent energy.

Kossuth had set the army on its feet, a Hungarian army. Batthyányi had been unable to prevent it. One might have thought that Széchényi, the "greatest Hungarian," would have welcomed the creation of a national army, for in this muddled world the sword is the best defence, the army the guarantee of peace. But Széchényi, the reformer, had never approved of this step. He was afraid that Hungary would still further widen the breach with Austria.

The emperor arrived in Vienna. His first action was to relieve his *alter ego*, the archduke-palatine, of his authority. The Vienna cabinet handed Batthyányi a memorandum containing a whole list of crimes of which Hungary had been guilty. Kossuth's finance measures, the plans for the formation of a national army, the sending of ambassadors to Frankfurt, these were all viewed as grave delinquencies. Kossuth was named as the moving spirit of these anti-Hapsburg actions.

Batthyányi importuned the cabinet and the court to be allowed to speak to his king. It is the last chance of a peaceable discussion, the last chance of stifling the menace of a second revolt at home. But he is denied an audience.

Too late! The court feels itself strong. It has no wish to compromise. It is determined on the restoration of absolutism.

In this difficult situation the much-abused Kossuth still looked for a solution. Fresh fighting, ending partially in the success of the Hungarian troops, showed how grave the situation had become. But even within the Hungarian camp there was danger: the officers who had taken the oath of allegiance to the emperor appeared half-hearted in their duty to the national army. Kossuth saw but one hope: a large deputation of a hundred persons must go to Vienna and once more beseech the king-emperor to save his throne and to allay excitement by coming to Budapest. The deputation was chosen and started immediately on the 5th September.

Kossuth had no objection to the hotheads of the Café Pilvax abusing him as a monarchist. Yes, he was a monarchist; he had never ceased to be one. Once again practical common sense triumphed over the promptings of his ideas; he wanted to avoid the shedding of blood. If the king would reaffirm the March constitution and acknowledge the nation's financial and military independence, then all would be well and there would be an end of all revolutionary activity. He did not ask what place there would be for himself in a contented Hungary. And even now the man who most feared and hated him, Count Széchényi, misunderstood his great rival.

This is the tragedy of Hungary in these years of crisis. As in one of Shakespeare's dramas, men of imposing stature tread the stage, but weaknesses and passions, errors and prejudices paralyse the energetic, confuse the wise, and fritter away the unity of the noble guard that should have advanced in brotherhood towards a common goal. Petöfi, in the glorious blindness of his youthful enthusiasm, hated Kossuth. Széchényi who believed that Hungary was born of the fair dreams of his own mind repelled Batthyányi who had taken the reins out of his hands, and yet he joined forces with him to cripple Kossuth's powers. His diary is full of apostrophes and grim forebodings. "Kossuth has lighted the fuse" and "I was a reformer. He has gone so far as to start an *auto de fé*." In May when the king's flight gave the optimists hope, he groans: "The future is pregnant with blood! Black clouds over the whole of Europe. They will soon burst. Blood will flow in rivers." And again: "I brought light, Kossuth fire," and in the last hour of crisis: "Kossuth's name appears to me in the history that is yet to be written in a sea of blood."

And this man, Kossuth, now waited anxiously in Pest for his "great deputation" to be admitted to the king at the eleventh hour, hoping to avert the sanguinary issue. Dreadful news drifted through. Jellasich openly declared that he would begin the war against Hungary with eleven battalions on the 14th September. How few days were left before this horror happened! Kossuth trembled. No news from Vienna. Again the deputation was refused an audience. On the other hand it was reported that Jellasich had occupied the port of Fiume on the very day on which the first Hungarian ship was due to leave the harbour.

The 8th September. At midday the deputation was to be received. At 11 o'clock they set out in Hungarian gala costume for Schönbrunn. Everything was in readiness for the reception. Life guards in full parade. A vast concourse of people. Then, on the stroke of twelve, the imperial state coach drove out of the palace. The guard presented arms. The delegates were allowed—to go for a walk in the palace park.

At last on the 9th September the audience was commanded. The emperor appeared in a black dolman accompanied by the empress who smiled graciously to the Hungarian nobles; she had insisted on wearing red, white and green ribbons in her hair. The spokesman of the deputation made a long address, humbly and anxiously begging the king to end the troubles by coming to Budapest. The king did not move a muscle and then when his turn came spoke the little piece that had been formulated for him: "I cannot come to Hungary for I am ill. I cannot yet sanction the laws passed by the Hungarian parliament, for I must read them first. If you have any other wishes My Austrian cabinet will deal with them. Furthermore I shall know how to guard the integrity of My Hungarian crown."

This was the end! Too late! Then the last straw: it was learnt that on that very day a personal letter from the emperor had been despatched to the traitor Jellasich in which he was expressly assured that His Majesty was aware that he had "never pursued any treasonable intention." His appointment as Ban was confirmed and he was reassured of special favour.

The deputation rushed back to their ships. And a strange thing happened. Those who had started out to reaffirm the idea of monarchy against the onslaught of the young radicals, now put red feathers in their hats, tied red ribbons round their sword-hilts and accepted red flags from the excited citizens of Vienna. And thus these Hungarian nobles in their gala costume drove through the streets of the imperial city like a horde of rebels, champions of those working masses from whom a whole world separated them.

Too late! Soon, too, the democrats in Vienna will be muzzled. Prince Windischgrätz has occupied Prague. How long will it be before he makes his entry into Vienna? Will he march on Buda, too?

After the return of the deputation every one in Hungary knew that the policy of conciliation had collapsed. Kossuth writes in his paper with such spirit and such lust for battle as he had not written for thirteen years, with the old fire and fearlessness of his "Farewell to my readers." "Are we going to sit still while the enemies of Hungary abuse the king's enfeebled health? No, we shall do nothing of the kind."

The following morning the rumour spread like wildfire through the city that Batthyányi's cabinet had decided to resign as a protest against the policy of Vienna. Crowds thronged the streets. Every one asked: "What next?"

IX

The First Victim

ARE REVOLUTIONS NECESSARY? DOES A REVOLUTIONARY UPRISING only accomplish the legal adaptation to an already changed social condition, as Lasalle thought, or do men, chosen by fate, consciously and of their own strength, transform the political picture as they wish? The most bloody revolution, that of 1789, disgorged from nonentity a quantity of figures who suddenly became the executors of a super-personal historical will. Certainly there were among them "revolutionary types," characters nature had trained for this hour of revolt. History teaches that the first advance guard of revolution, such as the heroes who first storm the palisades, are doomed to destruction. If the assault is beaten off, they are the victims; if it is successful, then the revolutionary troops push after them and clear those who have opened the breach out of the way. Revolution always follows the same pattern: the moderate, level-headed leader who still has moral obligations to the crumbling world is swept along by the truly volcanic force of freedom.

Now, after the emperor had rejected Hungary's last efforts for peace and had already secretly made military preparations against her, the age-long simmering revolt of the awakening Magyars assumed the character of revolution.

Count Széchényi, never in agreement with the new ideas and yet implicated by his love for Hungary, found himself drawn helplessly into this labyrinth. He feels himself hounded by destiny towards the precipice, hastening towards inevitable disaster. Ever since the first days of March he has been visited by sinister forebodings, the peril grows ever more threatening; its name is Kossuth. When Batthyányi begged him to join his ministry, he had no illusions as to what acceptance meant. As usual, he confided his premonition to his diary: "I have signed my death sentence. I shall not escape the knife." And he adds in comment on the tragedy of his fate: "The piquancy of the situation is that Kossuth at least will die for his opinions, but I shall perish for a doctrine that I have always fought."

He cannot sleep. Obsessed with fears and self-reproaches, he curses the day on which he presumed to awaken his country from its "Asiatic slumber." Added to his fears for the salvation of his soul is the anxiety that his life's work, the suspension bridge, which is almost completed will not be finished in time. In time—before the catastrophe, before his own candle is snuffed out. He spends the early morning hours on the bridge, counting and testing the chains waiting to be fastened in position. Once a chain snapped and this happening threw him into a veritable fit of despair. This chain became the symbol of his own fatal enchainment, a terrible omen of God's punishment. On the 25th August when the fourth chain was to be stretched, a midsummer hurricane burst upon the city—a sign of annihilation: "No work done on the bridge because of storm. Ha-ha-ha! The bridge will not be finished." He sees visions; he hears voices. On the 29th he notes: "Voices again. An ocean of blood. Feel I am damned. Beat my head. Confessed at seven this morning." And on the 30th: "No one sees the appalling catastrophe. Am filled with despair. Walk about the suspension bridge."

Indeed the Count, to the horror of the English engineer, Adam Clark and the workmen, walks about on the unfinished, loosely hanging girders of the bridge, stopping at dangerous places and staring into the depths below. With difficulty Clark conducted his friend back to terra firma. A rumour gets abroad that the Count has sought death in the river. He turns up again at a cabinet meeting. But on the 4th September he enters in his diary with a dreadful calm a confession which is the bald and cruel utterance of his own death sentence: "Slept four hours. Then again scourged by the Eumenides. Wanted to shoot myself. The servant disturbed me. Never has any man brought more confusion into the world than I. O God, have pity on me!"

The next day Széchényi rushed out of his house and down to the river, to his bridge. He was on the point of throwng himself into the Danube. An awful cry: "Blood! Blood! I see the name Kossuth written on the heavens in letters of blood!" Then he collapsed. A revolver falls from his hand. He has not pulled the trigger. His face is deathly pale, his expression petrified. His mind seems in darkness. The same day his friends placed him in the lunatic asylum of Döbling, near Vienna.

The revolution had found its first victim, just as the first days of the earlier revolt of 1835 had taken as victim the young hothead Lovassy. On the first day of the revolution Kossuth had lost his great opponent. But the news horrified every one, especially Batthyányi, who had so long revered Széchényi as the guardian spirit of loyalty.

The collapse of Széchényi ended the dramatic conflict of two decades between the two outstanding personalities who had raised awakening Hungary to historical greatness. Often smouldering and timidly disguised, then again naked and unconcealed, this conflict had accompanied the building-up of the national state. Had it hampered it? Certain is that the mighty figure of the Count had dammed Kossuth's revolutionary élan; certain is that the tirelessly creative magnate had obliged the upstart Kossuth to develop his powers to the full. The antagonist was great enough to check Kossuth's dazzling rise to power, important enough to compel Kossuth's magnificent self-education. Széchényi's jealous and uncompromising opposition forced Kossuth to make himself his peer.

The first serious attack of madness with its suicidal tendency lasted for several years, until at last in Döbling "the greatest Hungarian" was restored to lucidity and peace of mind. He never left the asylum and lived on there for years as "cured," senile and broken, until a fresh attack in a characteristic "unguarded moment" drove him to the fulfilment of his suicidal urge.

With Széchényi a great man retired into the shadows from the arena of events. In the history of the Hungarian revolution, so lavish of great figures, Széchényi is certainly the most interesting, Kossuth the most important. Széchényi soon sinks into oblivion in the consideration of his people and he had to wait for later generations to be once more appraised at his proper worth. But there was still one man who knew how to read the present with the incorruptible eye of wisdom: in London in exile sat Prince Metternich, himself now condemned to inactivity, but, as he said with a smile, "the spectator in his box." And Metternich was able to recognise the nature and the importance of the two men who had been antagonists up to the eve of the catastrophe. Metternich gave his opinion of them both to the two foremost statesmen of the coming epoch, Bismarck and Disraeli. To Bismarck (on the 5th July, 1857) he declared Kossuth to be "a great statesman of the revolution." Disraeli he recommended to use the tragic fate of Széchényi as material for a novel. Thus Metternich sensitively differentiated personal tragedy from historical greatness. Kossuth is the hero of the historian, Széchényi the subject for the psychologist.

X

Enthusiasm

THE RESIGNATION OF BATTHYÀNYI'S MINISTRY OPENED TO THE excited population the hope that now at last the man of the people, the real leader, would seize the helm. But the palatine, Archduke Stefan, who up till then had served the Hungarian cause heart and soul, announced that pending the appointment of a new cabinet he himself would take over the government. This audacious illegality threw the people into consternation. But —from now on all political events are inseparable from military— at the same time the news spread through the city that the commander of the Drave army found himself compelled to retire before the advancing troops of Jellasich. "Parliament resembled a huge catacomb, a place filled with frozen corpses" is the description recorded of the impression made by these two swiftly following reports. What was to happen now? The assembly was silent. But all eyes were turned expectantly on Kossuth.

Kossuth had relinquished his seat at the ministerial table. He sat, in order to emphasise his real political attitude, on the left benches, Batthyányi in the centre. Scarcely had the president of the assembly finished reading the palatine's message when Kossuth rose as if in answer to the anxious glances round him. Was he going to make a speech? Kossuth seized a chair and brandishing it above his head sprang on to the ministerial dais. With a crash he brought down the chair on the spot he usually occupied. "The palatine's letter is illegal!" he shouted, pale with anger. "I am still minister. And I should like to see the man who dares to give counter-orders to my orders without the endorsement of a responsible minister." The house broke into a storm of cheering. The assembly understood: at last the promise of real energy was breaking the crippling fetters of Batthyányi's policy of legality. But—and this fact compelled even the most circumspect to join in the cheers—Kossuth's revolutionary gesture was backed by an exact knowledge of the law. The king had not yet accepted the resignation of the cabinet; they were therefore still in office, therefore the palatine's action was illegal.

Now that the hour vehemently calls for action, Kossuth is the only one capable of forming a resolution. This is his greatness, this explains his power. And there is nothing of the demagogue in this decision. Once more Kossuth grasps with both hands at the protecting shield of loyalty, and once more it is a deep-seated human error, the childish trust he puts in others, that makes his decision a mistake. Replete with drama, the last scene is played. Its issue means life or death to the Hungarian nation, peace or war. "The king is ill, and not master of his decisions. Therefore he needs a proxy in Hungary, for only the mighty hand of a Hapsburg can still save our threatened land. Good fortune has given our country such a proxy: the archduke-palatine. The palatine shall be the king's viceroy, not by usurpation, or in defiance of the law, but by the will of the representatives of the people to govern jointly with the responsible ministry."

This was a brilliant move of a political genius, the expression of a policy which still held open the door to conciliation. But Batthyányi promptly rejected the proposal; he is tired of governing; he wants in this hour of danger that the government should be committed to one hand so that unity prevail. His words electrified the assembly. It is true the conflicts within the ministry must cease, a single will must decide—the will of the man who is capable of leading. And now, and not till now, after all other remedies have failed, it dawns upon the assembly that Kossuth alone can be this leader. "Long live Kossuth! Long live the dictator Kossuth!" cries the house and outside the waiting crowd propagates the cry throughout the city.

Kossuth has to come out on to the balcony of the House and show himself to the crowd. A roar of enthusiasm rises up to him, thousands of hands wave to him and many fall upon their knees to do him homage. An eye-witness thus describes the scene: "As the crowd bared their heads before him and he before the crowd, I feel that I am in the presence of a great man, I am conscious of the indescribable, mysterious breath of a great spirit. The people acclaim Kossuth dictator. Kossuth has only to reach out his hand. And what does he do? He stands calm and steadfast as a pillar; he lets the sea of voices surge over him. When the noise dies down, he begins in a firm, unfaltering voice: "First and foremost I declare my unshakable allegiance to my king." A tumult interrupts him: "We do not need a king." Kossuth continued: "But to you, my beloved people, to you, the land I adore, belongs my whole being. You must be saved. Trust me and have no fear." The people went mad with enthusiasm."

Kossuth went back into the assembly hall. The house elected him chief of the new cabinet. It is decided to send a deputation over to Buda to the royal palace so that the Palatine may confirm this choice. Meanwhile Kossuth immediately proceeds to lay before the house the most important laws which the situation demands. He formulates them extempore: the army must be made a real national defence force, the infantry must be called "Honvéd" (defenders of the fatherland); corporal punishment in the army must be abolished for good; the officers must be invited to enroll themselves in the new army. A bill to this effect is passed unanimously. The first hour's work of a new ministry. Kossuth has solved more problems than Batthyányi's ministry in six months. Hungary will wax strong through Kossuth's energy. But—a fresh denouement in this drama full of thrills—the deputation returned from the Palatine: he had refused to ratify Kossuth's appointment; he would rather leave Hungary than suffer this indication of mistrust towards himself. Nevertheless the House once more reaffirms its resolutions.

But in the evening when the House assembles for a night session Kossuth and his henchman Szemere are in their ministerial seats. Kossuth asks for another deputation to be sent to the Palatine to assure him that the election of a prime minister by the House without previously consulting him was in no way intended as an expression of lack of confidence. Kossuth dwells upon the unvarying nobility of the archduke's behaviour. Then Batthyányi rose to speak. He whom Kossuth had first recommended to the people as the first prime minister declared that the Palatine had meanwhile nominated him prime minister.

A vast silence fell upon the House, the dead stillness of a mortuary. This intrigue behind the scenes dumbfounded the spectators of the drama. Everybody knew that now the *élan* of the first hour must evaporate and Hungary would be again delivered over to the helplessness of Batthyányi, now in this hour of crisis. Kossuth rose to his feet from the prime minister's chair. He opened his lips to speak and then reeled, the colour left his face and it seemed as if he were about to fall. Szemere supported him; then helped him into his coat. Kossuth who was shivering with ague collapsed the instant he withdrew his arm; Batthyányi caught him as he fell. And amid the dumb excitement of the whole assembly Batthyányi led him out on to the balcony. There they remained while the minutes dragged, cooled by the gentle breeze of the September night. Then Kossuth came back, walking very slowly, and left the hall. No one followed him.

At last Batthyányi broke the silence. He informed the House that Jellasich had crossed the frontier and invaded Hungary.

Now events followed swiftly. Now the secret forces emerged into the daylight; the camarilla threw aside the mask. Count Teleki, the commander of the Drave army, refused to march against Jellasich. Jellasich issued a proclamation to Hungary, declaring himself the "executor of the emperor's will." The danger was grave indeed. But now, when the mischief seemed inevitable, a startling change came over Count Batthyányi: the proud magnate, the scion of national heroes, became a fighter. "I will contest Jellasich every foot of Hungarian soil," he declares and for the first time he has the House behind him.

But Kossuth became the soul of the resistance. Consumption has its grip on him, but still he works untiringly building up the army. From day to day his speeches strengthen the people's determination to resist. "Our freedom is guaranteed by the oaths of fourteen kings of the House of Hapsburg and all these fourteen kings have broken their oath!" And at last Kossuth dares to speak the word which preludes a new epoch, the second, sanguinary revolution: "Sons of the fatherland! Magyar people! I speak to you as a prophet. I have made many prophecies and I shudder when I see that all, all of them have been swiftly and horribly fulfilled. Yes, each of my warnings has became a fact, even the prophecy of the dreadful illness of the man—Széchényi—whose memory is linked with so many services, the death of whose intellect fills my heart with sorrow. What I foretold of the monarchy, of the Hungarian aristocracy, of Croatia, has all come to pass. I shudder; I feel as if the book of fate lay open before my eyes; the light darts through my soul like the lightning through the darkness." And now with the religious solemnity of his Protestant faith Kossuth calls upon the nation in the name of God to arm. "In the sacred name of our poor country, so perfidiously betrayed, I beseech you, believe the prophecy and it will be fulfilled. Arm, therefore, Magyars. For your country, for your homes, for the heritage of your forefathers, for the soil which nourishes you! The fatherland is all.

KOSSUTH—GUBERNATOR HUNGARIAE

From the Portrait Collection of the National Library, Vienna.

The grave-sad music of the Rákóczi march assembles the whole Magyar people—and then on against the enemy!"

The people obeyed this summons to a man. In wild enthusiasm, yelling "Éljen Kossuth!" a colonel Kis, with a handful of troops, repulses the advancing Serbs; the fanatical deputy Perczel forms the Zrinyi Corps, composed of Buda grenadiers, and leads them against the enemy; the Thurszky regiment goes over to the Hungarian forces. Kossuth rides post-haste through the country calling the people to arms. With fiery speeches he personally recruits the troops, 4000 in Cegléd, in one little town 3000 and in Kecskemét actually 12,000 men.

Now the Palatine also decides to enter the camp. But the Hungarian army is not yet organised, as yet no battle has been fought, and Jellasich scores a victory over the Palatine by diplomatic cunning. The Palatine had gone to meet the Ban as he advanced on to Hungarian soil; he had sent his chamberlain to demand a personal interview in the hope of inducing him to stop. A meeting was arranged. Jellasich had already reached the vine-clad hills that fringe the southern valley of Lake Balaton. The archduke went aboard his steamer; the place appointed for the decisive conversation was on the neutral territory of a ship's deck in the middle of the lake. But the Ban never came. It was said the Croat officers persuaded him not to trust the Palatine's desire for peace; but if Jellasich alleged that he who claimed to be a Hapsburg-loyal general believed the Hapsburg archduke capable of going back on his word, he proved by his action that he had planned this meeting as a trap; on that day the Ban's army turned Lake Balaton; no further obstacle impeded them; only a broad plain and then Budapest lay within range of their guns.

So through this eleventh hour desire for peace once more a day, an all-important day, was lost. If history may teach a lesson, then it must teach the student of this year, 1848, that the longing for peace, the clinging to loyalty, the tardy subservience to the letter of the law, which stigmatise every ideological viewpoint, cease to be political means as soon as the adversary in the political game disregards the rules. Already the smell of blood was rising over the plains of Hungary and still the government clung to the rules of loyalty at which the enemy scoffed. The consequences were disastrous and grotesque: Batthyányi hastened to Lake Balaton to lend the Palatine his support, but his well-intentioned absence gave nourishment to the wildest rumours and the cause of a dreadful act of blood. For the emperor had meanwhile appointed General Lamberg as commander-in-chief and commissioner extraordinary over all troops, and sent him, an intimate friend of Batthyányi, to Buda. No doubt in order to gain the necessary time for the policy of the camarilla until Jellasich stood before the gates of Buda. But the people, believing themselves deserted—Kossuth was in the provinces—thought that imperial troops were already on the march. Lamberg innocently drove down in an open carriage from the palace into Pest, with the good intention of presenting himself to the Diet. The news alarmed the radicals among the population whom Kossuth had always opposed. An armed mob met the Count's carriage as it crossed the bridge; they pulled him out; Lamberg fell on his knees and begged for mercy; a student from Székely ran him through with a sabre and the mob hurled themselves upon their victim and plunged their knives into the still quivering body. Then the armed peasants spitted the dismembered corpse on their scythes and bore their ghastly trophies through the streets. The remains of the imperial commander were hanged on a lamp-post.

Thus this bloody struggle of two sister peoples begins in horror. Perhaps it is part of the mysterious mechanism of this unnatural assault of armed forces against an unarmed people that defencelessness should break out into a fiendish and uncontrollable eruption. For only a few days later the exasperated people of Vienna behaved in the same way by murdering the Minister of War, Count Latour, in broad daylight in the open street.

Such were the excesses of despair. But Jellasich was moving forward. The Palatine recognised the error of his dilatoriness. The archduke was beaten; he had not the courage to report to his ministry; his role in the tragedy of which the first act was now being played was that of a weakling. He fled. In his desperation he fled to his imperial cousin and, on the 24th September, resigned his office. This noble weakling, this well-intentioned bungler, this slave of his good faith collapsed like Széchényi.

Until the last moment Kossuth had fought against abandoning the sheet anchor of legality. But now that Hapsburg had defied the rules he recanted: "The salvation of the country is the highest law, the means to this end are at all times legal. This is the only consideration we must respect. Our country must be saved." He had always fought against the fatal policy of waiting; now, when even Batthyányi had at last resolved to act, Kossuth wanted feverishly to accomplish what he had never had the chance to do. The whole land must rally to the Hungarian flag. The time was past for truckling to hesitant opponents; his duty was to be the artisan of history. And Kossuth sought out every corner of the land to play his part.

Meanwhile, on the frontier things were not standing still. At Kossuth's wish a new deputation headed by the old blind Wesselényi was sent to the people of Vienna. But the same Vienna which had acclaimed Kossuth rejected it; the Diet refused to receive the Hungarians. And then a surprising event brought fresh hope. The army under the command of Moga which had continued to avoid a clash with Jellasich's advancing forces gave battle. Between Lake Balaton and Buda there is a conglomeration of little lagoons to which the Hungarians have given the name Velence—Venice. Here the Croats were decisively beaten. Suddenly Jellasich's bubble reputation of invincibility was pricked; he proved himself to be a bad general. The troops of the young Hungarian army took fresh heart. Jellasich's advance was stopped. But again the unexpected happened: Moga, instead of pursuing the beaten enemy and annihilating him, granted him a three days' armistice which Jellasich used to flee to Sopron, taking six thousand of his men with him. The remainder of the army, a whole corps, deserted by their commander-in-chief, were taken prisoner by Colonel Perczel's three thousand men. The effect of this victory was great, as great as the anxiety to replace the irresolute in high positions by younger and more energetic men. Moga was accused of treachery. It is certain that he and part of his staff of old officers were not disposed to conduct the military campaign for Hungary's freedom.

Now begins the search for new men of military ability. As once the intellectual revolt of Hungary had produced poets and thinkers of genius, so now in this hour of need new leaders appear at the head of Hungary's army. Kossuth was the soul of this war of self-defence, but he knew that he must not be the general of an army, if he was to remain the leader of the movement. In the coming war it would be the care of the leader to stand over the generals with the greatest watchfulness. This would be Kossuth's hardest and most dangerous task.

At first it seemed as if this momentous hour had blessed the country with great men. Now, as at the siege of Toulon, the way is open for military genius. Perczel has earned his promotion; soon Dembinski, formerly governor of Warsaw, appears on

Hungarian soil; at this time too a Polish officer, Bem, who had fought in Davoust's corps under Napoleon, offered his services to the people of Vienna and assumed the military leadership of the October insurrection, but after the capture and bombardment of Vienna by Prince Windischgrätz, the general came to Hungary and organised a splendid army in Transylvania. And now a young officer who, tired of waiting in Austrian frontier regiments, had sent in his papers and devoted himself to chemistry, appeared at the Committee of National Defence and asked for a battalion. He was accepted, given the rank of major and the command of a small unit under Perczel. This young officer, Artur Görgey, like Napoleon before Toulon, perceives the opportunity to prove his military genius. In his search for new generals Kossuth finds him—and he, Artur Görgey, whose star is in the ascendant, becomes Kossuth's new, most dangerous and most feared antagonist.

Meanwhile, the conflict grows more and more acute. The emperor is back in Schönbrunn, enjoying the fine October weather in the palace park, while the camarilla about him push matters to a head. Prince Windischgrätz is now the right hand of the apathetic Ferdinand, the hope of the Archduchess Sophie, the fist of the reaction. He persuades the king-emperor to proceed to sharp measures against Hungary: the Diet is dissolved, all new resolutions declared invalid and, first and foremost, Jellasich is appointed commander-in-chief in Hungary and Transylvania. This decree of the 3rd October for the first time names the adversary; it denounces the moving spirit of the national revolution as the enemy of the House of Hapsburg. "To our great sorrow and indignation the house of representatives has allowed itself to be misled into grave illegalities by Lajos Kossuth." The insignificant lawyer of Monók who knocked in vain at the doors of the Buda palace seeking an official appointment has become the king's enemy.

But for Prince Windischgrätz who has laid Prague at his imperial master's feet Kossuth is not the only enemy: he is fighting on the side of the archduchess Camarilla—against the emperor himself. It is clear: the times need a strong man; the sovereign who must laboriously be driven to decisions, whose pen almost requires guiding so that he may be made to sign the necessary measures, can no longer be allowed to be a drag upon the wheel. The young archduke Franz Josef is already being coached in the part he will be called upon to play. On his eighteenth birthday he is to be declared of age and crowned emperor. During these days Prince Windischgrätz' brother-in-law, Colonel Prince Schwarzenberg, returns to Vienna from Radetzky's army in Milan. Schwarzenberg has the reputation of a Don Juan; a strikingly handsome young man of thirty, the lover of all the ladies of the aristocracy, a Byron in uniform, whom Metternich had removed to distant unimportant courts when he was still in diplomatic service. But he is notwithstanding a man of great acumen, brilliant intelligence and devoted to the ruling house. Windischgrätz recognises to his own astonishment that he is the man to guide the young Franz Josef, as chancellor in the new absolutist era. Metternich sits, the spectator in his box, far away from the conflict in the Hapsburg empire, but Schwarzenberg will carry on his tradition. This almost chance selection already decides the fate of Hungary, for military might needs the leadership of the politician, just as the Prussian army needed Bismarck. Kossuth had now another powerful opponent.

Meanwhile, Kossuth celebrated his greatest triumph. In Szeged he addressed the people who had flocked in from the surrounding plains in the most wonderful of all his speeches. In his words, burning with religious fervour, the fight for freedom becomes a sacred cause. From his lips speaks the spirit of Lamennais, the spirit of Luther, and overpowered by the greatness of the moment the people acclaim the man who undertook to make it a people.

XI

War and Winter

KOSSUTH HAS SWORN THAT HE WOULD NOT BE TAKEN ILL AGAIN. It seemed as if the strain he put upon himself improved his health. He was everywhere. He led the resistance both politically and militarily, overshadowing the ministry. At the beginning of hostilities he published a "Manifesto to the Peoples of Europe"; now he followed this up by sending ambassadors to every European capital to rouse the sympathies of the Powers for Hungary's fight for freedom. Count Teleki worked for him in Paris and his friend Pulszky in London. Men of consequence, principally Richard Cobden, took up the Hungarian cause and the British government recognised that the Hungarian question was of international importance. The ground for European intervention was prepared. This diplomatic action meant a great deal; it gave Hungary the hope that after a victory they might obtain a new regulation of the situation in the southern Danube area with the agreement of the Powers. If Hungary gained her independence, Austria would disappear as a great Power. The Holy Alliance would at last be broken up. A new grouping of the great Powers would result. Kossuth spread a wider net. The great democracies of the West, England and the United States, seemed to approve of his ideas. The name Kossuth appeared in the political leading articles of the Anglo-Saxon newspapers. Only in France opinion seemed to veer against him; Kossuth learnt with misgivings that the President of the Republic, Prince Napoleon, was secretly aiming at becoming emperor. Count Teleki reported that it was already being said derisively of the Prince-President that he was playing "the nephew, carrying on the uncle." No intervention by France? No help from the Italian states? But a friendly attention on the part of England, words of encouragement from the United States where Webster now embodied the tradition of this truly democratic republic. As in the day of his imprisonment the Anglo-Saxon spirit had brought him to maturity, so now the thought of these great democratic empires strengthened his determination.

For it was essential that, sooner or later, the small Hungarian army must obtain help from abroad. Windischgrätz had just surrounded Vienna with an army of a hundred thousand men and "purged" the insurgent capital of its die-hard democrats. Soon this huge army would unite with the armies under Jellasich's command which were advancing on all sides, aided by the minority groups in the frontier districts, the Saxons and Wallachs in Transylvania, the Serbs in the Bácska and the Bánát, and in the north the Slovaks. Hungary's effectives had to be divided. But in all the provinces the Magyar element rallied to the flag. Kossuth realised that an early and decisive victory was necessary to focus Europe's attention on the Hungarian cause. Vienna was bleeding from the hammering of its conqueror Windischgrätz. But Kossuth conceived the audacious plan of marching against Vienna, delivering battle to the numerically superior enemy and relieving Vienna. On the 20th October he appeared in the War Council of the army which Moga commanded, eight days before Vienna, half in ruins and in flames, surrendered to the emperor. Thereupon, Kossuth decided to cross the Leitha, the river that forms the frontier between Austria and Hungary.

This was not only a military act; it was the formal beginning of an offensive against Austria, if she—as she afterwards did—wished to mask the invasion of the Ban Jellasich as an "Hungarian internal quarrel."

This offensive was very nearly successful, but General Moga hesitated to strike. When at last, on the 30th October, he took the field with about fifty thousand men against eighty-two thousand imperial troops under the personal command of Jellasich near Schwechat, four hours from Vienna, Jellasich had had time to post his batteries on the heights. The young Hungarian army fought valiantly; but the attack was beaten off by force of numbers. Kossuth's hope that the people of Vienna, hearing the guns so close, would start another rising, was not fulfilled. On the 3rd November Kossuth had to inform the House that fortune had been against them: "From now on the army will confine itself to the defence of our fatherland."

But the battle of Schwechat had a decisive effect: Austria recognised the strength of her opponent. Now seemed the moment to carry out the camarilla's plans. On the 3rd December the imperial family united in Olmütz. The emperor Ferdinand abdicated. His brother Franz Karl, the heir presumptive, renounced his succession in favour of his son; Franz Josef who had been previously declared of age was crowned as emperor.

Now the way was clear for Windischgrätz. Prince Schwarzenberg remained at the side of the young emperor as the head of his government. Under the command of Field-marshal Windischgrätz began the invasion of Hungarian territory. What use was it that the Hungarians, presuming on their rights under the pragmatic sanction, refused to recognise Ferdinand's abdication and declared Franz Josef's coronation to be illegal? What if they objected that, according to the constitution, the king must have himself crowned with the crown of St. Stephen and must conclude a coronation contract—*diploma inaugurale*—with the nation before he could legally rule? The huge army advanced. Prince Schwarzenberg was already innoculating the young sovereign with the idea that the Hapsburg monarchy depended on a "single centralised state" and that all the succession states, Hungary, Transylvania, Croatia must be welded into one empire governed from Vienna.

To all sane judgment the war was as good as lost. What could the untrained Hungarian troops do against the tried armies of Austria which were pushing forward on every side? Kossuth did his utmost to choose the best among those officers who rallied to the national colours: he gave the Pole Bem the command of a corps in Transylvania and the young Görgey a corps in the main army under the command of Perczel. But still their effectives were not strong enough to check the enemy's advance. One thing alone gave Kossuth hope: the determination of the people who had reason to hope that this war might free them from ever from the Hapsburg yoke.

After the unsuccessful battle of Schwechat Kossuth saw that he must undertake a complete reorganisation. Just as in Austria the political and military leadership were in different hands, so he must have a generalissimo, capable of assuming responsibility. But, plain as this was, it was not an easy task to find the man. A stroke of the pen and the appointment was made—but the future depended on his choice.

The situation was further complicated by the fact that the war was being waged on four different fronts and that four separate armies must be organised. On the west Jellasich's army, now subordinate to Windischgrätz, was held up by the fortress of Komorn. In Transylvania Baron Puchner was operating with a nucleus of Austrian troops, soon joined by Roumanian and

Wallach insurgents. In the Bácska the Serbs were advancing under the nationalist leader Stratimirovitch, their only obstacle being the fortress of Peterwardein, while the mixed troops invading Hungary from Slavonia had yet to circumvent the fortress of Esseg. Four armies must be found to defend the kingdom of St. Stephen! The main problem was for the armies to maintain contact with each other, so that they could follow a uniform plan. But the success in forming effective units was counterbalanced by the disunion among the military commanders. Kossuth very soon recognised that the whole campaign must be co-ordinated under a single leader, a generalissimo. But where was he to be found? This realisation induced Kossuth, once his task of inciting the people to arms had been accomplished, to retire temporarily from the stage of politics until the situation on the various fronts should be decided.

But instead of a quick decision, the army command, having to face attacks on so many sides, was driven to defer the crisis until after the winter. On the southern front, after the initial successes of Colonel Kis at Perlas, General Mészáros, the Minister of War, now in command, was fighting with little fortune. Already Kossuth was contemplating coming to terms with the Serbs, in order to dispose of at least one enemy and to free one army. But—what tragic irony!—the Serbs had risen under Stratimirovitch because Kossuth, the father of the idea of nationalism, had answered them in the private audience in March with the dangerous challenge: "In that event let the sword decide between us!" Now, when the nationalist idea was threatened by the revival of absolutism and the centralist tendency of Schwarzenberg, Kossuth was ready to come to terms with Stratimirovitch. He might have been successful; for Stratimirovitch was after all a nationalist, like Kossuth, and an enemy of the Hapsburgs. But by this time the Austrian agitation had already replaced the Woiwode by Major-general Suplikac and given him the command of the Southern army, an Austro-Serbian army corps. There was no possibility of making terms with Suplikac; like Jellasich, he was an exponent of the Hapsburg monarchy.

In spite of several Hungarian successes under Damjanich and Kis, and though Suplikac died on the 27th December and Kis gained a victory at Neudorf on New Year's Day, 1849, he was defeated the following day. There was as little hope of a favourable decision in the Bácska as in Transylvania where most of the Saxon population, threatened with the loss of their time-honoured privileges by the union of Transylvania with Hungary, were making common cause with the Wallachs. It was true that the Székely troops were fighting tooth and nail, but General Puchner, who was old and ill, was waiting desperately to be reinforced by the Galician corps and on this front too no decision was reached.

Decision must come in the West where lay the main Austrian army. But after the battle of Schwechat no move was made. Prince Windischgrätz remained quietly in Schönbrunn. The year was drawing to its close. As if war were a matter of arithmetic, Windischgrätz had first to decide the victory on paper before he gave the signal for advance. And before that he must complete his work of enthroning the young emperor Franz Josef. At last, on the 15th December, Windischgrätz issues orders to Jellasich to cross the Hungarian frontier at Bruck an der Leitha.

The main army of the enemy moved forward. Will the Hungarian Danube army be able to hold up the advance? After his defeat at Schwechat Moga had been relieved of his command and replaced by Görgey. This young officer had no faith in his troops; "the much-vaunted Landsturm," he said derisively, "will only hold its ground if it feels a cannon in every pocket." Görgey dared not risk a battle. His army retired; it abandoned Pressburg; the left and right wings even suffered a sensible reverse. Perhaps the courage of despair might still have enabled the retiring army to hold up the Ban's advance on the road to Budapest. Was the capital really to be surrendered to the enemy without a fight? Now Kossuth—armed with full powers as president of the Committee of National Defence—urged Görgey to unite his forces with Perczel's army operating on the Croatian-Styrian border and to hold up the Austrian army with their combined forces. But this union never happened; for Görgey and Perczel were mortal enemies. Left to his own devices Perczel was routed at Mór on the 30th December. At the turn of this fateful year 1848, Budapest lay defenceless at the feet of the advancing Austrians.

On the 1st January Kossuth ordered the removal of the government to Debrecen. The citizens of the capital, the proud advance guard of the revolution, were filled with consternation. The evacuation was carried out with all precautions; even the banknote printing press, that most important instrument of civil defence, went with the government. The cautious Balogh pointed out that the crown of St. Stephen ought not to be left behind in the palace of Buda, but his advice was not followed. What use was a crown to a government in flight?

On the 4th January the army which Görgey had withdrawn to Budapest evacuated the city. On the 5th the Austrian army entered Buda. On the same day Széchényi's suspension bridge which was to have been the symbol of a new life for the Hungarian nation was completed—but the first to cross it were the victorious Austrian troops.

XII

The Enemy within the Camp

THE SHADOWS OF THAT JANUARY NIGHT PRESAGED DEFEAT. WAS the revolution after twenty years of preparation really to be ended within twenty days of Jellasich's advance? So it almost seemed and deep discouragement brooded over the land. If this tragedy were now inevitable, it would be the tragedy of loyalty; it was too late to repair the shilly-shallying of Batthyányi's ministry. And now once more Batthyányi, in his unimpeachable honesty and fanatical credulity, accompanied by the archbishop, heads a deputation of the most distinguished persons in the country to Field-marshal Windischgrätz's headquarters at Bicske. He, the prime minister appointed by King Ferdinand, wishes to make it clear that this war has been forced on Hungary; that no one wanted anything else than Hungary's rights under the pragmatic sanction.

But the prince declared: "I do not negotiate with rebels." Batthyányi returned to Buda; he was not the man to flee. If the soldier Windischgrätz refused to negotiate, the politician Schwarzenberg will surely preserve justice. Batthyányi waits. He little knows that Prince Schwarzenberg will pursue his aim of choking the last breath of freedom even more arrogantly and coldbloodedly than Metternich. Who respected the noble behaviour of a man who believed steadfastly in justice? Not Windischgrätz; not Schwarzenberg, nor yet the young emperor. Windischgrätz enters Buda; his first official act is to order Batthyányi's arrest. Batthyányi is the victim of his faith in justice.

The black and yellow flag floats on the City Hall of Buda. Windischgrätz takes up his quarters in the palace, already surrounded by those magnates who have always viewed the revolution as an outrage. Jellasich, in a magnificent hussar uniform, parades his guard before the prince and then billets himself in the palace of Count Károlyi. Prince Lichtenstein, on Jellasich's staff, insists on occupying Kossuth's house. Prince Windischgrätz loses no time in declaring Kossuth and all his adherents outlaws.

Görgey withdrew his army northward into the hill towns of the Tátra. No news came from Debrecen. Prince Windischgrätz could afford to remain comfortably in Buda: Austria's victory seemed assured.

In Debrecen what had Kossuth to propose? He too was a prey to the general helplessness. His influence in the Diet was on the wane; he seemed to be losing his own confidence. But a strange piece of news roused him from his inertia. General Görgey had issued a proclamation to the retiring Danube army: "The army is exclusively defending the constitution sanctioned by King Ferdinand. It must be consulted in any negotiation with the enemy, and the result of such negotiations must be submitted to the army for approval."

What was the meaning of this presumption on the part of a soldier? Had Görgey done this only to reassure the old officers of the army or had he secretly some other purpose? He was now a man of first importance, the hopes of Hungary relied on him. But who was this Artur Görgey?

Kossuth mistrusted him. Twice already this young officer had focussed attention upon himself. At first he had been attached with the rank of major to a Hungarian unit with orders to guard the crossing of the Danube not far from Budapest. He was stationed on the island of Csepel in the middle of the Danube. On the 29th September, during the first skirmishes with Jellasich, he stopped a mailcoach and arrested the passengers, Counts Eugene and Paul Zichy. As they were coming from Stuhlweissenberg there was reason to suspect that they were the bearers of a message from Jellasich to the Austrian General Roth. And actually there was found on Count Eugene Zichy a letter from the Ban recommending him to General Roth. A crowd of armed peasants who had collected on the river bank threatened to lynch the Count. These were the days of most violent embitterment, the first clamouring for vengeance, which had led to the murder of Lamberg in Pest. Of course Görgey was doing his duty as an officer in protecting the Count from the fury of the mob. But this duty performed what did Görgey do? He instituted a court martial for the trial of Count Zichy. Two young officers are soon found to complete the necessary tribunal. Copies of Jellasich's proclamations have been found on the accused; Zichy's defence is that they were smuggled into the coach by his servant. And the letter of recommendation to General Roth? Zichy explains that, as his estates are in Stuhlweissenberg, in territory now occupied by the enemy, he had need of such a letter in the interests of his officials and peasants. But Görgey sentences him to death. Count Eugene Zichy was hanged on the nearest tree on Csepel island.

The effect of this sentence and execution was enormous. Only a few members of the government protested that the major should have handed his prisoner over to the civil courts of Pest. But the population of the capital cheered this energetic action. At last a man who did not flinch before a magnate! At last an officer of the Austrian school who had shown that he could be depended on! In point of fact Görgey's first action gained the confidence of the people in the new army. Not every one rejoiced that this war had begun with an execution. The hanging of a defenceless man seemed to sensitive minds a symbol of horror, a dreadful Mene-Tekel. But what were such sentimental emotions beside so infectious an example of energy and ruthlessness! The name of Major Görgey was on every tongue.

Who could have suspected that this ambitious officer was acting according to a clearly conceived plan? A plan which could surely only have been inspired by Napoleonic instincts. If no opportunity offered for spectacular promotion, he would create an opportunity. Görgey was Colonel Perczel's subordinate. In Görgey's opinion Perczel had made a military mistake in granting the defeated General Roth a three days armistice. Görgey disobeyed the orders of his superior officer. Covered by the instructions of the Committee of National Defence he acted on his own initiative. This was an audacious thing to do as if he had been court-martialled the penalty would have been death. And Perczel did threaten to have him shot. But Görgey had acted cleverly. His object, as on the occasion of his first intrusion into the limelight, to rouse an echo for his behaviour in Pest, succeeded. On the 6th October, when he had not been an officer of the Hungarian army for more than a few weeks, he addressed a report to Kossuth in which in the light of a superior knowledge he drew his attention to the bad state of Perczel's army. "The Committee," he observed, "appears to be in ignorance of what is going on in the camp." This is not the language of an anxious patriot but of a future dictator. But the Committee was neither a general staff nor a War Ministry, it was at best a rather ineffectual excrescence of the hour of crisis intended to bolster up Kossuth's position as prime minister. Görgey's disobedience to Perczel was as deserving of punishment as this undisciplinary complaint. But—Görgey got away with it.

Now in the first days of actual warfare there was enacted a

scene unparalleled in an army during war-time. Perczel summoned his officers together for a council of war and called upon Görgey to defend himself. Görgey defended himself in a speech, overwhelming his commanding officer with accusations and insults. He expected, as he writes later, that Perczel would challenge him to a duel. A duel between officers at the front? Perczel is a soldier; he has no need of a theatrical sensation to enhance his prestige. He does what his duty prescribes; he calls the guard and gives the order to shoot Görgey.

If this order had been carried out, perhaps the fate of the war, the fate of Hungary would have turned out differently. This episode reveals the character of the principal actor in the next phase of the war; it already shows his power, which he owed not only to his energy and brains, but still more to his enigmatical personality. The execution of Zichy was only technically illegal; he had deliberately purchased prestige at a comparatively small risk. But now he was gambling with his life, but he won. Several officers at this council, particularly the junior officers, sided with him. The affair lapsed; nothing survived but Perczel's hatred. Two days later Kossuth promoted Görgey to the rank of colonel.

For one instant Fate had warned the nation against this man. For one instant death threatened this man who combined presumption, disobedience, craft with great ability. And yet no one heeded the warning. But Kossuth's fatal error was always to misread character. And now particularly when he had little time to make decisions, when his only guidance in judging men was instinct, he made more and more mistakes. He had trusted Szabó who embezzled the monies of his company; he had made Batthyányi prime minister over his own head; now he trusted Duschek who controlled the national finances and was to cheat him and the country most disgracefully; he trusted Madarász who later stole the jewels of the Count Zichy whom Görgey hanged; and he trusted Görgey. Admittedly the dearth of capable officers was a valid reason for retaining the services of a man of such energy and ability. But now Kossuth failed to detect the tone of Cæsarean ambition which spoke with shameless clearness from Görgey's report of the 6th October. For this young officer had the impudence to write: "I would point out to the Diet that the proper leadership of an army requires military knowledge as well as the gift of rhetoric and good intentions." This was Görgey's first thrust at Kossuth. But soon after Kossuth gave Görgey the command of the Danube army.

It was then the necessary collusion between Görgey's corps and Perczel was frustrated by the enmity of the two commanders. And other enmities followed. Kossuth only felt a vague mistrust of Görgey but as he was unable to substantiate it he did what was imperative at the time: he left this efficient general in the most important post.

At first nothing appeared to justify this confidence. Görgey had retired into the mountains and nothing was heard of him except his proclamation. But Görgey was making good use of his time to gain the allegiance of officers and men, so that he could rely on them, not only to follow him into battle, but also to support him politically. Gradually Görgey's troops began to be spoken of as a "praetorian guard" that wanted watching.

Kossuth was moving heaven and earth to put new forces into the field. Among the junior officers he found a young man of twenty-eight named Klapka and proposed giving him Mészáros' command. For one of Austria's best officers, General Schlick, had invaded Hungary from Galicia, repulsed Mészáros and occupied Kaschau, the capital of Upper Hungary, even pushing forward as far as Eperjes. Of Görgey there was no sign. He did not move from the inhospitable valleys of the mountains where he was protected from any molestation by the enemy. So Schlick was able to rest his army in Kaschau. One day however, on the 17th January a patrol reports having sighted Hungarian troops. They belonged to Klapka's corps which had taken up a position in the Tokay hills, preparatory to an attack. Schlick is driven back and forced to evacuate Eperjes. Simultaneously Görgey emerges from his mountain fastness and a division storms the pass through which Schlick's army must retire. The juncture of Görgey's and Klapka's armies is completed. On the 9th February Schlick abandons Kaschau and retreats into Galicia.

This was the first victory. At the same time Perczel guarding the passage of the Theiss at Szolnok in a valiant offensive drives back Ottinger's redoubtable cavalry brigade beyond Cegléd.

These important successes revived the courage of the government in Debrecen. But they also re-alarmed the Committee of National Defence. Görgey victorious? Kossuth thought it expedient to offset the man that he mistrusted with a new commander of rank. He found him in Dembinski.

This choice of Dembinski who was set over Perczel and Klapka was again militarily sound, but once more Kossuth's character judgment was at fault. For Dembinski, a Pole, who had distinguished himself in the Polish fight for freedom, was obsessed with political ambition. His aim was the liberation of Poland and the revolt of Hungary only a convenient means to that end. He did not understand the Magyar officers and his orders were ambiguous and contradictory. A conflict with Görgey was inevitable.

Now Görgey began to agitate against the Committee in Debrecen even more violently than before; Dembinski's unpopularity allowed him to show his hatred of the "clerks in Debrecen." But his ceaseless agitation, his opposition to Perczel and now this fresh tension with Dembinski were to cost the army and the country dear. Görgey's enmities were already prejudicing the efficiency of his army; they actually prevented a decisive victory against Schlick in the battle of Kápolna on the 26th February.

Thanks to the energy of the Committee the Hungarian army had been able to strengthen its effectiveness very considerably; it now numbered 120,000 men. Kossuth might now have followed his first inspiration and placed the whole army under the command of one man. The Minister of War Mészáros shared his mistrust of Görgey; and soon an order of the day, issued by Görgey to "his" army justified this mistrust. Görgey, as soon as he learned of Dembinski's appointment as commander-in-chief declared: "I call upon all officers to accept this apparent humiliation with the same indifference as I voluntarily subordinate myself to the orders of Lieutenant-General Dembinski." Dembinski immediately altered the plan drawn up by Klapka and Görgey, by so doing he enabled the Hungarians to capture Kápolna, but there was no decisive victory. Dembinski was as cautious a general as Windischgrätz; as the troops were advancing to the attack he unexpectedly ordered a retirement to the Theiss. Nevertheless Kápolna was a magnificent confirmation of the efficiency of the Hungarian army. On the 1st March Görgey, in defiance of Dembinski's orders, crossed the Theiss. This fresh act of insubordination called for Kossuth's intervention. Once again Görgey was threatened with a court martial. But again he got away with it. The best officers, such as Klapka and Aulich, supported Görgey and declared that they would no longer accept orders from Dembinski.

Thus Kossuth discovered the higher command divided into a camp of enemies. It was a grave moment when he stood face to face with this young would-be Cæsar to judge him. It was no longer a question of mistrust; there was no mistaking Görgey's talent as a general or his dictatorial ambition. Again Kossuth had to make the decision: whether political or military reason should prevail. And Kossuth, the politician, decided against the warnings of his political conscience. He decided for Görgey.

This decision proved Kossuth's true greatness. Never for one instant did he forget that, as long as the danger lasted, it was his duty to entrust the life of Hungary to the army. Everything else was subservient to the prosecution of the war, and as Kossuth was trying at the same time to invigilate the conduct of the war, he implicated himself in an inextricable conflict. Kossuth confirmed Görgey in his command and dismissed Dembinski. But his words to Görgey after this decision show his premonition of its political danger: "Brother, tell me what you want. Confide your wishes to me and I will work for you. Do you want to become dictator of Hungary? If so, I will help you to it. Do you desire the crown of power? You shall have it. Only save Hungary."

Görgey replied with a sneer that he wanted nothing but his command. But he continued to depreciate Kossuth in the eyes of his army. Kossuth spent the night in the camp; Görgey in full uniform lay down on the threshold of his tent, ironically pretending to be his bodyguard.

Kossuth's words have often been interpreted as an offer of the Hungarian crown. But Kossuth had no crown to give. In his view King Ferdinand still wore the crown of St. Stephen and Hungary was in the field, not against him, but against the camarilla, not against the House of Hapsburg, but for the upholding of the pragmatic sanction. There is no doubt that Kossuth even then thought of giving the supreme command for the duration of military operations to the one man among his generals who was filled with a Napoleonic lust for power, but nevertheless seemed to him indispensable. Important, but not decisive victories had been won. Both of them, Kossuth as well as Görgey, thought that a decision in the field would decide the government of Hungary. Görgey was well aware that his genius enabled him to outshine all rival generals; only diplomatic cleverness—as he once said himself—would allow him to override the only opponent of any consequence—Kossuth. There can be no doubt that Görgey desired victory, but in the hour that followed victory he meant to make himself dictator. Kossuth left the camp; the bout with his new antagonist remained for the time being undecided. On the 6th March Kossuth returned to Debrecen.

On this day the die was cast, not in the camp at Tiszafüred, but in Kremsier, the seat of the Austrian Diet; Count Stadion proclaimed a "constitution," a work which was to realise Prince Schwarzenberg's plan: the creation of a seventy million empire, the abolition of all frontiers between the succession states, Hungary and all the other parts of the Hapsburg monarchy, and to found a unified empire. According to this constitution, approved by the emperor Franz Josef, Hungary ceased to exist as an independent state. The government in Vienna already believed that Hungary which was still unsubdued was in its pocket. The name of Windischgrätz guaranteed the final triumph of Austria's might.

Hungary was to become a part of Austria? This constitution completely shattered the pragmatic sanction. For the crown of Hungary was only hereditary by contract with the House of Hapsburg. This contract had often been disregarded, by Ferdinand's abdication it had been disgracefully evaded; now it was impudently torn up. On this day Hungary's war had a new meaning. The victory for which Görgey and Kossuth alike were striving would now mean something more than the annihilation of the new reaction. It would create a new dispensation in the regions of the Danube for centuries to come.

XIII

Victory

A MIRACLE HAPPENED: MARCH BEGAN WITH A SERIES OF HUNGARIAN victories. It seemed indeed, as Kossuth declared enthusiastically in Szeged, that the 17th March, the anniversary of the constitution, was to be the birthday of a liberated Hungary. He himself, working at the organisation of the army with indefatigable fanaticism, had again literally conjured up fresh troops by the mere force of his oratory in the remote and hesitating peasant areas; he now sent them into the field to reinforce the separate armies at the front. He sent them to help Perczel who was now in command of the fourth army at Szeged. The general, at last free of the daily bickering with Görgey and independent commander of a strong corps, advanced with incredible audacity on the southern front. Ten days later he relieved Peterwardein, dismissed those old officers who were suspect of loyalty to Austria, and on the 3rd April surprisingly stood before the Serbian fortress of Szenttamás. Now the young army had to stand the test of an assault. With bands playing, singing the "Kossuth Song," the enthusiastic troops stormed the fortress. The Serbs fled across the frontier. The Bánát was cleared of the enemy.

But there were other great leaders, brave corps and fearless officers rivalling Görgey's praetorian army. The Pole Bem, now called by his men who loved him "Little Father Bem," had had a difficult task in Transylvania. Continually harried by the enemy, molested by the insurgent minorities, Saxons and Wallachs, he had to make forced marches through mountainous and thickly wooded country in order to repel, now here, now there, the enemy's attacks. Things looked black when, on the 2nd February, a Russian corps under General Lüders reinforced the enemy, evidently intent on forcing a decision, for the Czar had decided to interfere on the south-eastern front, so that later he could have his say in the final regulation of this area and to lend emphasis to his policy of provoking Turkey. On the 3rd March the irresolute and ailing General Puchner, with this important support, might have defeated Bem at Segesvár, but Bem by a clever stratagem had slipped through his fingers, captured the poorly defended town of Hermannstadt and was ready to give Puchner battle. Now an extraordinary thing happened; the old and experienced campaigner lost his head as Bem counter-attacked; he fled incontinently with his whole staff, abandoning his army to the advancing Bem. Twenty-five thousand Austrians and twelve thousand Russians fled across the frontier. Transylvania too was free.

But notwithstanding the decision rested with the Upper Danube army. After the battle of Kápolna the supreme command had been given to Vetter, but Vetter reported sick and Görgey assumed the command that was rightfully his. He too took the offensive in March. On the 5th March the corps of General Damjanich—by birth a Serb whom love for Hungary made the most ardent defender of his adopted country—surprised Ottinger's cavalry corps at Szolnok and wiped it out. The Hungarian hussars charged into the enemy's ranks with such bravery and fury that they captured the whole of their artillery. Meanwhile Prince Windischgrätz sat undismayed in the palace of Buda, smiling and studying the new constitution, sure of victory, just as if there had been no war going on at all. But after the victory at Szolnok three powerful corps were in the field; Damjanich at Cegléd, Aulich at Tiszafüred and Klapka at Tokaj. On the 20th March Görgey gave orders for the attack.

Thick mist lay over the grey-blue shimmering hills of Tokaj, the vine-clad slopes breathed the peace of early morning. At every point along the wide horizon Honvéds suddenly appeared. At the same time hussars charged, scattered the Austrian troops and hurled the great Schlick back on Erlau, Kaschau and Eperjes. The victorious army followed up its victory. At last, on the 2nd April, the decisive action began. "The Hungarian hussar" —to cite a contemporary account—"the best cavalryman in the world overrode the enemy like a wild boar trampling corn." Now Jellasich himself with the main army had been beaten. He attempted to unite with Windischgrätz who had hurried into the field and with Schlick.

On the broad plain, from Gödöllö and Hatvan as far as Cegléd, only a few hours from Budapest, the Austrians formed a ring; the "three great generals," Windischgrätz, Jellasich and Schlick, were in command. The artillery was concealed in the wooded hills behind, the cavalry occupied the plain. Now a decision must be forced. It was a battle which offered small chance of victory to the attacker. What is courage against the mathematical certainty of a carefully calculated position?

But, as the great chess-player extricates himself from an unfavourable situation by a daring move, Görgey launched his hussars against the enemy entrenchments. The Austrian infantry stood firm, aiming their rifles at the faces of the charging cavalry. But then, at a short distance from the ramparts, the cavalry divided and swerved, attacked the surprised Austrians on both flanks and hewed them down, meanwhile the picked troops of the Honvéds dashed forward against the centre. This victorious stratagem was the beginning of the decisive battle of Isaszeg. It ended with the complete victory of the Hungarians. The imperial army fled till within a short distance of Budapest.

Windischgrätz made a stand in front of Pest. The Hungarians had their flank protected on the west by the fortress of Komorn which had been in turn invested and assaulted but had held out desperately. On the 10th April Görgey attacked the main body of the army at Waitzen. The enemy's flanks were turned, the battle was won, and simultaneously at Nagysarló the Austrian corps besieging the fortress of Komorn was defeated. Komorn opened its gates to its victorious brothers. Meanwhile Görgey pushed on across the Danube and threw back Schlick's corps on Raab almost driving them across the Austrian frontier.

This was complete victory. And on the 25th April Aulich, the commander of the second corps, was able to send a message to the citizens of Pest to say that he was marching with the victorious Hungarian army to drive out the garrison, left in the fortress of Buda under Hentzi, and to deliver the capital. "We bring you the greatest blessings: Freedom, independence and peace!"

Hungary was free, from the Transylvanian frontier and from the Carpathians to the Danube.

This colossal victory relieved the whole country from the agony of fear and doubt. For since the flight of the government from Pest the opinion that the struggle was hopeless had gained ground. Even in Debrecen the Assembly of Deputies became a prey to faintheartedness and panic. It seemed that Kossuth used all his powers of oratory to infuse the will to victory in vain. No one any longer believed his words. Only a small band remained loyal to him, those whose radical opinions Kossuth himself had never before approved. But the Diet was not the country; it was no longer even the mouthpiece of the nation. The provincial towns which Kossuth had fired by his great speeches, the villages where the peasants cheered their emancipator, these formed the following that believed in the leader. It was from their midst that he recruited the continually needed drafts of men, from the reflection in their trusting eyes in the darkest days he won back faith in his mission. This war was a war for his ideas; this victory was the fruit of his energy. Certainly the military genius of Görgey and the talents of the other officers had brought about the decision on the field of battle. But Kossuth's spirit lived in the young troops. It was "Kossuth's Song" they sang upon the march.

Let the generals quarrel—the soldiers, the peasants' sons and the men from the provincial towns knew but one leader: Kossuth. While in Görgey's eyes the "gasbag of Debrecen" shrunk into a figure of no importance and he alone, "the man of action," was the instrument of destiny, for the army and the people this victory was Kossuth's victory. But Kossuth himself knew that he had only given the nation its faith like a quickening flame. He knelt on the battlefield of Kápolna and gave thanks to God. He remained with the army during the decisive battle at Gödöllö and only after the victory at Isaszeg did he raise his voice: "Our valiant army is driving from your frontiers the enemy who dared to say that Hungary has ceased to exist and never will exist again. Our valiant army is driving from your frontiers the enemy who even in flight plunders as footpads plunder. Months ago I prophesied that Hungary's freedom would blossom out of tyranny. And so it is." Now is the time to remind the nation of the idea that it is fighting for. Victory is complete, but the war is not yet ended. How long ago was it that Windischgrätz had arrogantly declared that he would not negotiate with rebels? Now the Vienna cabinet sends Prince Lobkowitz as mediator to Debrecen. Prince Windischgrätz was speedily dismissed by the emperor who learned the news of his defeat in Olmütz. He hastened to Buda, leaving behind only the garrison under General Hentzi, but not forgetting to take with him on his retreat his prisoners, and first and foremost Count Batthyányi. In Debrecen Kossuth's "call from Gödöllö" had restored courage to the fainthearted who had always pressed for making terms with Windischgrätz. Lobkowitz came to Kossuth "in the name of the king

Franz Josef." "Who is this Franz Josef?" Kossuth asked the prince. "What? Do you not know that King Ferdinand has abdicated?" replied the prince in astonishment. "Does not Your Highness know that in Hungary a king cannot abdicate and another sit upon his throne without the connivance of the nation and the observance of the constitution?" So the conversation of the mediator with Kossuth ended without result. Victory had created a new situation. Now Kossuth meant to realise the idea for which Hungary had been fighting: Freedom.

But Görgey was not silent. Whose victory was this? Was it the victory of the soldiers? Or was the man who had only talked while others bled to be allowed to claim his share in this victory? On the day on which Komorn was relieved, Görgey too issued his proclamation to his comrades in arms: "Our bravest men would not have dared to expect so much. You have been victorious and you must win further victories. Remember this when the day of battle comes again." For Kossuth the army was the flower of the nation; for Görgey: a praetorian guard. In the hour of victory the general seeks to win this army for himself, to alienate it from the man who had created it. And thus—an unexampled spectacle in history—on the very day of victory, the shadows of a new peril darken Hungary.

The beaten Austrian army was in retreat. Dismay seized the government in Vienna, the gagged democrats rejoiced. "To Vienna!"—this must be the watchword. "Austria is within our reach like a ripe fruit!" cries Kossuth. Now is the time to grasp it, to end the work begun.

But things happened otherwise.

XIV

The Pinnacle of Power

IN ALL THE EXCITEMENTS OF THE PAST WEEKS KOSSUTH HAD HAD the strength to let the momentous decisions which had to be made wait patiently upon the claim of mature consideration. The "constitution," devised by Schwarzenberg and granted by the emperor Franz Josef, deprived Hungary of all her rights, cast her back beyond the times of Metternich, even beyond the tragic days of Eperjes. But Kossuth had trained himself to wait, a discreet spectator, accompanying the fighting troops with hands folded in prayer. He had knelt on the battlefield of Kápolna and the whole army had paraded in a square; the grave mounds were decked with flowers, the melancholy notes of the tárogató, the Hungarian shepherd's pipe, more plaintive than a human dirge, hymned the sorrow of the survivors. Then Kossuth had come forward. The colours dipped. Bareheaded, with the voice of a deeply affected preacher, Kossuth thanked the army and its leaders, thanked God for the salvation of Hungary. The army surrounded this man whose faith had foretold prophetically this day of victory in silent gratitude. Still Kossuth, the politician, was dumb. But now that the decision had been reached, he too had come to his decision. Hungary had become strong. Nowhere else had the Austrian army been defeated; the passionate insurrection in the Italian provinces, befriended by all the states of the peninsula, blessed by the Pope Pio Nono, had been quelled by Radetzky; the Slavonic movement of the Czechs had been strangled by Windischgrätz; in Croatia and the Servian Bánát the nationalists had long since been forced to submit to Austrian leadership. And, strangely enough, those who had complacently incited the minorities against Hungary, now looked with admiring wonder at the leader Kossuth who alone stalked through the danger with head erect, never swerving from his purpose. Even in Bohemia Kossuth's name became popular; the incredible happened; one night an "Eljen Kossuth" was chalked up on the wall of a public building in Prague, and young Czech leaders nailed Kossuth's picture on the walls of village taverns, and even Kollar preached against the folly of his compatriots who by their conflict with Hungary had delivered themselves into the hands of the Hapsburg reaction. Kossuth could celebrate the triumph of his ideas, as well as the military victory, on his return to Debrecen on the 14th April.

On the 14th April Kossuth addressed the Diet. Those who had but yesterday opposed him, cheered; but no one knew that a grave and momentous hour had begun. The gentle bearing of the preacher of Kápolna is laid aside; he faces the House with the calm of the fencer who is about to give the final thrust. Szemere, his confidant, alone knows that it will be the death blow to Hapsburg.

What would have happened if Windischgrätz had conquered Hungary? He had crushed Prague, he had bombarded Vienna, here he would have hanged the leaders of the revolution; would he not have done what the bloodthirsty Austrian general, Baron Haynau, had just done to Brescia and made Budapest, Debrecen and Szeged, Eperjes and Arad the scene of savagery and slavery? Was there in this system of tyranny of a dynasty that ruled callously over many peoples, as if they were foreign subjugated colonies, room at all for men of clemency and understanding? Was not the English observer right who called the Hapsburg régime "a despotism mitigated by good manners?" Already Europe had begun to delve with horror into Austria's history: Richard Cobden described for England the calvary of Hungary under Hapsburg rule, in Paris Lamartine had expressed his sympathy with liberated Hungary. Kossuth knew that now the moment had come to throw off this tyranny for ever. Hungary must be severed from the Hapsburg crown.

Kossuth proclaimed this separation: "The House of Hapsburg-Lothringen has by the war against Hungary torn up with its own hands the Pragmatic Sanction and dissolved every tie of mutual obligation between itself and Hungary. Therefore the House of Hapsburg is for ever deposed from sovereignty over Hungary and declared to have forfeited the throne and to be excluded and banished in the name of the nation." This resolution is followed by an appeal to the conscience of Europe: "We inform all the peoples of the civilised world of this fact, in the firm conviction that it will accept the Hungarian nation, as the youngest but not unworthy brother, into the ranks of independent nations."

The Diet met in the church of Debrecen, the "Calvinist Rome," and after Kossuth's declaration the sacred building rang with cheers. But who was to stand at the head of the state? Behind the scenes there had been a curious struggle of which those present were unaware. Szemere pressed for the realisation of the republican idea. Kossuth however carefully avoided the word "republic" to which, it seemed to him, there clung too much historical ballast. Nevertheless the constitution—which was to be considered temporary—was essentially republican: it prescribed for a president (*gubernator Hungariae*) at its head, a president such as János Hunyadi, the father of King Matthias Corvinus, had been. This president was responsible to the responsible ministry. But in the hour of birth of this "temporary republic" the final form had not yet been found. The main question was to find a strong hand to guide the helm in the conflicts still to come. Naturally Kossuth was elected governor-president and, it must be remembered, unanimously. Now he had reached the pinnacle of power. The little lawyer of Monók was the successor of the Hapsburgs, the ruling president of Hungary.

But: power creates opposition. The victory was not yet fully exploited before adversaries appeared within the camp. It had always been thus. But the curious thing in the story of Kossuth's life is that his opponents always sprang from the ranks of those whom he himself had chosen. He had given Görgey a commission in the army; he had raised Szemere from obscurity. At Kossuth's wish Szemere was elected prime minister. Kossuth could not guess that Szemere's first act would be to join forces secretly with Görgey to bring about Kossuth's fall. Görgey rebuffed Szemere. He wanted to lead the attack against the all-powerful president alone.

Now, in this story so rich in surprises and dramatic episodes, begins the most shocking episode of all: the struggle in the dark that wantonly gambled with disaster. In the dark: for Görgey did not refuse the portfolio of Minister for War when it was offered him. He acted as if he were Kossuth's man. But at the same time he undermined Kossuth's power, he incited his staff against him, he spoke of the declaration of independence as "Kossuth's folly." He agitated secretly. But when he presently revealed his opposition to Kossuth, the assembly in Debrecen shouted with one accord: "We want no military revolt! No dictatorship of the sword!" Görgey drew in his horns; he reflected. In his memoirs he admits: "Outside the Diet I had to concentrate on robbing the party of the 14th April of its weightiest supporters." This day, so he says, brought to him the realisation that Kossuth was ruining the country.

Why? What was gnawing this general whom Kossuth had

always mistrusted? Had he really thought that, if he returned victorious, he could usurp political as well as military power? Or was he one of those who feared that Kossuth might abuse his power to seize the crown?

After the victory of Isaszeg and the relief of Komorn Austria lay at the feet of the victorious army. The president Kossuth ordered Görgey to cross the Leitha and advance into Austria before the beaten enemy should have time to rally and panic-stricken Vienna devise new tricks. It would of course be a good thing if a small force could recapture the only fortress still held by the enemy, the capital Buda. Perhaps it was unconsidered to declare this wish to Görgey. Perhaps this only too comprehensible longing of Kossuth's was inspired by the wish to enter the fortress where he had languished in the cause of freedom as president of a liberated nation. What a brilliant symbol of the ultimate victory that would be!

But at the zenith of his power Kossuth experienced the first defiance of his orders: Görgey refused. He alleged as an excuse that he had not enough munitions to pursue the enemy. Not enough munitions? But Kossuth, the magician, found them. Now Görgey asserted that he must employ all his forces in order to take the fortress of Buda in a few days. He was the commander-in-chief; he must decide. Kossuth must yield to him—But afterwards Görgey admits in his memoirs that he had no mind to carry the offensive on to Austrian territory.—And so the victorious Hungarian army marched on Buda. The troops assembled in Pest, riotously welcomed by the civil population. But General Hentzi was a loyal soldier. He threatened to defend Buda to the last man. Already the cannon on the heights of the palace hill were spitting fire. A plucky captain hazarded an attempt to blow up the suspension bridge. The mine blew him to pieces; Széchényi's bridge held.

Hentzi's resistance lasted seventeen days. At last the troops under Klapka stormed the fortress. Hentzi died in the victorious Görgey's arms. On the 21st May Görgey was able to send the message to Debrecen: "Buda éljen Görgey." On the 5th June Kossuth, accompanied by all the ministers and members of the Diet, entered the capital. The bells rang, the streets were strewn with flowers, the president's carriage was drawn by four white horses and followed by a regiment of hussars.

But the next day already the new peril loomed. The capture of Buda had taken seventeen days, forty days had elapsed since the relief of Komorn. Forty days! Did anyone believe that the Vienna cabinet would not make good use of them? The young emperor Franz Josef had gone post-haste to Warsaw to ask the Czar Nicholas I personally for military intervention. The Holy Alliance no longer existed; but the insubordination of Hungary, the insurrection of a people, the victory of the rebels alarmed the autocrat of Russia. On the 21st May the Russian interference was decided on. Two hundred thousand Russian soldiers were hurried by forced marches towards the frontier. The Austrian army was again ready to invade Hungary. And the emperor entrusted the supreme command to the man who had already shown that he could deal most summarily with rebels, Baron Haynau. This choice showed at once Austria's intention of incorporating Hungary with the Austrian empire, and furthermore to crush completely the independence movement by relentless persecution of all "rebels." For Franz Josef too it was a fight for an idea: absolutism or constitutionalism. The two autocrats in Vienna and in St. Petersburg were bent on annihilating the last enemy of their omnipotence. Two empires, the still powerful Austria and the mighty Russia, had to unite to pulverize Kossuth's Hungary. This was indeed a tribute to Kossuth.

This alliance sealed the fate of the Hungarian revolt. Whatever happened afterwards, however valiantly the brave and well-led Magyar armies fought, against the invasion of such powerfully armed forces the little country could no longer defend itself.

Kossuth was accompanied on his triumphal progress to the Buda palace by a crowd drunk with happiness. His wife Therese at his side felt the happiness of that hour; it had been her vaulting ambition to see the man she worshipped on the pinnacle of power; it was she who had often whispered in the ear of the man who loved her that it was his mission to lead the people he had made a nation. Perhaps the envious gossip-mongers were not altogether wrong when they asserted that Kossuth's wife had even flirted with the idea of seeing her husband crowned. The crown of St. Stephen? It reposed in the palace of Buda, now again guarded by a guard of honour. Therese may have had dreams and let her tongue wag a little imprudently. Kossuth was silent. He knew what ominous storm clouds were gathering. He stood on the heights of Buda's hill and looked down as president upon the land and people which acclaimed him as their liberator—and yet he knew that this moment when he would fain have said: "*Verweile doch, du bist so schön!*" would not last.

XV

The Crusade

KOSSUTH BELIEVED IN THE POWER OF HUNGARY TO REPULSE EVEN the united armies of the enemy.. The ideologist Kossuth—and it is this that may be called his tragic culpability—was the victim of his faith in his idea even at this hour. If the Russian empire attacked the Hungarian nation, moreover without a declaration of war, must this not awaken a cry of horror throughout Europe? Liberal Europe which had long eyed the despotic countries with latent hostility? Foreseeing the possibility of a Russian invasion, Kossuth had sent his ambassadors to the European courts, Pulszky to London, Count Teleki to Paris. When would they report that the great Western Powers were protesting against the Russian intervention? That they were hurrying to Hungary's aid? But the Powers were silent. Now in the hour of peril the president of independent Hungary turns to the peoples of Europe with an appeal: "After the victory of the young Hungarian army over the tried Austrian army the House of Hapsburg, united with the Russians, is for the second time attacking Hungary, the land of the martyrs of national independence." And with great dignity and characteristic pride he declares: "We shall not lay down our arms. God is righteous and omnipotent, He breaks the might of the presumptuous. But we address an earnest appeal to the constitutional governments and peoples of Europe. A great responsibility rests upon you. Awake, you peoples, before this monstrous danger! You proud nation of England, have you forgotten the principle of non-interference you yourselves laid down? You are not only defending the sacred interests of liberty and humanity, but you are aiding the victory of the oppressed. The proud British flag is threatened with ignominy. God will withdraw from it His blessing, if it be false to the cause to which it owes its victory. You, Republic of France, have you forgotten the principles that you proclaimed at your birth?" In this tone of solemn adjuration and warning Kossuth appeals to all liberal peoples. "For we shall fight until we have shed the last drop of our blood."

The echo of this "Manifesto to the Peoples of Europe" was faint enough. A few individual spirits were stirred and shocked by this document. But the governments remained deaf. Kossuth's hopes dwindled. Hungary stood alone.

Now Hungary's own strength must save the nation. Again Kossuth addressed his people. He calls his country to arms, to a "crusade." Now is no longer the time to conceal the danger. The death struggle has begun. The peasants stream in from the country, fourteen-year-old boys enlist as volunteers, differences of rank and of religion no longer matter, the people, once again in arms, are linked together in one great brotherhood.

But this fight was decided before it was begun. How idle it is to estimate which of the mistakes that were committed were most responsible for the speedy collapse. Certainly it was a fatality that Dembinski as commander on the Carpathian frontier should have omitted to occupy the mountain passes in time. Certainly the intolerable bickering of the generals completely destroyed the last possibility of a co-ordinated defence. Certainly Kossuth whom even Klapka had begun to warn against Görgey should have made up his mind to relieve him in the supreme command by a more reliable general. But it was simply the superiority of the enemy that decided the issue. Already on the 20th June Görgey, despite a desperate resistance, was driven out of Raab. He was outnumbered by eight to one. The Austrians entered the town in the presence of the emperor Franz Josef, plundered it and exercised martial law. Hungary learned that in this fight no quarter would be given. Of what use was the Honvéds' bravest counter-attack? "The Russians stood like granite, immovable. No sooner had the artillery mowed them down than fresh reinforcements filled the depleted ranks."

Gloom and confusion, the forerunners of defeat, prevailed in Pest. After the first lost battle, Kossuth relieved Görgey of the supreme command, again appointing Mészáros and Dembinski, but this excited Görgey's praetorians who sent a deputation to Kossuth. Görgey retired from the War Ministry and the supreme command, but remained the commander of his own army.

On the 2nd July Budapest again lay open to the advancing enemy. For the second time the government had to flee to Debrecen. Again the removal was carried out in precipitate haste. The oddest baggage was taken with it: munitions and stores, banknotes and bars of gold, the banknote printing press and a few chattels belonging to the fugitives. But in a special chest Kossuth took with him a mysterious load; it must have been a heavy object and valuable as gold, for he never let the roped box out of his sight.

Meanwhile Görgey endeavoured by bold attacks to throw back the Austrian corps. But he was driven back himself at Vác. On the 11th July Haynau entered Buda. The suspension bridge was repaired—that was Haynau's first concern—and across Széchényi's bridge trotted the Cossack squadrons! The townsfolk gazed in horror at the foreign cavalry. At this moment they realised their fate; the Russians scared them more than the dreaded name of Haynau who was now master of the city. The Cossacks in Buda! Surely this was the beginning of the end.

The crusade continued. The animosity of the generals which had its origin in petty ambitions grew to open mistrust; and now at last Kossuth was infected with the fear of Görgey. Görgey himself had moments when he admitted to himself, as he writes later, that "I did not fail to appreciate the situation in which I had placed Kossuth. I saw moreover that he as governor had only two alternatives: either to resign or to get rid of me." A Napoleon would have rendered harmless the man who at the head of his praetorian army threatened the unity of the government. But such acts of firm resolution were not in Kossuth's character. He had been a dreamer, he had schooled himself to be a thinker, fate had made him the chosen leader in this fight that he had never wanted, but he had never been a "man of action" in the realistic sense that Görgey was. If Kossuth had been possessed by ambition, as his enemies and Görgey claimed, he would have taken advantage of this moment to "get rid of" the dangerous enemy within the camp. But Kossuth hesitated, questioning his right to remove a great general at this time of crisis. If he should again be victorious. . . . But Görgey was not victorious, and in the president's entourage the voices multiplied which held Görgey responsible for the defeats.

There now began a grotesque guerilla warfare between the civil and the military leaders. In both camps childish accusations were made. Görgey never tired of belittling Kossuth to his officers. He accused Kossuth of having ordered him to retake Buda out of vanity, and that "he had sat in the royal box in the National Theatre and held a truly dynastic court with his family until the day of the flight to Debrecen." But in Debrecen Görgey was ridiculed for having chosen that moment to appear in a brand-new gala uniform, and suspected because he put no restraint upon the captured Austrian officers in his camp at a time when Haynau had published a proclamation showing that

KOSSUTH IN TURIN

From the Portrait Collection of the National Library, Vienna.

there was no chivalry to be expected from Austria. It was rumoured that Görgey was in contact with his brother-in-law, then Austrian Minister of War, and was secretly making terms with the enemy. Kossuth did not believe this rumour, but he saw more and more clearly that Görgey's object was to get rid of him, and so he addressed a sharp scarcely veiled warning to him from Debrecen: "If any wretch tried to make himself an autocrat, I would kill him with my own hand." But despite these sudden outbursts and his increasing hatred of the man, Kossuth complied with his duty: he backed Görgey as long as he felt he must.

It was not long before the Russians were close to Debrecen. The government withdrew to Szeged. Again the banknote printing press, weighing six tons, and the mysterious chest accompanied it on its wanderings. Again the Diet opened in Szeged. From here Kossuth sent a deeply moving appeal to Görgey: "Dear Artur, let us not cherish any resentment against each other now. I know that no one loves Hungary more than you. Let this conviction preserve between us the harmony we need in order to save our country." But even this effort failed; for Kossuth's prime minister, Szemere, the man that he had made, was now in Görgey's camp. Now, when Kossuth's power seemed threatened, Szemere dared to intervene; in a letter which is an appalling documentation of the want of union he charges Kossuth: "Do not live in the illusion that you do not covet power. But at least admit that you are not the only one capable of saving Hungary."

The circle of hostility was closing in round Kossuth. This war within war was terrible; the more so because its stupidity is clear. Szemere no longer hesitated to join forces with Görgey; without the knowledge of the Ministry over which he presided he wrote to him on the 25th July, practically whining for the general's favour and accusing Kossuth of every possible mistake. "The Ministry," he concludes, "considers that it is Kossuth's duty to the nation to resign." And now also Duschek whom Kossuth had made Minister of Finance allies himself to the elements of disruption; he refuses to issue any more paper money, thereby imperilling the provisioning of the army, and finally, after Austria's victory, he hands over all the reserve stocks of "Kossuth money" to the enemy.

While all this was going on below the surface Kossuth undeterred sought for a plan to save the situation. The reports of his ambassadors read unfavourably; no country was moving a finger in Hungary's cause. Everywhere the Hungarian troops were defeated, only the valiant Bem held Transylvania against an overwhelming offensive. Kossuth's sole desire was to save Hungary, not his own authority. He had from the first avoided making Hungary a republic, as Szemere had wanted. The "temporary constitution"—this was his far-seeing idea—permitted a return to a monarchy. Only the Hapsburgs were to be debarred from re-ascending the throne. Kossuth looked round the German princely courts to consider who might be worthy to wear the crown of St. Stephen. And, strangely enough, he first hit upon a member of the ducal House of Coburg whose history was to be so closely linked with that of South-Eastern Europe. But there was no time left for such a step. Now Bem too was compelled to evacuate Transylvania and in the battle of Temesvár everything was lost. The Russians poured across the frontier. Haynau threatened to become the destroying angel of Hungary. And then Kossuth conceived his boldest and absurdest plan: to offer the crown of Hungary to one of the Russian grand dukes! Then at least the Czar would save the defeated country from the worst.

But it was too late. On the 11th August the government had to remove to Arad, protected by the army which took up a position close to the town to await General Schlick's advance. Kossuth sat in a little house in a side street waiting for Görgey. In this hour of crisis all the generals assembled at the president's quarters and at last Görgey himself entered the dark and narrow room. The Russian Count Rüdiger had already sent envoys to Görgey summoning him to surrender unconditionally. Görgey had replied to the Russian commander that he was determined at all costs to save Hungary which the Emperor of Austria in alliance with the Czar of Russia intended to destroy. "We shall therefore be obliged to fight until our peaceable fellow-citizens are saved from the danger of subjugation, or until we ourselves perish in this unequal fight." This answer was conveyed to the Russian field-marshal Prince Paskiewitsch; the Russian advance continued.

Görgey's reply proves beyond doubt that he was actually as firmly resolved to save Hungary as Kossuth. He was no traitor. But he believed that Kossuth was opposed to any reconciliation with the enemy. Now, at the meeting of the generals in Kossuth's lodging in Arad, Görgey declared for the first time openly that Kossuth's person made any agreement with the enemy impossible. In his opinion the 14th April—Kossuth's deposition of the Hapsburgs—had ruined any hope of a favourable peace. Görgey showed that he paid no heed to Szemere's insinuations; he despised this schemer so much that he pointedly ignored his presence at headquarters. By his friendly treatment of the Austrian officers he had purposely tried to keep open the way to a reconciliation with Austria. And yet it was from the Czar alone that he expected magnanimity; it was with him alone that he was prepared to enter into negotiations.

On the 10th August Görgey met Kossuth once more in private conversation. The two men who had fought each other and quarrelled with each other made no reference to the past. They discussed the possibility of a fresh offensive, a last forlorn hope against the advancing enemy. Rumours of a victory of Dembinski's army at Temesvár had filled Kossuth with new hope. If this rumour were true, Görgey was ready to renew his attack. "But if the Austrians have been victorious at Temesvár?" asked Kossuth.—"Then I shall surrender," answered Görgey. And Kossuth: "And I shall shoot myself." Görgey, the cold, irreconcilable antagonist, turned to Kossuth: "You must live. You must flee. For one day your hour may come again."

Deeply moved, Kossuth looked into the general's face. What did his expression betray? His eye shone with boldness and determination. Was not that a message of hope? The situation was desperate. On every side the enemy was pressing in against the last strip of Hungary which they still occupied, against the small, poorly armed ring that defended Arad. Only in the south, at Temesvár, critically near the headquarters at Arad, Dembinski still harried the enemy. Only one line of retreat remained open: to the south-east, via Lugos, by the narrow route between the mountains that led to Orsowa on the Danube, Orsowa, the frontier of the Turkish Empire.

"If you believe that you can save Hungary, then I will place all authority in your hands," said Kossuth at last.

"I will save her," replied Görgey calmly.

That night the manifesto was formulated: the proclamation to the nation in which Kossuth announced his resignation and handed over all his powers to Görgey. "May Görgey love his country without self-seeking, as I have done, and may he, in his efforts to secure the welfare of Hungary, be more fortunate than I."

The very next day Görgey informed General Rüdiger that he was ready to surrender. He appealed to the magnanimity of the Czar in the hope that he would intercede with the Emperor of Austria for indulgence to the Hungarian nation.

The crusade was at an end. Kossuth had retired into the shade. Perhaps now fate would be kinder to Hungary.

XVI

The Spirit of the Maccabees

IN SZEGED, A FEW DAYS BEFORE THE CATASTROPHE, THE SPIRIT OF revolt stirred once more in Kossuth's mind. In this last hour a creative act must speak for the vision which had guided him and led him to the edge of the abyss. No matter that to-morrow would bring defeat—history judges differently from the present. Through all the past year Kossuth, hurrying from camp to camp, from place to place, burdened with his daily task, occupied with cares of equipping and provisioning the army in the field and harassed by worries over the command, had had no breathing-space. The power was still in his hands. The Diet still followed him. His decision would become law.

Kossuth had been allowed no time to realise his ideas; all the time he had been in power he had had to fight. Now he meant that the annals of history should at least record what his aim had been.

What a ghastly fatality! Kossuth had fought for the abolition of class differences, for the emancipation of the peasant serfs, for religious equality of rights. But it was left to the Austrian tyrant, the Minister Bach, to realise many of his ideas—of course from very different motives. But in this ultimate hour of collapse he meant to show by a visible sign the spirit which had inspired the insurrection under his leadership. And so it was at his wish that the prime minister Szemere rose at the last historic meeting of the independent Diet in Szeged to give the Jews of Hungary their emancipation.

Such was Kossuth's conception of the word "people." A sincere co-operation of all parts of the nation that should extinguish class barriers, proletarian prejudices, and all the differences of nationality. And it was as a symbol that Hungary had become a people, despite the defeat that threatened her, and that what was left of her survived Kossuth's own collapse, that the emancipation of the Jews from their degraded status was to be made law.

At the beginning of the revolution the Jews who in the cities still lived shut off in their ghettos had answered the call to independence. The great Hungarian poet Jókai whose novels give a true picture of the times, wrote: "At that time when every national community with which Hungary had shared her freedom rose in arms against their fatherland, the Jews were ready to sacrifice their lives, their money, their brains, in defence of the Hungarian nation and for constitutional liberty; the one race that was kept beyond the pale of the constitution, those very Jews who alone were denied equality of rights in this their country."

The able-bodied Jews had flocked to the National Guard to fight for their country's newly won independence. They had lived for centuries as close neighbours of the Magyar race, more nearly related to them than the Roumanians or the Serbs, the Croats or the Slovenes who should have fused with the Hungarian people after the revolution. In the distant past, under the old Hungarian kings, they had attained the highest honours; Laki Thüz for example had become Ban of Croatia. Now they hoped in an independent Hungary to be given their rights as citizens. They organised a special guard of their own, but after the rioting of the 19th April they were no longer allowed to bear arms. Kossuth had protested against this provocation. "Until to-day Jews were not allowed to join the National Guard; although the law allowed it, human intolerance and benighted stupidity forbade it." And yet in spite of this first rebuff the Jews insisted upon fighting in the army. "Love of country when once it has taken root in a man's heart cannot be eradicated." At the beginning of the war the rabbi Löw Schwab issued a proclamation to his brother Jews: "Your country calls you to defend honour, unity and right. Up! Answer the call with a joyous heart, with fiery zeal and with the courage that scorns death! Show yourselves true sons of Hungary, worthy descendants of the Maccabees!"

On Kossuth's orders the Jewish volunteer troops were now enrolled in the army. General Klapka admits: "A twelfth of our corps consisted of Jews. Every battalion had Jewish volunteer platoons. They distinguished themselves by their bravery. Many of them fell on the field of battle, a large number were promoted from the ranks, such as Ignaz Eisenstädter, Henrik Lévai, Doctor Rotfeld and many others. Many of the Jewish officers were decorated for valour, such as Captain Arányi Mór who led a daring attack which saved his commander, Count Leiningen, from being taken prisoner at Cibakháza, Hazai,

Just who distinguished himself as staff captain in Komorn, Schlesinger of the Komorn garrison and Leo Holländer."

Their bravery was acknowledged by the whole army, that is by the nation at the front. Now when Szemere on Kossuth's orders introduced the bill which gave the Jews equality of rights, its acceptance was a foregone conclusion. Szemere pointed out that "the persecution to which the Jews have been subjected was never instigated by the Magyars, but by immigrants, particularly by the German populations of the cities." He went on: "What do we owe to those who have rewarded our callousness with fervent love, and have shed their blood and sacrificed their goods and chattels for our country and her independence? Those who are persecuted and oppressed, not as we, but far more than we have been." For, as Windischgrätz had done after he re-entered Buda, so now Haynau had already inflicted the severest punishment on the Jewish population. From all the benches of the Diet a shout arose: "Long live our Israelite patriots, our gallant brothers!" And so the law recognising the Jews as true Magyars was passed amid wild enthusiasm.

The result of this act of magnanimity on the eve of defeat was that the victorious Austrians wreaked a dreadful vengeance on the Jews. But human actions have far-reaching effects. Hungary had become a nation, and whoever was ready to stand up for the spirit of this nation was a member of it. Kossuth knew that his day was done. But he was justified in hoping that he would retain the love of the nation he had created and united.

XVII

Defeat

ONE BATTLE! PERHAPS A SMALL VICTORY! THIS WAS KOSSUTH'S prayer. He had resigned, he had made room for Görgey. Now he was just an ordinary citizen, a Magyar, one of the millions who were now secretly praying for a favourable turn at the last moment. Would Görgey risk another battle with his sixty thousand men? There was still time, Kossuth thought, to reorganise resistance. He had gone with all speed to Lugos by the only road still open, to the foot-hills of the Transylvanian mountains where Bem's corps had retreated. Ought not Bem to take over the supreme command? This eternal question of the supreme command! Now when the army consisted only of routed units it needed a Bonaparte to save the situation. Kossuth knew that it was beyond his powers. And Görgey remained inactive. Kossuth sent a message to Bem advising him to make a stand before Lugos, in the hope of holding up Jellasich's force of eighty thousand with his five thousand men. And Bem accomplished the incredible: for one day his little band held up the whole army of the allies. But this 13th August was no more than a day of grace, for on the same day Görgey in Világos had asked General Rüdiger to state his conditions for capitulation.

Kossuth knew that this was the end. There were still strong fortresses in Hungarian hands, but they too would fall, one after the other. The end! The war was lost! The gallant Bem was still fighting at Lugos, but this forlorn hope served no purpose except to keep open the last way out for those whom Görgey had abandoned: flight or a voluntary death.

Kossuth broke down. It was not his old malady nor physical pain that prostrated him; it was grief. Why had he always held himself in reserve? Why had he not fought as a private in the ranks? He might have fallen in battle and been spared this day of bitterness. A few days ago, on the 31st July, when Bem had attacked the greatly superior Russian General Lüders at Schäsburg, his adjutant, a young officer who had often been reprimanded by the pedantic War Minister Mészáros for wearing his collar unbuttoned without the regulation tie, stood beside his commander in the hail of bullets. This queer fellow was Bem's bravest comrade. When the army halted to rest after long marches he would lie down by the camp-fire and scribble his thrilling verses on scraps of yellowed paper. What had befallen Sándor Petöfi, the poet of liberty? He had not returned from the battle. In the small hours of the morning hussars searched the battlefield strewn with dead. There they found their "little father Bem" who was believed dead lying severely wounded in a ditch. But they had not found Petöfi. Kossuth had scarcely ever seen him, but he loved his poetry. Petöfi died at the age of twenty-six; he was spared the knowledge of the fate that awaited Hungary. In the woods of Lugos Kossuth, with death in his heart, spoke the lines of Petöfi, filled with the foreboding of death, but also with the pride of the happy warrior:

"My mind is tortured by one haunting dread,
The thought that I may one day die in bed;
That I may languish feckless in repose,
To fade and wither like a canker'd rose;
That, as this candle gutters in the gloom,
I too must peter in my lonely room.
Merciful God, let me not die this way,
Nor rot and wither thus in slow decay.

O let me be a rock by lightning split
That crashes with the storm that smashes it!
O let me be a rock 'mid summer's green
That thunders echoing in the deep ravine!
And when at last the nations of the West
Throw off the yoke by which they are oppressed,
And when with firm-set, anger-reddened face
The people break the tyrant's rod of grace;
When towards heaven its banner is unrolled
Whereon the sacred emblem is enscrolled:
        World liberty!
Then may I too stand in the battle smoke,
Rejoicing, and when my last words are spoke
And drowned by clash of steel or cannon's roar,
Then let me lie there where my charger bore
My corpse across the Puszta to the spot
Where victory was ours because we faltered not."

Kossuth longed for death. Was there still a hope left? Görgey, he heard, had signed the capitulation. The Russians were advancing. He had to make his decision.

He fled to Orsowa, the last Hungarian town on the Danube, on the frontier of Wallachia and Serbia which was under Turkish rule. Here he decided to await events.

But many others fled, like him, the best generals, and finally, the gallant Bem himself. After the surrender of the army it was useless to resist.

Görgey had thought that nothing was to be gained by further bloodshed. On the 11th August the Russian field-marshal Prince Paskiewitsch informed the Czar Nicholas I: "Hungary lies at Your Majesty's feet. The rebel government has laid down its powers and transferred them to Görgey. But Görgey with the main army has made unconditional surrender before the Russian army. I am happy to report that the only condition is that Görgey may be allowed to capitulate to the Russian army."

Görgey believed that by commending himself and his army to the mercy of the Czar he would receive honourable terms. For the Austrian commander-in-chief, Haynau, was a morbid, spiteful man who both in Italy and Hungary had pronounced and carried out the harshest sentences. Surely the Czar whom Kossuth had offered the crown of Hungary for one of his grand-dukes would not abuse his victory.

Alone and silent, sullen as ever, Görgey waited for General Rüdiger. His officers approached him. They besought him to go on fighting. His prætorians who had followed him loyally for a year were bubbling with excitement. General Schweidel was the first to tackle Görgey; Nagy-Sándor begged him with tears in his eyes to alter his decision. Görgey silently led the way up the hill towards the castle where his headquarters were. There on the terrace they waited for the Russians' answer. At last a black mass appeared on the horizon. It was Rüdiger's corps advancing to disarm the Hungarians. Suddenly the clear voice of one of Görgey's adjutants broke the oppressive silence: "Gentlemen, do not deceive yourselves: we are surrendering at discretion." These words roused the greatest indignation. So this was how Görgey told his officers that they were delivered up to the mercy of the enemy! Görgey stemmed the tide of mutiny by threatening to shoot any man who resisted the surrender. The officers withdrew; they thought their commander a madman. How was he dressed? As if for some great occasion. He who had always worn a simple field service jacket to-day wore a brown gold-braided tunic; his wounded head was bandaged with a Turkish scarf. He stood with his hands clasped behind his back and stared with set lips into the distance. Or was he smiling?

Görgey's mysterious behaviour drove several officers to desperation. One cavalry captain swore that he would ride out with his squadron and fight the oncoming Rüdiger to his last breath. Görgey replied: "I will have you shot first." Again silence. Then shots were heard in the park. Three, four, five. Görgey did not move. An officer rushed on to the terrace and reported that five officers had just taken their lives. All present wept. Görgey remained dumb.

At that moment Csányi, the old civil commissioner who had for a long time represented the government with the army, appeared upon the scene; he declared that he would not allow Görgey to abuse the powers that Kossuth had surrendered to him by this cowardly capitulation. He threatened, nay, he ordered Görgey to go on fighting; for it was only on this condition that Kossuth had resigned in his favour. Görgey answered coldly: "I will have you put in irons." Csányi could say no more. But he did not leave the camp, although he could have fled. He remained—and he was to be one of the first whom Haynau hanged.

On the road that runs past the mill at Világos thirty thousand men stood to arms, with a hundred and forty-four cannon. The August sun blazed down upon the silent army. A colonel in a war-tattered tunic kissed the regimental standards and they were then passed from hand to hand and every Honvéd kissed them in turn. Then the colonel burned the flags. The hussars stood beside their horses, in their light blue dolmans and scarlet shakos. Only Görgey sat his horse alone, waiting for Rüdiger. At last the Russian general appeared with his staff, his corps behind him. Görgey rode to meet him. The two generals saluted. Görgey did not address his troops. The surrender followed, slowly, almost mechanically, in ghastly silence. Now and again shots rang out and Cossacks silently carried away the lifeless bodies of suicide Honvéds. The hussars' horses were herded together, the rifles piled on carts. It was late evening when the disarmament was finished. Görgey and his army were the prisoners of the Russians.

Only Bem escaped across the Turkish frontier after his stand at Lugos. One by one the fortresses capitulated. Komorn alone held out. General Klapka, who commanded the fortress on the Danube, withstood all the assaults of the besieging army, in defiance of Görgey's orders to surrender. And now by his heroic defence of Komorn Klapka became one of the most famous generals of his time and even in England, where personal bravery has always been admired, children were christened after him—e.g. Jerome K. Jerome. Furthermore, Klapka was the only commander granted honourable terms.

After the capitulation at Világos Paskiewitsch urged the Czar to treat the captured officers with clemency. The Czar lost no time in informing Franz Josef of the victory, meanwhile ordering that the prisoners should be well treated and assuring Görgey that he would guarantee his life and liberty.

It seemed therefore as if Görgey's idea of surrendering to the Russians had been the right one. However much the people might murmur against him and his officers curse him—Görgey had capitulated because he was convinced of the uselessness of resistance and to prevent further bloodshed. As an officer he could rely on Paskiewitsch appreciating his behaviour. He had surrendered at discretion; but the Czar was not the Austrian emperor, Paskiewitsch was not Haynau. The Cossacks might have been guilty of occasional excesses, but the Czar's generals had never sanctioned such inhuman reprisals as the sadist Haynau. Görgey acted as a soldier, not as a politician.

He could not know that the entourage of the Emperor Franz Josef were incensed at the victory of the Russian troops. The Russians had been called in to help the Austrians, not to win the war. Already in April, when there was first talk of Russian intervention, the then commanding General Velden had issued a warning: "The help of Russia would be a complete moral defeat of Austria, an admission of her impotency before all Europe." Prince Schwarzenberg saw in Görgey's gesture a still more humiliating moral defeat. He knew that Haynau's instincts would lead him to savage retaliation, but if Görgey had thrown himself on the mercy of the young emperor, perhaps Schwarzenberg might have got rid of the compromising Haynau, as he actually did, a year later, on the first opportunity. But now he demanded the surrender of the captured army as Austria's right. And the Czar complied; the prisoners were handed over to the Austrians. Görgey alone had the Czar's promise; he was exiled to Klagenfurt.

Now there was nothing to restrain Haynau's savagery. Thirteen generals were sentenced to death and were hanged or shot on the 6th October at Arad. At the same time Count Batthyányi was sentenced to death in Pest. Hungary's first prime minister paid the penalty—of his loyalty. The only crime that could be brought up against him was that he had sent an independent Hungarian embassy to the Diet of Frankfort. The Count was resolved not to undergo the shame of an execution; on the morning of the 6th October he was found in his cell with an opened artery. But he was still alive. Still breathing, he was dragged to the scaffold where the gallows had been erected. The hangman had difficulty in lifting the sagging body to place the rope about his neck. And so Haynau who was present had him shot "so that he should not die before his execution."

The young government of Franz Josef believed this manifestation necessary to bolster up the failing might of Austria. The death sentences were determined on and approved in Prince Schwarzenberg's office in the Ballhausplatz. The horrified aristocracy, the officers of the Austrian army, appealed to Schwarzenberg to exercise clemency and not to carry out the Arad sentences. But Schwarzenberg replied: "Clemency? By all means, but we will just do a little hanging first." Batthyányi's trial was followed with consternation by the nobility. Two lenient sentences were quashed by Haynau. When it was known in Vienna that he had been condemned to death, the nobles begged the emperor not to permit this infamy to be carried out. No one believed that the young monarch would initiate his reign with such atrocities. But Franz Josef let things take their course. The execution of Batthyányi and the Polish Prince Woroniecki, the aged president of the upper house, Baron Perényi, and the minister Csányi humiliated the Hungarian nation, but strengthened its hatred against the House of Hapsburg. The war was ended, the Hapsburg was victorious, but he had not conquered Hungary.

The revolution had been quelled, but not the patriotism of the Magyars.

XVIII

Farewell—for Ever

AS LONG AS ARMED RESISTANCE HELD OUT THE SMALLEST HOPE Kossuth had not left Hungarian soil. The invasion had separated and disorganised the armies still in the field, but Kossuth placed his hopes on the resistance of the fortresses which might be made rallying bases for the scattered Honvéds. On the 14th August Bem was fighting his heroic battle to keep open the one possible line of retreat, the road from Lugos to Orsowa.

The fleeing ministers met in Orsowa, all except Duschek who proceeded straight from Lugos to the Austrian camp to hand over to the enemy the reserves of paper money, the so-called "Kossuth notes," and gold. Kossuth had entrusted the cash in the government's treasury to Görgey and so after the capitulation of Világos this too fell into the enemy's hands. He only managed to send a small remittance to his wife who had remained in Pest with his two sons and his aged mother. He himself had nothing.

The collapse threatened to crush his spirit. In the night of the 17th August he wandered through the poorly fortified town, alone. The war was over. Hungary was once more in Austrian hands. For the first time he felt lost and the memory of the 5th September of the previous year haunted him. At the beginning of the war Széchényi had broken down; had he not been right in his prognostication of the end? Like Széchényi in the depths of his depression Kossuth could not but cry: "I am to blame! I alone!"

But he is not Széchényi. His nature is stronger; he has other reserves of strength. He feels that the future needs that he should live. He is physically ill; his cheeks are sunk, his hair is grey, he looks years older; but his vitality is stronger than might be suspected. In this hour of despair he clutches at the straw of a lie: Görgey is to blame! Görgey is the traitor! And at the first moment of repose, at Vidin, Kossuth issues his famous manifesto to the world in which he arraigned Görgey as a traitor. He does not mention that the war was lost the day the Russians agreed to interfere. He still believed that Bem could defeat the Russians. Kossuth wrote to him, urging him to hold the Hungarian fortresses at all costs. Did he dream of returning to the army? But already the Austrian troops were within a day's march of Orsowa. One day was left to flee across the frontier. Kossuth had not forgotten to prepare for an eventual flight to Turkey, for himself and for the foreign volunteers, the Italian, Polish and German legionaries, who had joined the Hungarian war of independence.

On the morning of the 17th August the prime minister Szemere and the high officials of the government, assembled in a wretched peasant cottage in Orsowa, learned that Generals Perczel and Dembinski had already been driven back across the Turkish Wallachian frontier. Once more they sent a courier to Görgey before deciding on the last step, flight. At last Görgey's answer came. He still said nothing of the capitulation at Világos, but—and this shows what was in the wind—he ordered the ex-president to hand over the crown and the crown jewels.

The crown? The crown jewels? Szemere pricked up his ears. No one knew that Kossuth had brought them with him; no one had had a chance to look inside the mysterious chest that the president had carried with him from place to place and never let out of his possession. Szemere had suspected that it contained money, gold to provide for the difficult days of exile. Görgey's summons was refused. Szemere asked Kossuth whether he really carried the crown jewels with him. Kossuth admitted it.

An hour later—the firing of the approaching enemy cavalry was already audible in the distance—Kossuth entered the miserable tavern near the bridge of Orsowa. On the far bank of the Danube floated the Turkish flag. It is still daylight, but only a meagre light filters through the narrow windows of the bare room of the inn. The frugal meal is over. The leaders of independent Hungary sit in silence, waiting. Now Kossuth opens the heavy chest and takes out of a brown sack the crown of St. Stephen. It has been the emblem of Hungary since the year A.D. 1000 when Pope Silvester II presented it to St. Stephen; the crown was Hungary itself, whose members were the nation and the king. Although Verböczy's interpretation of the constitution and the Hungarian revolution may have been filled with a new meaning, the crown preserved its symbolism intact. The diadem is ornamented with fifty-three sapphires, fifty rubies and hundreds of pearls. The cross in front is bent, for in the days of the Turkish invasion the crown is said to have been damaged in its wanderings from camp to camp. The bent cross is a reminder of the sufferings of the Magyars. The hunted ministers gazed at this holy relic in this tavern room at Ostrowa, on the boundary of the Turkish Empire. Nothing spoke more eloquently of defeat and humiliation, despair and horror of the future than this shameless display of the abducted crown, orb and sceptre in this place.

Szemere burst into a paroxysm of laughter. He picked up the crown; no one hindered him. Kossuth leaned against the wooden wall, shaken with weeping. Then to put the final touch of grim absurdity to this Shakespearean scene, Szemere flung about his shoulders a military cloak, turned inside out, so that the red lining looked like purple in the dusk; he found a half-broken mirror in the wall; he placed the crown upon his head, took up the orb and sceptre, and paraded like a mountebank before the looking glass. No one laughed. All stared at him in silence. The crown wobbled on his head as he pranced about the room; then as he reached the mirror, an ague seized him. One of the others saved the crown from crashing to the floor.

At last the dusk drew on. Kossuth quietly left the inn, the sacred jewels in a parcel under his arm. He walked along the river bank until he found a boat. Then he rowed out to a lonely stretch of bank, overgrown with bushes and at the foot of an old tree he dug up the loose earth with his hands and buried Hungary's crown. Did he believe that now no king could legally rule over Hungary, because only coronation with the crown of St. Stephen could invest him with the rights of kingship? But Franz Josef had never asked to be crowned king; he ruled by virtue of his might.

Night had fallen by the time that he returned. The last night on Hungarian soil. On the morning of the 18th August his loyal band of followers gathered round him. Several battalions had meanwhile reached Orsowa in flight. The guns announced the nearing of the enemy's troops. The men drew up round Kossuth in a square spontaneously, as they had done so short a while ago on the battlefield of Kápolna. As then, Kossuth fell upon his knees, bent down and kissed his native earth. The soldiers bared their heads. There were no cheers. Kossuth closed his eyes. How long ago was it that, when he had shown himself to the crowd in March of the great year 1848, a young man had run towards him with the cry: "I fall on my knees to you, as to a God, Lajos Kossuth!" And Kossuth, the same man, bent with his superhuman efforts for his country, had now to make his last speech of farewell. But the eloquence of the great orator became a stammering; gradually he regained the mastery of his voice, but his emotion was even more moving than his words. "Forgive me, Hungary, forgive me who am now condemned to wander far from here because I strove for your welfare. Forgive me who can no longer call anything free save this little strip of your soil where I now kneel with a handful of your loyal sons. Forgive me that so many of your sons have shed their blood for you because of me. I wanted a free nation, enjoying a freedom that only God can give. My principles were those of George Washington. I love you, Europe's most loyal nation."

As Kossuth spoke the troops had fallen on their knees. Now they rose. Kossuth led the way across the bridge. On the other side waited the commander of the Turkish Ostrowa brigade. They stood on foreign soil. Turkish troops occupied the bank and barred the crossing of the Danube. The Austrians entered Orsowa. But they found Kossuth no longer there.

PART FOUR

A SECOND LIFE

I

A War of Letters

MR. JAMES BLOOMFIELD OF MANCHESTER PRESENTED TO THE GUARD at the gate of the Turkish fortress of Orsowa a laissez-passer made out by the Hungarian Minister of Foreign Affairs, Count Casimir Batthyányi, for the traveller had lost his passport. Mr. Bloomfield was on his way home to England via Constantinople. His description: Protestant, age forty-seven, tall, pale, blue eyes. Mr. Bloomfield encountered no difficulties; the guard presented arms; an officer in Turkish uniform appeared, saluted and addressed the traveller from Manchester as "Your Excellency." The whole of Orsowa had been waiting for President Kossuth.

Gradually his companions followed. Then the Turkish brigade occupied the river bank. The Hungarian emigrants were in safety. What was to become of them? "I care nothing for my personal safety; I am tired of life," Kossuth had written to Bem. It was a good thing for him that he had plenty to do. But what influence had his name here in a foreign country? The name of a defeated rebel? A visionary?

It was a good sign that Karagiorgevics, the Prince of Servia, invited Kossuth and ten of his ministers to be his guests in Belgrade. Many Serbs had fought against Hungary; the people still hated the Magyars and actually insulted the Polish and Italian legionaries who fled to Serbia. But the prince was otherwise disposed; he had political vision; he knew that the victory of Russia would break up the crumbling unity of the Ottoman Empire. But Kossuth did not accept the invitation to Belgrade. His goal was Constantinople, the city of the Turkish Sultan, and at the same time the diplomatic centre of the Balkans. The next stop was Vidin, the fortress on the Danube. The Pasha of Vidin was expecting him. On the boundary of the two districts Kossuth thanked his hosts of Orsowa in suitably florid language.

The Pasha received the fugitives with oriental cordiality. But soon the question became urgent when would they proceed to Constantinople. The Pasha had received no orders from the

Sultan to further their journey, but he had been instructed by the powerful general Omar Pasha from Bukarest to keep the Hungarians in Vidin. Five thousand Honvéds had arrived and had encamped outside the fortress walls. Kossuth and his companions were lodged within the town. This was taken as a mark of special consideration, until they saw the airless, dilapidated quarters reserved for them. In the dusk Kossuth could hear the soldiers singing Hungarian folksongs in the camp. He would gladly have been amongst them. But he felt that he must keep his distance; that he must still keep up the fiction of being president.

In the camp there was growing discontent. The food was bad. There was no pay. The soldiers bartered their horses and last possessions. Poverty and idleness were hard to bear. Quarrelling and brawling destroyed the last vestiges of discipline and comradeship. Even Bem became moody and sought to wear away the time by drinking. He too grew quarrelsome; on the 30th August he wrote irritably to Kossuth—he wrote, he did not go to see him, "J'ai l'honneur de vous dire que je n'avais pas un sou chez moi." And speaking for his comrades: "Ce ne sont pas des fuyards qui aient lâchement abandonné leur patrie, mais des braves qui ont combattu jusqu'au dernier moment. . . ." Thus began the exile: disaffection in the camp and the uncertainty as to when this distressful situation would end sapped energy and courage.

But misfortune is the best antidote to discontent. The injustice of fate awakens the determination to resist. In the hour of need Kossuth always found fresh strength; grief had prostrated him, necessity set him on his feet again. Three years of imprisonment in Buda had not crushed his spirit; now in the stifling emptiness of Vidin he rose to the occasion. It was his duty to carve out the future for himself and for those who depended on him.

A new fight was beginning. With what weapon was a destitute and homeless fugitive to fight? Could he find a weapon? Yes, his pen. He now used the power of his rhetoric in a new form; no longer as an orator, nor as a journalist, but as a letter-writer. A war of letters began, a war without a parallel. Letters broadcast to all the world; moving, provocating, argumentative. Letters coloured with humility when they were meant to move the Sultan; simple, straightforward when he sought to analyse the situation with political logic. His letters gave Kossuth back his poise.

What hope was there? What end had he in view? The most immediate step was taken first: he had to arouse the compassion of the Sultan in order to alleviate the misery in the camp. Kossuth's letters were successful; the Turkish General Omar Pasha gave orders that "they were all to be well treated, particularly General Bem." The Sultan contributed to their relief. But the men remained sullen and disheartened. Kossuth had to encourage them with speeches. He often rode through the wide-spread city of tents and the sight of him brought new hope.

Hope of what? Of a return to Hungary? Yes, but it should be a bloody return, a return by force of arms. Kossuth still believed this possible. The fortresses, he thought, were still in Hungarian hands. If he could only raise a new army, Turkish troops perhaps, would not the country rise again as in the first days of independence? Kossuth clung obstinately to this plan. Fortunately the man he had made ambassador to Constantinople was Count Julius Andrássy, Etelka's son, who was devoted to him. He wrote to him incessantly, urging him not to lose contact with the ambassadors to the Western Powers. Surely now at last England and France must see that Hungary's fight was also the fight for maintenance of the balance of power in Europe; would they look on while Russia celebrated victories, Russia who had for a long time been stretching out her hand to seize Constantinople? Kossuth was the first to recognise that Russia's intervention was merely a cloak for the imperialistic tendency of Czarist policy; to bestride the Bosphorus and to destroy the Ottoman Empire. But Kossuth had no time to wait for Andrássy. He still had his "diplomatic agents" abroad, Pulszky in London, Count Teleki in Paris. On the 12th September he sent them his "statement of accounts." He admitted that he had always hoped for European intervention and counted on the protest of the democratic Western Powers against the invasion of the Czar. He had been mistaken; the Powers had not raised a finger. But was it now too late? "It would be too late if the subjugation of Hungary were complete. The grave does not yield up its booty. There is no example in history of a resurrected nation. It did not even happen with Greece. Galvanisation is not life. . . . But once Hungary's subjugation is accomplished, then Europe will follow its old practice and accept it as a 'fait accompli'." Therefore he besought Pulszky to leave no stone unturned in London.

London was Kossuth's hope. Lord Palmerston, the British Foreign Minister in Russell's cabinet, must be won over completely. Palmerston, impetuous, fire and flame for any noble cause, the friend of Lord Byron in his youth, nicknamed "Lord Firebrand," had always shown his sympathy with south-eastern nations in their fight for independence. But what is sympathy that is confined to words? Now when England was pursuing a policy of splendid isolation, Pulszky must point out to Palmerston the danger of Russia's victory which made Austria a satellite of Russia, whereas a young and powerful Hungary would be a protective barrier on the East. Kossuth was clever enough to mark down Russia as the only enemy of Europe, peace and liberty. He foresaw that Russia would kindle the next European war. "The Turk feels instinctively," he writes, "that his own fall is linked with ours. The Pasha of Belgrade wept at our defeat; he foresees that the Turks cannot keep their foothold in Europe for longer than two or three years at most. Even Turkish children prayed for our victory." And he warns England "to see the symptoms of decay in Turkey and to abandon her policy of weakness towards Russia."

Within little more than three weeks of his flight the defeated and deposed president of the Hungarian free state was altering history. The English people in numerous meetings expressed their enthusiasm for Kossuth; a Kossuth group was formed in parliament; Richard Cobden, Lord Nugent and other important members of the House of Commons supported him. It was possible that in England the fate of Hungary might yet be decided.

But time pressed. Austria feared Kossuth even in victory. On the 28th August Austria demanded of the Sublime Porte the extradition of Kossuth and his companions. Russia followed suit a few days later. Now the exiles were in serious danger. The best advice Count Julius Andrássy could give was that the fugitives should be converted to Mohammedanism, for the Sultan would never hand over the "faithful" to the infidel. A letter from the Sultan himself reiterated this advice. To many the danger of extradition was preferable to a change of faith. But conversion to Islam guaranteed the officers a commission in the Turkish army. Without hesitation Bem and sixteen officers of high rank decided for conversion; they made their confession of faith in the mosque of Vidin; they were given new names; as Turks they were separated from their comrades; they were given appointments in the Turkish army.

Kossuth himself had rejected Andrássy's advice with indignation. But the first blow against the unity of the emigration had been successful: the camp was split.

Palmerston had secretly agreed with Napoleon III to bring pressure to bear upon the Porte for the protection of the Hungarian emigrants; a fleet of warships was in readiness to proceed to the Bosphorus when Thiers brought about a change in the French policy. "To start a war for a *polisson* like Kossuth looks as if England found pleasure in setting the continent in flames." Napoleon followed Thiers' advice; he sent General Lamauricière to St. Petersburg to appeal to the Czar's magnanimity. Lamauricière succeeded in arranging a compromise between St. Petersburg and the Sublime Porte by which Kossuth was permitted to remain in Turkey, but only in Turkish Asia Minor where he seemed as innocuous as Napoleon in St. Helena. Meanwhile, however, Lord Firebrand had acted on his own initiative; he committed a breach of treaty by sending a British fleet through the Dardanelles. This occasioned a sharp protest from Russia and of course the Tories attacked Palmerston in parliament. The fate of Kossuth was beginning to divide the Powers.

Kossuth knew nothing of all this. Still tireless in his letter-writing he wrote to the British ambassador to the Sublime Porte, Sir Stratford Canning, to ask his help against the threatened extradition. "Extradition or conversion to Islam is the alternative of a certain death." And again he displays his politica acumen. "What does Turkey stand to gain? Can she avoid a war with Russia?" Kossuth concludes by saying that he and those with him placed themselves under the protection of England and France.

Kossuth works with unexampled energy; he is now writing letters, astonishingly enough, in four languages: in German to Andrássy, in Hungarian to his friends, in French and English to the ambassadors. On the 20th December, as his fate is still undecided, he addresses a direct appeal to Lord Palmerston which an adventurous English journalist who has visited him at Vidin undertakes to deliver. He sums up the causes of Hungary's plight in one sentence: "What tyranny began, treason achieved." He "conjures" Palmerston "in the name of God," to grant the exiles an asylum in England.

But meanwhile the Austrians delivered a direct attack upon the camp at Vidin. On the 13th October the Austrian General Hauslab appeared, charged with the mission of winning back for the Austrian army some at least of the officers and men. All who returned to their allegiance were promised a free pardon. His arrival caused a new dissension in the camp. For the men, living as they were in direst misery, he was their saviour. Three thousand five hundred men, but only twenty officers, followed him. That evening three boatloads steamed up the Danube towards Orsowa.

The emigration was crumbling. Did Kossuth guess that in the end he would stand alone? Utterly alone? But presently news reached him of the results of Lamauricière's *démarche* in St. Petersburg. The Sultan assured those who remained in exile complete liberty and decent pay. Kossuth's hopes rose; he was full of plans. He was now living in the comfortable palace of Vidin. But orders were given for the camp to be removed into the interior, to Schumla. Kossuth distributed among the men a large sum of money given by the Sultan, and on the 29th October the whole camp assembled in the garden of his palace where Kossuth appeared among them with all the dignity of a president in office and was once more greeted with cheers. He made them a speech disclosing his hopes: all the English newspapers had espoused the Hungarian cause; in the event of war being decided on against Austria and Russia, they would all return together up the Danube where hundreds of thousands of volunteers would flock to join them; fourteen British ships had appeared in the Dardanelles. "There we shall be hospitably received until the outbreak of war."

Kossuth confidently hoped soon to renew the war. Therefore, being a shrewd psychologist, he made a point of playing his role of leader even in exile. He had to defend his authority against Bem who was now openly agitating against him and against Perczel who had succeeded Bem as camp commandant. And the camp decided for their president.

The removal to Schumla interrupted Kossuth's political activities. On the 1st November the renegades who had embraced the faith of Islam left Vidin under the command of Bem, the women already wearing the yashmak. On the 3rd November the Hungarians who remained with Kossuth started on the twenty-day march across the mountains to Schumla. There Kossuth was housed in the finest house in the town. He sat, day in day out, at his writing-table, but always ready to receive any of the soldiers who came to him for advice. Winter set in and the men suffered from the bitter cold in their billets in the dilapidated houses with paper windows and broken doors.

Kossuth was still obsessed with the idea of a European war against Russia. He foresaw that a naval action by England and France in the Black Sea would not be effective without co-ordinated help on land. Poland, Hungary and Turkey must combine in attacking Russia. At last the Sublime Porte seemed to realise the necessity of resistance. For, in spite of the agreement of St. Petersburg, Prince Radziwill had appeared in Constantinople to renew the Austrian demand for the extradition of the Hungarians. The Sultan refused. But the more public opinion in England decided for Kossuth, the more determinedly the government in Vienna strove for his destruction.

And now began a grotesque melodrama, stage-managed by the Austrian secret police, with all the stock characters, the traditional accomplices of villainy, spies, hired assassins, and an adventuress. Turkey swarmed with Austrian spies, in all possible disguises, as journalists, as commercial travellers. Even foreigners were roped into the service of espionage. Kossuth in exile seemed to the Vienna government even more dangerous than before; his success with the Sultan—for Palmerston's order to the fleet to enter the Dardanelles was Kossuth's success—made it clear that the spirit of this determined rebel was not broken. What matter that spies reported that Kossuth was down with fever and could not live long in the unhealthy climate of Schumla? Vienna needed certainty and haste.

One incident dissipated any doubt that Kossuth's name was still a menace. Baron Haynau, the victorious general, had been retired by Prince Schwarzenberg, for when he found this man's sanguinary reputation an unnecessary embarrassment, Haynau had gone to London on an official visit. Palmerston ignored him. Haynau stayed in London for his own amusement. One day, it was the 4th September, 1850, he visited Barclay's brewery. As he was being shown round, the personnel began to evince a curious interest in the visitor and suddenly the workmen crowded together and gave Haynau a good thrashing. Was it his imagination or was it true that they shouted: "That's for Arad" ? Half an hour later he was taken in an ambulance to hospital. An hour later the whole of London knew that the workmen of Barclay's had in their own fashion avenged the outraged sense of justice of the civilised world.

This, too, was Kossuth's doing. He must be got rid of. And now Vienna actually had recourse to assassination. A writer named Jassinger consented to kill Kossuth. He started for Turkey, amply provided with money, excellent credentials and exact instructions. But this highly paid assassin behaved like the veriest tyro. In Constantinople he recruited twelve Croats "armed to the teeth," and with these auxiliaries took the train for Schumla. An observant Hungarian officer, a lieutenant

Bardy, had already overheard this amateur murder club boasting in Constantinople and had hastened to Schumla to warn Kossuth. When the assassins arrived in the town they were promptly disarmed and arrested. After this the Sultan had Kossuth's house put under armed guard and Kossuth allowed one of his servants, the Arab Halil, who was devoted to him with an Oriental fidelity to act as his personal bodyguard. This swarthy giant rode behind Kossuth with two loaded pistols in his belt, slept on the threshold of his room and when the governor had visitors Halil lowered, like the Moor Fiesco, behind the curtains to watch over his master.

Kossuth was now protected from Schwarzenberg's hired assassins, but not even Halil could protect him from the last, and greatest danger. The Vienna plotters had still a third card up their sleeve: the "adventuress," the "fatal woman," in the language of a later age the "vamp." The spies had correctly reported to headquarters in Vienna that Kossuth had relapsed into depression. In December with the Balkan plains lying deep in snow Kossuth grew desperate. His letters are full of bitterness: "I am beginning to be a very sick man. The misery of my country, the changing clouds on the political horizon, the complete uncertainty as to the fate of my dear wife and my children, have so undermined my nervous system that I spend whole days in delirious fancies. Have you no news for me of my family? None? It is horrible." And again he complains: "This place swarms with Austrian spies and agents, regular plots are hatched and subventioned with money."

He is on his guard. He is well protected. Only his closest friends have access to him, first among whom is the young Dembinski, nephew of the general, who since Vidin has been his constant companion. Now his pretty wife, Emilia Hogl, joined her husband in exile and her advent came as a welcome relief to Kossuth, who was wearying of the quarrelsomeness of his exclusively male society. She alone understood him; her presence comforted him. And when the young officer went to Constantinople to discuss important plans for the future, the pretty Dembinskaja became Kossuth's companion. She read his most secret thoughts, she knew how to rake the embers of his ambitious dreams. In his depression he had lost the faith that he could still do something for the liberation of his country. Dembinskaja revived his hopes. She was not inactive; she used her connections in Vienna and Prague to work for him; and one day, immediately after the New Year, she was able to inform him that the opponents of the new régime were eagerly awaiting Kossuth in Vienna. He had only to go there, incognito of course; he could travel by one of the English ships lying in the harbour of Varna, land in Trieste and reach Vienna from there. His devoted Captain Blana had given him the same advice: "If he put on civilian clothes and travelled unobtrusively in a Turkish cart to Varna and there went straight to the British Consulate, ten thousand Turks could not stop him. For British ships were anchored in the harbour." Escape! How good that would be! And, not to escape to save his life; not to exchange his miserable quarters for comfort—but escape in order to take into his own hands the reins of a new revolt which was already organised. Kossuth was ready—and the same night Austria's best spies reported to Vienna that Kossuth had swallowed the bait. Dembinskaja would deliver Kossuth into the hands of the secret police.

And now a miracle happened. The *deus ex machina* arrived in the nick of time. Kossuth still hesitated to leave Schumla before he knew for certain what had happened to his wife and children. Then, on the 15th January, his wife suddenly appeared in person. She had got through, furnished with a British passport. Kossuth fell into her arms. The drama planned by the Vienna secret police had a surprise happy end. Dembinskaja left Schumla.

Ever since her husband had left her without a word, the fugitive of a lost cause, Therese had been through dreadful times. She had been imprisoned for a while; even Kossuth's old mother had not been spared; it was thought that when he heard of her arrest he would hand himself up although there was a high price upon his head. But the news never reached him cut off from the world in Vidin and Schumla. Finally both women were released. Kossuth's faithful spy, the Baroness Beck, who had crossed the enemy's lines during the war in a hundred ingenious disguises to carry messages to Görgey or to Komorn, visited Therese and encouraged her to risk the journey to Schumla. The British helped her with a passport and admiring friends with money.

After Therese's arrival Kossuth was a different man. His mind recovered its clarity; he worked more methodically and extensively. He sketched a picture of the future of Europe, a prophetic picture which was only too soon to come true, in the Crimean War. His analysis of the European situation, his prognosis of the impending collapse of the Ottoman Empire and of the aspirations of Russia, were startling. But he himself knew that his prophecy was nothing more than shrewdness and imagination. "Educated in the practical school of a stormy life, I have gained a sure insight into the future. This is no gift of divination on which I pride myself; it is merely historical logic which teaches me that from certain causes certain results must naturally and inevitably follow." Kossuth saw that the increased Panslavistic activity of Russia would demolish Turkey. The last moment has now come for the Sublime Porte to begin the war with Russia. The idea of Panslavism was a menace to the world; it aimed at a transformation of the Continent. "But ideas can only be combated and defeated by ideas." From this profound train of thought Kossuth arrived at a completely new realisation which meant jettisoning his own idea, that of pure nationalism. He had held up to the small nations the ideal of independence. But in the process of fighting for his idea he perceived that one nationalism postulates another and becomes the enemy of that other. Must that be so? Can there not be a society of nations with due stress upon their national idiosyncrasies? Now, on the threshold of the year 1850, Kossuth gives birth to the idea of a league of nations. "The idea of Panslavism can only be countered by the idea of federalism," he writes, "that federalism which guarantees small nations against foreign domination. This idea will and must prevail, especially in Germany, in Italy, and most of all in Eastern Europe. For federation means liberty, Panslavism slavery."

Therese's presence was responsible for a great change in her husband's mode of life. Her way of thinking was sufficiently English for her to know that "manners maketh man." She had forced him to surround himself with a certain pomp and circumstance when he was governor, and now she insisted on ceremony. She no longer allowed visitors to call on him indiscriminately. She organised his life as officially as if he had still been in power. By so doing she upheld his prestige, with the Honvéds, with the Turks, and not least with himself. He rode abroad on splendid horses, he virtually held court, and the Pasha had less compunction in paying him the high pension allowed him by the Sultan. And so, too, the Turkish government was induced to grant a regular subvention for the officers and men. Therese knew that Kossuth would still have a great role to play. Already friends in England were urging him to do everything possible to leave the Turkish camp. But there was no hope of that. Four weeks after his wife's arrival he had to leave Schumla for Asia Minor. The spot chosen for his internment was Kiutahia, the capital of Anatolia. Therese accompanied him and shortly after his arrival in Kiutahia a ship brought him his children. Now life was tolerable and work easy.

Kossuth realised that in the next war there would be no room for a leader who was not also capable of directing military operations. So he took up the study of military text-books. "I am lapping up strategy by the spoonful," he writes. More and more clearly he sees George Washington as a political ideal.

It was not only in the free countries of the West that Kossuth was a name to conjure with. A visitor to Kiutahia reported to Pulszky in London: "Since Napoleon no name had achieved such wide-spread fame in the East as Kossuth's." And this observer describes Kossuth as he found him: "I believe that Kossuth has as shrewd a knowledge of human nature as his favourite poet Shakespeare to whose bust he bears a certain facial resemblance. To complete the portrait I only need to add that he has the chin and mouth of Lord Byron, and the eye of Napoleon Bonaparte as Delaroche painted him."

His vitality restored, Kossuth composed his "Proclamation to the free people of the United States of North America." This proclamation produced a great impression. The Senator of the State of Mississippi, Foote, moved in the Senate that the government should offer Kossuth and his comrades an asylum and send a warship to Asia to fetch him with the Sultan's consent. The motion was carried unanimously with great enthusiasm. Kossuth was compared to Lafayette; preparations were begun for a ceremonial reception. Kossuth wrote to Pulszky in a tone of new hopefulness: "My day is not yet done."

Weeks passed before the Sultan gave his consent to Kossuth's departure. Meanwhile the American frigate *Mississippi* cruised up and down the Bosphorus. At last, on the 18th August the Sultan granted his permission. The news was acclaimed with delight in England and in America, with horrified amazement in Austria and Russia. Kossuth's release alarmed Austria to such an extent that the Austrian government actually broke off diplomatic relations with the Sublime Porte. The Sultan's humane behaviour threatened to kindle a war.

Kossuth, his wife and children, Count Casimir Batthyányi, Countess Perczel and forty comrades went on board. The frigate hoisted the Hungarian tricolour. The captain welcomed Kossuth as "President of Hungary." In Smyrna the United

States consul-general came on board the ship to hand Kossuth two thousand dollars on behalf of his government. Kossuth refused the gift.

Now followed a triumphal voyage through the Mediterranean. All the world wanted to see Kossuth. In Marseilles a huge crowd had assembled on the quay to welcome the champion of liberty.

In the hardships of his Turkish exile Kossuth had not realised that he had become famous in the Western world. He had lost his fight, but he had won the sympathy of the world. But Kossuth was to learn in Marseilles that acclamation is one thing, politics another. The Prince-president Napoleon—already preparing to make himself emperor—forbade Kossuth to land in France. Kossuth was astounded. Had not Prince Louis Napoleon as Carbonaro championed the same idea as he? At the same time Kossuth learnt that Austria had devised a new method of showing her anger at the release of the rebel against which she could do nothing. Kossuth and thirty-five other sentenced rebels were hanged in effigy in Pest.

Napoleon could debar Kossuth from landing in Marseilles, but he could not prevent the Marseillais from going to Kossuth. Thousands went on board the *Mississippi*. An enthusiastic shoemaker, named Jean Jonquil, plunged naked into the sea and swam out to the frigate in order to be the first to wring Kossuth's hand. When Kossuth asked him in astonishment how he had been able to swim such a distance, Jonquil replied: "Where there is a will, nothing is impossible." The shoemaker's answer became Kossuth's slogan. He uttered it in his speech to the citizens of Marseilles in which he expressed his gratitude to the French people. He also addressed himself to the working classes of France in a newspaper article, announcing his sympathy with them. The social struggle was about to begin in France; Kossuth, the pupil of Lamennais, consciously sided with the underdog. And so the stop at Marseilles, although Kossuth never went ashore, was of great political significance. In the coming struggle the workers of France could cite Kossuth as their spiritual leader.

The frigate proceeded on its voyage to America; but Kossuth left it on the coast of Spain. He was determined to pay a visit to the country which had been the first to take up his and Hungary's cause. His comrades went on without him; they would meet again in New York.

On the 23rd October his steamer reached Southampton. He set foot in England, the "land of justice."

II

Paradise England

ENGLAND AT LAST—"PARADISE ENGLAND," AS KOSSUTH CALLED it in his letters to Pulszky. The refuge of the exile, the asylum of the persecuted, the home of justice. The Continent was in convulsions; devoured by the old European disease: hatred and disunion. England was peaceful. England was strong. In every capital of Europe rulers trembled for fear of the revenge of the oppressed. In the Opéra Comique in Paris the Prince-president Napoleon narrowly escaped assassination by a bomb which killed a hundred innocent victims. In Vienna, not long afterwards, in February, 1853, the Emperor Franz Josef was severely wounded by a knife-thrust in the neck. Everywhere political troubles led to individual revolt. Only England was an island of civilisation; the land of political morality.

About 1850, London sheltered a host of foreign revolutionaries. Forty thousand Germans alone had found asylum there, countless Poles, three hundred Hungarians, and many Italians and Russians, all hoping, working, plotting. Freiligrath was in London, Mazzini, Herzen. Karl Marx sat in a London garret with Friedrich Engels preparing the "world revolution." And at the same time, almost unnoticed, in Eaton Square lived the most famous of the emigrants: Prince Metternich. The man of the past and the men of the future alike breathed the free air of this paradise England.

Pulszky who had so skilfully awakened England's interest in Kossuth knew at once that Kossuth would inevitably be drawn into this vortex of nationalist revolutionaries and would be overwhelmed by it. When he went on board his ship at Southampton to be the first to embrace his friend, he already had a letter for him from Mazzini inviting him to a "conference." President Napoleon's *coup d'état* was expected daily; the emigrant revolutionaries must act. And so Kossuth found two Englands: the paradise he longed for, and the emigrant volcano.

How would Kossuth decide? Which England would he choose? When the steamer entered the Solent, the quarantine boat brought on board the Mayor of Southampton, Pulszky and Lord Dudley Stuart. Pulszky handed Kossuth Mazzini's letter, and Lord Dudley Stuart a personal letter from the Foreign Minister, Lord Palmerston, inviting him to his house in London. Kossuth put both letters in his pocket unread. A huge and enthusiastic crowd was waiting on the quay. He had first to show himself to the English people. He had time to read his letters, to make his decision later.

Preparations had been made to give him a magnificent reception. The municipal council of Southampton offered him an address of welcome, congratulating him on his release from an unjust internment and expressing their admiration of his statesmanship and personal character. When he came down the gangway, followed by his wife and two children, a cheer went up all round the harbour. They were conducted with difficulty to their carriage which was decked with the Hungarian arms and colours. All the streets were packed with people, all the windows occupied. The bells were ringing. In front of the Town Hall working men lifted Kossuth out of the carriage and carried him into the building. Presently he appeared on the balcony. The crowd cheered. Slowly shouts of "Silence!" drifted to the back of the crowd. At last Kossuth was able to speak.

"I beg you to excuse my bad English," he began hesitatingly, almost embarrassed at hearing himself speak the language which he had learned in his prison cell in Buda but never had an opportunity of speaking. "Only seven weeks ago I was a prisoner in Kiutahia, in distant Asia; to-day I am a free man!" Renewed cheering. The Mayor raised his hand. The crowd hushed. Raising his voice, Kossuth continued: "I am free because England willed it so. England which the genius of humanity had chosen as an enduring memorial of its greatness, and the spirit of liberty as its happy home." His emotion choked him; he was scarcely able to go on. He apologised for his emotion, "a natural consequence of so impressive a change, so dazzling a contrast." He ended quickly: "May England always be great, glorious and free! But may England, though the most glorious, not be the only country wherein freedom dwells! It is a glorious sight to see a queen upon the throne that represents the principle of freedom. Help me to express my feelings by giving three hearty cheers for Her Gracious Majesty."

That afternoon at a banquet given in his honour in the Town Hall Kossuth made another speech. He spoke extempore and so in the spirit of the English language that only the subject-matter of his speech reminded his listeners that he was a Hungarian. All the county was present at the banquet. Requests for invitations were so numerous that the Mayor had to engage a special "secretary for the organisation of the Kossuth banquet." The invitation cards were ornamented with oak leaves, olive branches and vines, the emblems of strength, peace and hospitality. At this banquet, a few hours after his arrival, Kossuth announced that he "hoped to see the sympathy of the English people for Hungary directed into a practical channel." He had not come to be entertained nor for his own personal safety. He intended to live, to make his home in exile the sure haven of this mighty island empire, yes—but he intended to live for his country; he intended to begin without delay the work that would lead him to his goal: the liberation of Hungary.

If Kossuth had been the vain man his enemies tried to make him out, he could now have offered his vanity the greatest triumphs. He was certainly affected by his reception in Southampton; its cordiality overwhelmed him, the respect shown him by the greatest in the land delighted him, but, in the very first hour, Kossuth had decided: against comfort and repose, for fresh activity. Against his personal welfare, for his tortured country. It was not in order to enjoy his life that he had survived the crisis. Revolution, war, defeat; this was the first chapter of his life. Now began the second: new work, a second life.

Kossuth opened the letter which Lord Dudley Stuart had brought him after the banquet. Lord Palmerston's invitation touched him deeply: but—he refused it. As Lord Palmerston's guest he would have been obliged to political neutrality, to silence; but he wanted to be free. He admitted openly: "I have political aims in view in England. I wish to appeal to the people as the defender of my oppressed country."

The emigrants in England, from Metternich to Marx, had been received as guests. Kossuth was welcomed as a hero. Never before had England given a foreign statesman such a reception. The address offered him by the Municipal Council of Southampton was followed by a similar address from the townsfolk with 1100 signatures; Palmerston's invitation by others on the same day from the Lord Mayors of London and Birmingham in the name of their cities. Wherever he appeared, the crowd cheered him. Everything looked most promising for the success of his mission.

The next morning, the 24th October, he moved out to the Mayor of Southampton's country house; Pulszky took the children with him to his home near London. Kossuth's next stop was Winchester. Special cheap trains were run from London for the thousands who wanted to see Kossuth before he came to London. The Mayor arranged a brilliant luncheon to which were invited the Hungarian emigrants, Lord Stuart, the American Consul, the editors of the leading English newspapers and—Richard Cobden—Cobden whose works Kossuth had read during his imprisonment in Buda. Cobden's presence was for Kossuth the highest possible compliment. And Richard Cobden who, more than anyone, had informed the general public about the causes and the aims of Hungary's struggle for independence, spoke twice at this banquet. "Our friend," he said, "is still a stranger in England, but no doubt he is aware that here, as in Austria, the enemies of public liberty are the same." He warned Kossuth not to be deceived by his triumph; opponents would appear and would heap abuse upon him as whole-heartedly as he was now being overwhelmed with honours. "But such attacks will fail of their effect in England, so long as we stand on the side of truth and justice."

On the 28th October, after a stay of one day in London where acute pains in the chest forced him to consult a famous specialist, he had returned to Southampton for another banquet. He went back to London immediately after the banquet. It was one o'clock in the morning when he started for the station. It was raining in torrents. Kossuth was frozen; he was coughing. But it took him half an hour to reach the station; the crowd had waited in the rain, they followed him on to the platform.

It was the same story in London. Banquets, receptions, ovations. How long ago was it that Queen Victoria had invited Prince Louis Napoleon to her table at Windsor? Then the proud aristocracy had retired to their estates; now they returned to London to see Kossuth. Kossuth was the man of the hour; he was at the zenith of his fame.

Two things contributed enormously to Kossuth's popularity: his amazing mastery of English and his magnificent oratory, and his comprehensive and exact knowledge of conditions in England. A contemporary, and incidentally an opponent, Butler, characterises him as a speaker: "The statesmen and the crowds of two continents listened to his eloquence with open mouths and moist eyes. And yet he does not resort to any flowers of rhetoric to attract the attention of his auditors;

he does not exploit any class prejudices for his own ends; he does not promise the poor any Utopias, nor does he attack the rich. He is always simple, earnest and considered. He stands there calmly, with the supreme dignity of true greatness and utters nothing but the truth. And yet he carries away his audience and fires even the indifferent."

Kossuth's appearance helped him. His bearing, Therese's influence, completed the picture that won him the sympathy of the Anglo-Saxon world.

Three hundred towns of England begged Kossuth to be their guest. How could he cope with this? He had promised to hasten to the United States whither his loyal comrades had preceded him on the *Mississippi*. His departure was fixed for the 20th November. In these four weeks, regardless of his health, he had to hurry from town to town, from one banquet to another. On the 3rd November the Trade Unions of London paraded in his honour and escorted him in a procession, carrying banners inscribed with the slogan Kossuth had borrowed from the swimmer in Marseilles, to the party offices.

Kossuth was very diffident about explaining his ideas to British workers. He was no socialist; he never had been, in the sense in which the Trade Unions understood the term. In Marseilles he had declared for the working classes in order to strengthen their resistance against the reaction under Louis Napoleon. England was a different affair. Here he had to prove his political tact and statesmanship. He was well aware of the situation of the working classes in the industrial towns; but he had not come to England to grapple with England's problems, but to enlist England's help for his cause. This speech to the Trade Unions had to be a diplomatic masterpiece. "No one has a greater right to count himself among the working classes than I," he began. "I inherited no wealth from my father, and all my life long I have had to work for what I needed. I believe that it was this that first gained me the confidence of the people; thus I knew their sufferings and their desires, for the very reason that I was poor myself." But at this point, honestly professing his creed, he diverges from the socialist theory: "Therefore I was able to devote myself successfully to the struggle to obtain political and social rights for my people; not for one class, not for one caste, but for the whole people. My people have been martyred for the liberty of Europe." But England is the land of liberty, and therefore Kossuth extols the English constitution. "England loves her queen and she has every reason to love her." This speech has often been misunderstood. Karl Marx vehemently condemned it and later theoreticians, such as Szabó, have contrasted it with Kossuth's declaration in Marseilles and qualified his renunciation of socialism as opportunism. But Kossuth was not, and never had been, the champion of a class. In his own words he had fought for the freedom of his people.

In everything he undertook Kossuth's main thought was Hungary. Wherever he appeared, he spoke for his country, soliciting allies in the fight for Hungary against Austria and the young emperor Franz Josef, whom he named "the beardless Nero." When he arrived in England he had every reason, as Herzen said, to "buoy himself with the most sanguine hopes." Palmerston was at the Foreign Office, and Palmerston had declared with all the weight of his personality for the cause of freedom. When, after Haynau's chastisement in Barlcay's brewery, the Austrian ambassador, Baron Koller, demanded satisfaction, Palmerston had replied that "by visiting England Haynau had shown such a want of tact that the excitement of the working classes was quite understandable." The savage executions at Arad, and still more the revenge taken on Count Batthyányi had raised a storm of indignation throughout England. These were Haynau's crimes. Palmerston was not the man to pardon them. And though Koller took his answer as a grave affront and the Queen urged Palmerston to omit the offensive sentence, he refused. His note almost led to the fall of Russell's cabinet, for the prime minister agreed with the Queen. Finally Palmerston had to retract his insult to Haynau to the Austrian ambassador. But the whole of England laughed over this moral chastisement of Hungary's conqueror. But it added a new incentive to Austria to discredit Kossuth.

Palmerston's invitation to Kossuth to be his guest had been a second affront to Austria. Lord Russell again protested, but Palmerston replied: "There is a limit to all things. I refuse to be dictated to as to whom I shall receive in my house, and whom not." Again Russell complained to the Queen. But Palmerston sent his invitation by Lord Dudley Stuart. The working classes to whom Kossuth was a hero now sent an address of thanks to Palmerston; in it they referred to "the absolutist monarchs of Europe" as "hard-hearted tyrants and despots, hateful and loathsome murderers." This was too much. Lord Russell expected Palmerston not to accept this address. Surely he would not embroil England with a foreign power for the sake of this Hungarian emigrant? But Palmerston hated despotism as Byron had hated it. He was a man who had ideals. And so he thanked the working men of London for their address, and even went so far as to declare that it had "flattered him extremely and given him great satisfaction." Now the Queen's anger burst upon him. The Tories raged. The Whigs were jubilant. But he had made himself impossible in Russell's cabinet and on the 22nd December Palmerston was dismissed.

Kossuth's first interviews with Mazzini had convinced him that only by a combined action of the two revolutionary nationalist leaders could they achieve their ends. In his "Appeal to the friends of Italy," he declared his readiness to join Mazzini in preparing the liberation of the Italian and Hungarian peoples. Kossuth redoubled his energy. He spoke up and down the country, agitating for his cause, and everywhere he met with a like enthusiasm. His cry, "Oppressed nations of Europe, be of good cheer and do not lose heart," re-echoed far beyond the shores of England. Kossuth was become an ever greater menace.

The weapons of the secret police had failed in Turkey. But there still remained a fourth weapon: slander. Suddenly there appeared in *The Times* letters by "an objective observer," accusing Kossuth of every crime in the calendar, theft, embezzlement, depravity and avarice. His English friends immediately rallied round him. The *Daily News* proved that the attacks came from the pen of the Vienna correspondent of *The Times* who had been tutor in the house of Prince Metternich. Enormous demonstrations took place. Protests poured in against this mischievous behaviour of *The Times*. England's greatest newspaper was threatened with the loss of its subscribers because it had attacked Kossuth. Lord Stuart put himself at the head of Kossuth's defenders. This "avaricious" man had refused a gift of two thousand dollars from the American government in Kiutahia, and had likewise refused a loan which Lord Stuart wanted to make him. In all England there was only one opinion; everyone saw in him, not only the idealist, the great orator, the statesman with prophetic vision, but also the noble character that Herzen has described, the pattern of a gentleman. Kossuth emerged from this campaign, instigated by the Vienna police, triumphant. He could now accept the invitation of the United States with a clear conscience. He had won England. On his return from America he would begin the action against Austria.

III

In the Land of George Washington

THE SHIP WAS NAMED THE "HUMBOLDT." IT BORROWED ITS name from one of the most illustrious figures of the century. When Kossuth and his wife Therese, accompanied by Pulszky and several comrades of the emigration, left the harbour of Southampton, the Mayor and Council appeared officially to give their farewell greeting to the distinguished guest who had won the hearts of all classes of the country. The coast battery fired a salute of twenty-one guns in his honour.

The thunder of a hundred guns greeted the ship on its arrival. The quay was dense with people as far as the eye could see. All the dignitaries of the city of New York were there in full force, with the reporters of the great American newspapers at their heels, enormous crowds lined the streets along the route the procession was to follow to the City Hall. On the railing of the ship leant a woman famous for her beauty. Was not this reception meant for her? Had she not often enough received the homage of the Old World? The incense of admiration and the intoxication of success were things familiar to her. Had she not had the great men of her time, bankers and ministers, princes and generals, at her feet? Yes, even the king himself, Ludwig I of Bavaria, who had made Munich the fairest city of Germany, had honoured her. But Lola Montez, the most famous dancer of the day, was overshadowed by the other passenger of the *Humboldt* who had remained quietly in his cabin throughout the voyage, absorbed in books and papers, the thinker Kossuth. She had tried, without success, to attract the attention of the man of whom she had heard so much in England. She had not been able to get near him. Pulszky kept her away from him so as to give no grounds for "malicious rumours which might injure his good name." Once, when Therese was lying seasick in her cabin, the beautiful dancer had succeeded in scraping conversation with the governor of Hungary on deck. "I am an emigrant, like yourself," she began in German.

"*Auch mich hat das Schicksalsjahr* 48 *von Haus und Hof vertrieben.*" Kossuth could not help smiling. "*Vom Hofe, ja,*" was all he said. Indeed the March revolution in Munich had banished the king's mistress from the court. Ludwig I had to separate from her. (It did him no good, for he was driven into exile just the same.) Lola Montez too had gone to London. Now she stood aside, she had to wait, unnoticed and pushed into the background, until the people of New York had welcomed their illustrious guest.

And what a welcome it was! Kossuth's most brilliant reception in England, that of Manchester, where half a million people packed the town, was nothing in comparison with his triumphal entry into New York. The streets were black with cheering crowds, the Hungarian tricolour entwined with the Stars and Stripes floated from every window. Mr. Walker had been right: only Lafayette had been accorded such a triumph. Walker's words had spread throughout the States, preceding Kossuth and carrying his fame to the farthest corner of the Union: "We look upon Kossuth as the champion of constitutional liberty and the rights of a brave, oppressed people." Walker knew his fellow-countrymen; he knew how they whose public life was based on the principles of liberty and self-determination would acclaim the man who had gone into battle for the principles of George Washington in the old continent of Europe. "No language can describe," prophesied Walker, "the stir which Kossuth's reception will make in America, or the gratitude which will warm every heart towards him." And so it was.

The *New York Daily Times* of the 12th December, 1851, reported in the most sensational manner imaginable "The Kossuth Dinner in the Irving House." The headlines: "Kossuth's Great Speech"—"The Doctrine of Non-intervention" indicated at once the importance of the occasion. The list of those present named, besides the Mayor, countless "distinguished individuals," such as the Governor of Connecticut and General Watson Webb. Kossuth entered the banquet hall at the side of Mayor Kingsland. The Reverend Bethune said grace. Then addresses were read out from Daniel Webster, Henry Clay and other important political celebrities who declared their close sympathy with Louis Kossuth. Kossuth replied to the Mayor's address of welcome in his "great speech." "It is a fine saying of Montesquieu's," he began, "that republics should be founded on virtue. And this virtue, as it is hallowed in the Christian religion, commands: Do to others as you would wish others to do to you." By way of a moral, theological, even philosophical digression Kossuth comes to the political question: non-intervention, the central problem of his activity.

The banquet itself surpassed anything that New York had ever seen. On the tables were masterpieces of the confectioner's art: a statue of Kossuth in sugar, the Statue of Liberty, and Kossuth's entry under the triumphal arch; and "a particularly amusing scene," according to the *Daily Times*, represented "Haynau's thrashing in Barclay's brewery."

The reception in New York was only the prelude to a triumphal procession through the States; banquets, torchlight processions, fêtes of every sort in every city. In the true spirit of American enterprise up-to-date business men were soon manufacturing and throwing on the market hundreds of thousands of "Kossuth hats." In every railway station, at every street corner Kossuth biographies were on sale and were bought like hot cakes. Everywhere "Associations of friends of Hungary" were formed who met with the sole idea of helping Kossuth and furthering his plans.

Well might Kossuth write that he would find in the States the backing for his coming campaign. For this reason alone he submitted to the strain of these festivities, this fatiguing puerile display, which must end by ruining his health. But enthusiasm was the surest guarantee of success. This was a rich country and the independence movement needed money. Money meant: arms. Kossuth knew that he had no choice but to cover the length and breadth of the United States to enlist new supporters for the fight to come. He landed in America on the 6th December, 1851; he left it on the 14th July, 1852. In less than eight months he toured the country and spoke in every town of any size, tireless, never discouraged, never shirking the tedium of the receptions, even though the exertions often proved too much for his strength.

But the over-exhausted organism does not always obey the iron will. In Philadelphia he had a breakdown; on Christmas Eve, 1851, he collapsed and had to be carried to bed. Therese and his friends were anxious. He was pale, he had a serious cough and fever. Nevertheless, he had to get up on Christmas Day for a reception. He forced himself to be well. A procession fetched him from the United States Hotel and escorted him to the Independence Hall, the building in which the Declaration of Independence was proclaimed on the 4th July, 1767. The Mayor Gilpin, the man who was originally responsible for the

American government's invitation to Kossuth at Kiutahia, honoured the guest as one of the greatest living contemporaries. The citizens of Philadelphia vied with one another in giving him small souvenirs of the occasion. The commander of the Pennsylvania militia, Colonel Page, presented him with a golden Maltese cross; in the centre was a miniature of George Washington framed in pearls, and from the clasp hung a gold locket containing a most sacred relic—a lock of Washington's hair. On the back were engraved the words: "To Louis Kossuth the Patriot of Hungary and Friend of Humanity from an American Volunteer.—There is no difficulty to him who wills." Kossuth's slogan, the motto of the swimmer of Marseilles, had swept the States.

The day after Christmas Kossuth had a second attack of fever. His old lung trouble, which had never been cured and scarcely even treated, laid him low. His programme of festivities had to be altered. Opposite the hotel room in which Kossuth lay sick a huge picture was set up: it was a cartoon depicting the goddess of liberty with her heel upon the prostrate Hapsburg's neck. The town was illuminated with Bengal lights in the Hungarian colours: red, white and green. A prize was offered to the schools for the best essay: a speech of welcome to Kossuth. A thirteen-year-old boy won the prize; he appeared in Kossuth's sick-room and recited his speech. Kossuth was deeply moved. "If this is your youth," he remarked, "your country will always preserve its freedom."

But in the evening he had again to muster up his strength, for the citizens of Philadelphia were giving him a banquet. And there, despite his illness, Kossuth replied in one of his greatest speeches. On New Year's Day the President received him in the White House at Washington; a few days later he was the President's guest. But the greatest honour was accorded him on the 7th January; he was invited to take part in a session of Congress in the Capitol. Before him only one man had been vouchsafed this honour, Lafayette.

On that day the Capitol was filled to the last seat. The member for Ohio, Mr. Carter, greeted him as "Governor Louis Kossuth." All present rose. The session was interrupted in order that the members might be presented to their illustrious guest. This high honour proved to Kossuth that this truly democratic people were on his side. No matter how the reaction in Europe entrenched itself, the New World would bring about the victory of liberty.

Kossuth had won the United States—the land of George Washington. How often had he repeated Bezerédi's catechism: "Who was the first man?—George Washington." And now with all the ardour of conviction he recited the second question and answer: "What form of government is the best?—The republican." In these two years of exile Kossuth had pondered a great deal over this problem, which form of government was the most desirable. In the early days of his quarrel with Austria he had fought religiously for the upholding of the constitution. (Richard Cobden stressed this point.) The development of the struggle taught him that the Hapsburg monarchy must always tend to disregard the spirit of the constitution and to paralyse its real meaning, liberty. For one brief moment he had flirted with the idea that another dynasty, a Coburg or a Russian grand duke, might be a better guarantor of the constitution of Hungary. In his "Declaration of Independence" of the 14th April, 1849 he had tried to sever the bond with the Hapsburgs for ever. But if, according to the old constitution, all power was invested in the crown of St. Stephen, then it was time the old constitution were altered.

In England Kossuth had been permitted to experience the blessings of a monarchy, a monarchy, to be sure, which had developed in the course of centuries of struggle into a peculiar institution. Kossuth had been quite honest when he told the trade unions of London, who expected from him a profession of socialism, that England was fortunate to be a monarchy. But he saw also that no form of government could be judged theoretically, according to abstract principles. Whatever constitution best guaranteed true liberty to a particular country was the right form of government for that country. Therefore Kossuth said to his London audience: "The fact that England is a monarchy is no reason for hating the republican form of government in other countries which have other needs, other desires and conditions." And here for the first time he formulates a political ideal for his country: "Hungary desires to be a free, independent republic—but a republic founded upon the rule of law and civil discipline, security of person and of property—in a word: a republic like that of the United States with the inherited institutions of England."

Kossuth ended his tour through all the States of the Union, touching almost every town of any importance, New Orleans, Charleston, Richmond, Albany, Salem, Worcester, Boston. The subject of his speeches varied. He treated them all with a like mastery. He spoke on despotism, on trade, on the "Balance of Power," on "Present Day Democracy," infusing every topic with the same lucidity, opening new perspectives, pointing the way towards the future. He always knew how to adapt his speeches to his audiences. "The Hungarian whirlwind," says Butler, "united all present to a single body of admirers prostrate at Kossuth's feet. No other before him has ever spoken as he has to American statesmen. Every word of his poetical acknowledgment of the moral greatness of America had an immediate effect upon his audience. The speaker's picturesque appearance, his archaic English which he learnt from Shakespeare, his vibrant and penetrating voice, his artfully chosen instances, all this created a powerful effect."

What were the results achieved by these stupendous exertions, these amazing triumphs? The immediate success appeared enormous. Kossuth was justified in harbouring the greatest possible hopes. He believed that he could reach his goal.

What was his goal? Nothing less than the reorientation of American foreign policy! Kossuth asked for intervention: he dreamed of being able to decide the United States to an armed intervention against Austria. Was not this fantastic? But Mr. Walker, whose utterances carried a great deal of weight in America, had, in his famous letter answering the invitation to the Kossuth banquet in London, definitely announced this change in foreign policy in favour of Hungary: "Millions of my fellow-countrymen will consider it a glorious privilege if they are allowed to take up arms against a world, for and with England, under her and our flag. But the threats of absolutism will not intimidate English hearts." This declaration expressed the private conviction of the former Secretary of the Treasury of the United States. Kossuth, thus encouraged, undertook to convert the whole country to this conviction.

A colossal undertaking! He knew the gulf that separated America, in matters of foreign policy, from all the muddles of Europe. On the 2nd December, 1823, President Monroe had enunciated the doctrine that the United States would brook no interference from Europe in their affairs. Now Kossuth was demanding interference in European affairs. It almost seemed as if he would achieve his object. The great day in Washington, when he was received in the White House, made it seem as if his dream were coming true. Next to Kossuth at the banquet sat Daniel Webster, the most important figure in American politics, then in charge of foreign affairs. Webster had had to defeat the attack of Kossuth's adversaries. Austria had not been idly looking on at the activities of this dangerous emigrant. She sent her diplomatic representative, Baron Hülsemann, to Webster and to President Filmore to raise a protest. Hülsemann left no stone unturned, stopped at no slander and insinuation in his efforts to get Kossuth expelled from the United States. But Webster remained unperturbed; his energetic attitude defeated Austria's manœuvre. Webster became the Palmerston of the United States.

At this banquet, given by the Senate in the National Union Hotel, after the customary toasts, Kossuth rose to make his great speech. Never had he spoken more brilliantly. He praised the constitution of the Union which he had carefully studied and which so much resembled the Hungarian municipal system, the self-government of the counties. He gave a new interpretation of the historical mission of his nation, in which for the first time his Protestant piety found undisguised expression: "We Hungarians became the rampart of the West. We saved Christianity for the future reformation of Luther and Calvin." He deplored the decline of liberty in Europe—for he had already received the news of Napoleon III's *coup d'état*: "Europe is henceforward no abode for free nations. And yet I look to the future full of hope and confidence. I have faith in the principles of republicanism." The effect of this speech, even in America which had produced so many great orators and possessed in Webster one of the greatest, was unprecedented.

Now Webster, heedless of the protests of Baron Hülsemann, rose to reply: "This much I can say, that Hungary is certainly better able to regulate her own affairs than if they are ruled by Austria." Thus he took sides with Hungary. Nay more, he had been so completely convinced by Kossuth that he concluded his speech with the declaration: "Independence for Hungary! Hungarian control of Hungary's affairs! And Hungary as an individual nation among the nations of Europe!" Webster was then a man of seventy, he died soon afterwards; one of his last political statements was this pronouncement for Hungary's independence.

Kossuth knew that the first essential to political action was money to defray the cost of war. How else could the citizens of the United States show their sympathy than by contributing generously to the Kossuth Fund? A Cincinnati banker alone subscribed ten thousand dollars. Soon an enormous sum was in Kossuth's hands. He immediately ordered arms and munitions—for the whole sum. Many people shook their heads when they heard of this. Was this homeless, penniless refugee keeping nothing for himself? Kossuth had declined to accept the money that Lord Dudley Stuart held at his disposal; he did not touch one cent of the "Hungarian National Fund." He believed in the war that he was planning; for it he sacrificed this fortune.

He was so inconsiderate of himself that he actually refused the high remuneration offered him by rich people in Chicago if he would speak at private gatherings. He was no professional lecturer. He spoke: only for Hungary.

The New Year began, spring arrived, then summer. He had now toured the States from north to south, from east to west. He had received a delegation of the Red Indian tribes and the slaves of the southern states had hailed him as the prophet of emancipation. To be sure Kossuth had never departed from his political principle of not interfering in the internal affairs of the country whose hospitality he was enjoying. However, he could not check the effect of his personality and speeches on all citizens of the Union. The slave question was just beginning to excite the politicians. The country threatened to be divided into two camps, the south against the north, naked egoism against the doctrine of humanity. In this imminent struggle which was growing more and more acute—and was soon to be fought out in civil war—Kossuth was unwittingly the auxiliary of the side of justice. Abraham Lincoln's famous speech in Gettysburg was an echo of the ideas that Kossuth preached.

Kossuth's influence was great—his success was small. His objects were acclaimed, his demands approved, his speeches cheered—but nothing was achieved. Innumerable associations were formed bearing his name. Religious cranks interpreted his utterances in the spirit of the New Testament. Every society that stood for the principles of liberty chose Kossuth's name as a symbol. To this day there are still Kossuth Societies and Associations in all parts of the States from New York to California. Louis Kossuth lives in the memory of the American people as an evangelist of liberty. He was the forerunner of Walt Whitman as the prophetic interpreter of democracy. But when at last he returned to New York it was already July. He no longer hoodwinked himself: he was a prey to disappointment. What was the meaning of this enthusiasm. Politically the Union was inflexibly busied with its own troubles. Kossuth had received money, he had found fame and honours. But not help. Not the intervention he had counted on.

In New York sad news awaited him. The Belgian chargé d'affaires informed him that the Austrian government was at work in Brussels, where his aged mother and his sister had taken refuge, trying to prevent the renewal of their permission to stay in Belgium. Finally the King of Belgium, to avoid incurring the enmity of Austria, had been forced to have the ladies examined by his own physician, and only the authoritative certificate of the king's medical adviser that they were both seriously ill saved them from expulsion. This was how the government of the "beardless Nero" sought to take its revenge. Kossuth was appalled. He wanted to return to Europe. Here he had nothing more to hope for. On the 9th July a desperate letter reached him from his mother. He must get back, as speedily as possible. When did the next boat leave? The *Africa* on the 14th July.

And on the 14th July, 1852, unnoticed by the others, two passengers went on board the ship, bound for Southampton, Mr. and Mrs. Smith. The *Africa* sailed. The houses of New York slowly disappeared, the New World remained behind beyond the horizon. Louis Kossuth and his loyal companion Therese who had been welcomed by cheering crowds departed incognito, as quietly as if they had been ashamed, disillusioned and distressed.

IV

The Great Hope

ON HIS RETURN FROM THE UNITED STATES TO LONDON, KOSSUTH wished to live in complete retirement. He had his two sons and his daughter Vilma with him, Therese managed the household. He set about finding a means of livelihood. He did so quite openly, making no secret of his poverty. He had refused presents, he had spent the fund on munitions. He accepted an offer to write articles for a Sunday paper. The articles were good, but they attracted little attention. Napoleon's *coup d'état* had altered the European situation. Kossuth was right when he once wrote in exile: "Europe is always ready to accept a *fait accompli.*" Palmerston was out of office; the Tory government aimed at a peaceful understanding with Austria and France. But Kossuth seized every opportunity to air his views; even this Scotch Sunday paper which provided his daily bread must serve this purpose. And so it came about that Englishmen soon found his opinions out of date. He only stirred enthusiasm when he spoke at meetings.

The complete retirement suited his nature. He passed his days and nights studying the European situation. Meanwhile in the garrets of the emigration the mysterious agitation went forward with increased intensity; Mazzini was the focus of a constant plotting. In 1853, a year after Kossuth's return, Mazzini brought off his revolution in Milan. It was bloodily suppressed. Mazzini's friends were thrown into Austrian prisons. The Frenchman, Ledru-Rollin, followed the Italian's example; his accomplices perished in Cayenne. Only Kossuth held himself aloof from this agitation. Like Garibaldi, he expected nothing from these puerile attempts at assassination, but everything from a strategically planned, military rising. And yet it happened once when Kossuth changed his lodging that he had to submit to an examination of his luggage. His frequentation of Mazzini's society had made him suspect.

Had England changed her attitude? Or was it merely that his sanguine hopes were not being fulfilled? Kossuth worked indefatigably. He read the news from Austria. What had happened there? At first, after Hungary's defeat, the aristocracy had made overtures to their conquerors. But the system of the new reaction, the era of Bach, managed to freeze off all classes by its unexampled arrogance and severity. With one exception: the Hungarian clergy. Austria's savage treatment of Hungary appeared even to the loyal councillors less an injustice than a stupidity. The cleverest among them, Humelauer, wrote in a private letter to Prince Metternich in May, 1850: "The Schwarzenberg-Stadion cabinet is a catastrophe compared to which the revolution was a mere mishap." The old Prince Windischgrätz's warnings were of no avail. The young emperor blindly followed Schwarzenberg's dictation and Humelauer had to remark: "The initial sympathy for the young emperor had completely evaporated." Even with the officers of the army the government succeeded in making itself unpopular. Count Grünne, the most important of the emperor's advisers, carried on his private intrigues against the general staff, and when urged to raise the pay of junior subalterns he replied contemptuously: "For twenty-four gulden a month I can get all the subalterns I want."

Kossuth could hardly help being jubilant. Every weakness of Austria strengthened his hopes. But Austria had her powerful ally, the Czar. Would Kossuth's prophecy be fulfilled? Would the Czar—as Kossuth had so insistently dinned into the ears of the Western Powers—attempt the destruction of the Ottoman Empire? Kossuth's letters should have taught the cabinets of London and Paris the consequences of a Russian invasion of Turkey. Now they learnt the lesson—from war.

For, exactly as Kossuth had foretold, the Russian troops crossed the frontier of Moldavia on the 3rd July, 1853; the Czar came forward as the "protector of the Christian subjects of the Sultan." He simply informed the governments in London and Paris. He was sure of help in Vienna. War in South-eastern Europe! Kossuth's hope seemed to be fulfilled. Now at last he could decide England to intervene. Prince Paskiewitsch, the conqueror of Hungary, marched into Bulgaria. Austria mobilised. France and England sent troops to Turkey. The Crimean War began. The question was: Would Austria come to the help of Russia? Franz Josef hesitated. Schwarzenberg, an apt pupil of Metternich, advised him that he had a higher duty than gratitude and loyalty to an alliance: the safeguarding of Austria's future. Hapsburg's interests demanded that Russia should be kept out of the Balkans. In March, 1854, an alliance was concluded between London and Paris and the Sublime Porte. Now Schwarzenberg's counsel prevailed. Two days before his death, he induced the emperor to throw in his lot with France and England, although he had cynically to admit: "We shall astound the world by our ingratitude."

On the 2nd December, 1854, Austria joined the alliance of the Western Powers. But Franz Josef followed a policy of vacillation. His armies occupied Moldavia and Wallachia, but he did not participate in the war. The threat of his armies was enough to divide the Russian forces. And so the taking of Sebastopol sealed Russia's defeat.

The chance was gone. Kossuth had to wait for a better one. But fresh clouds were moving up in the political sky. That perpetual crater Italy again burst into eruption. Another conspiracy of Mazzini's. Austrian officers were murdered in broad daylight in Genoa. Again the revolt was ruthlessly suppressed. Kossuth recognised that Austria could only be driven out of Italy by an alliance with Victor Emanuel and the clever, cautious policy of Cavour. Meanwhile the experience with Austria in the Crimean War had disposed Napoleon III more and more favourably to Savoy, especially as Victor Emanuel had taken part in the war against Russia. Kossuth was ready to come to an understanding with the emperor of the French, the moment he was the enemy of Austria.

No one in Vienna wanted war. The police system in Hungary, introduced by Bach, had increased the antipathy to the court. Kossuth knew this. Then Klapka suddenly arrived from Italy with the news that everything was ready for war. Kossuth immediately took the initiative. Count Teleki was still in Paris, and was an intimate adviser of Prince Bonaparte, who formed a kind of collateral government at the court of his imperial cousin. Prince Bonaparte was married to Victor Emanuel's daughter, and urged common action by the two houses. But Teleki had parted company with Kossuth; he had fallen under the influence of Szemere who was openly agitating against Kossuth. But what were petty rancours at a moment such as this? Kossuth created a National Directorate of three equal members, inviting Klapka and Teleki to form the other two. Now the movement was provided with an organ with which Cavour and Bonaparte could negotiate. Teleki was enthusiastic over Kossuth's plan. But how were they to place an army in the field in the event of war? "The best speculation," said Kossuth, "is to send fifty thousand men to Hungary—then an additional army of two hundred thousand enthusiastic Magyars would at once volunteer." These plans which Teleki and Klapka laid before Prince Bonaparte found a hearing and the astonishing thing happened: the emperor of the French summoned Kossuth to Paris. To a conference. To sign a pact as between equal partners. This was the greatest moment in Kossuth's second life.

Teleki and Klapka accompanied Kossuth to the Palais Royal. The Prince received him immediately. They spoke quite openly.

The Prince: "It is the emperor's intention that Hungary shall become an independent state. He has no other aims. There is only one condition he desires to make: that you do not set up a republic, but remain a constitutional monarchy."

Kossuth: "I find that very natural. A constitutional monarchy entirely corresponds to the traditional tendency of my nation. Hungary's whole past is monarchical, and a history extending over a thousand years leaves a deep impression on the character of a nation. I am myself a republican, but I am, first and foremost, a patriot. I place my country above my theories. However I should like to know what choice for king of Hungary would most readily meet with the emperor's approval."

The Prince: "The emperor leaves that entirely to your judgment."

Kossuth: "Naturally we cannot contemplate disposing of the crown of Hungary. We have no right to do so. But I know my nation, I know that gratitude is part of their character. Therefore I can lend emphasis to my conviction that my nation would offer the crown of St. Stephen to Your Highness."

The Prince rose, bowed deeply and replied: "I deeply appreciate this honour, but I beg you, let there be no further suggestion of this between us. We Bonapartes have learnt much from the history of our uncle. We have not only learnt what we should do, but also what we should not do. And in the latter category belongs the rule that no member of our house must accept a foreign throne. Allow me to say frankly that the throne of France is something which our family is not disposed to risk even for a crown so brilliant as St. Stephen's."

Kossuth: "Very well, let us leave that care to the future."

The crown of St. Stephen which Kossuth tried to promise to Prince Bonaparte and which he had buried at Orsova had actually been found. Had one of his companions in Orsova been the agent? Szemere, or one of his friends? In any case the crown, which had once been recovered from the Turks, returned to Buda from its second adventurous journey undamaged.

Although Kossuth was ready to sacrifice his "principles" for his "idea"—his republican conviction for the liberation of Hungary—even though he was prepared to give the crown to Prince Bonaparte and to retire into the background, as he had always done—he was determined to carry through the practical action himself. Life had taught him that he was lost the moment he left things to others. He wanted to be general and diplomat. And it was natural that Prince Bonaparte should wish to negotiate only with him, for Kossuth was: revolutionary Hungary. Colonel Kis would recruit a Hungarian army from the ranks of the emigration, General Klapka would command it. But Kossuth reserved the supreme command for himself, and this appeared quite natural. For ten years he had kept awake the faith in this war of liberation, he had stirred the world's enthusiasm for it, he was about to conclude a bargain with Napoleon—the ex-governor of Hungary with the reigning emperor of France. Kossuth stated his conditions and the princely negotiator agreed to all his precisely formulated "guarantees." Kossuth demanded: "The unfurling of the imperial French banner on Hungarian soil in the company of as large an army as the emperor should consider necessary for the protection of the martial honour of this banner. Secondly: A proclamation from Napoleon to the Hungarian nation, acknowledging the Hungarian nation as allies in the war against Austria, to enforce the declaration of independence of 1849." The acceptance of these conditions was essential before Kossuth was willing to engage in war in Hungary and for Hungary. Whatever other compromises he was prepared to make, his purpose was unchanged.

That night at eleven o'clock Kossuth was received in the Tuileries by Napoleon III. The emperor showed himself thoroughly informed by Prince Bonaparte. He understood that Hungary would take part in the war, provided that the emperor carried it from the Po to the Danube and the Theiss. "The Prince has been your faithful interpreter; he has been very eloquent in pleading your cause. This arrangement is not without precedent in the history of my house." The emperor went to the table and unfolded a roll of parchment. "Here is the original of the proclamation which my uncle addressed to the Hungarian nation in 1809." Kossuth knew it, he recited it by heart. Yes, Napoleon had invited the nobility of Hungary on the field of Rákos to choose their king, independent of the Hapsburgs. Then the nobility had remained loyal to the defeated House of Hapsburg. But now it was difficult to feel gratitude towards the dynasty. The emperor showed himself a politician. In England, after Palmerston's resignation, a Tory government, friendly to Austria, was in power. It was necessary to overthrow the Derby cabinet. Kossuth declared that he would undertake to bring this about.

Napoleon looked up in astonishment: "You could do that?"

Kossuth: "Yes, sire. I am a penniless exile, but I know the position of the parties." And Kossuth developed his tactics: he would induce the Lord Mayor of London to preside at a great meeting where Kossuth would make an appeal for England's neutrality in this war. "I have no doubt that everywhere in the country resolutions will be carried corresponding to my wishes."

The Emperor: "What you have told me is very interesting and very important. I beg you to carry out this action. The assurance of England's neutrality will remove the main difficulties to the realisation of your patriotic wishes."—This historic interview ended by Napoleon saying: "*C'est entendu!—Au revoir en Italie!*"

Was Kossuth boasting when he assured Napoleon that he could influence the attitude of a pro-Austrian England? That he, the defeated exile who had been burnt in effigy, could compass the fall of the Tory government behind which stood the Queen herself? Certainly Kossuth had already been responsible for the fall of one government; but Palmerston had been overthrown because of him, not by him.

However Kossuth set himself to carry out this apparently impossible task. If he were successful, he would prove to Napoleon that he knew England's political situation as well as he understood the character of the English people. But what faith he had in the power of his oratory! Had not the newspapers ceased to ask him for articles because they were out of date?

Time pressed. After Cavour's rejection of the Austrian ultimatum, the Austrian troops began their march. Kossuth returned to London on the 8th May. A few days later appeared Queen Victoria's proclamation that the government of Great Britain desired to observe strict neutrality for the whole duration of the war. This made Kossuth's mission more difficult. This proclamation was exactly what Napoleon wanted, but he wanted it assured by a change from a Tory to a Whig government. Kossuth did not hesitate. With the help of Gilpin, M.P. for Northampton, a tireless friend of Kossuth's cause, the campaign for his meetings were organised. When the Tories heard of it, their press protested that it was impossible that Hungary could any longer be behind Kossuth, seeing that the Emperor Franz Josef had appointed a Hungarian, General Gyulai, as commander-in-chief. But a general is not the people, replied the Whigs.

KOSSUTH AS AN OLD MAN

From the Hofrat Constantin Danhelovsky Collection, Vienna.

Besides no one knew that the emperor had forced General Gyulai to accept the supreme command against his will; Gyulai recognised that the task was too big for him, but the all-powerful Grünne had replied: "What an old fool of eighty, like Radetzky, could do, you will be able to do." Of course it presently transpired that Gyulai was only keeping his place warm for the real commander-in-chief: on the 29th May Franz Josef unexpectedly arrived in Verona and personally assumed the supreme command. Like his opponent, the Emperor Napoleon, the Austrian Emperor wanted to play the soldier. The ambition of these two rulers had one beneficial result: it brought this amateur war to a swift conclusion.

But there was still the danger of an intervention. Kossuth went systematically to work. In London, in Manchester, in Bradford, everywhere Kossuth repeated the triumphs of his former speeches, enhanced by the compelling force of his own enthusiasm. But the elections did not result in a clear majority. Gilpin promised Kossuth to do everything to defeat Derby's government on the sole question of foreign policy. In allusion to the outbreak of war, the Queen, in her speech from the throne at the opening of parliament used the words "armed neutrality" instead of "unconditional neutrality." Lord Derby declared that, although he cherished no sympathy for Austria's system of domination, he was of the opinion that this war "was not being waged for the liberation of Italy, but for the territorial expansion of Sardinia." This gave the Whig party a handle as the party of peace. If the government were defeated, Lord Palmerston would be called upon to form a cabinet. Palmerston had given a written pledge "to accept the absolute neutrality of England as the basis of foreign policy," and further—this was Kossuth's greatest triumph—"even in the event of the war being extended from the banks of the Po to the banks of the Theiss and the Danube."

The opposition motion of no-confidence was carried by a majority of thirteen votes. Lord Palmerston had been dismissed from the Foreign Office because of his sympathy for Kossuth. Kossuth's political interference in England made Lord Palmerston Prime Minister.

This was Kossuth's greatest political triumph. A good omen for the action which could now be taken in hand "*Au revoir en Italie!*" Kossuth hastened to arrive in Italy. After the indecisive battle of Magenta on the 22nd July, the Hungarian legion was at last put into the field. It numbered four thousand men under the command of Colonel Ihász. It was called the "Hungarian army in Italy" and Ihász was given his command "in the name of the government of Piedmont" by General Klapka. Kossuth arrived in Genoa on the 22nd July. He immediately visited the legion in camp at Aqui. Kossuth was sixty. His hair was grey, but the fire in his eyes was not extinguished. When he appeared in the camp, a storm of cheering greeted him; the men crowded round him, with cries of "Our father Kossuth"; every legionary wanted to shake him by the hand. "Even the toughest faces were wet with tears of joy." This army would stand the test.

Kossuth had kept his part of the bargain with Napoleon. What now stood between him and his goal?

On the day after the battle of Magenta the Austrian army at Solferino again attacked the enemy. Benedek, afterwards commander in the war with Prussia, was victorious on the right wing; but the left wing and the centre were repulsed. Now was the moment for the high command to make a decision. But Franz Josef, a tyro in commanding armies, lost his nerve. He ordered a retreat. This tragic comedy of Solferino gave the other amateur general, Napoleon III, an unexpectedly sudden and decisive victory. What now? The most important object had been attained: the nephew had established his military genius, at least in the eyes of his people. Was he now to continue the war because he had promised Kossuth to extend it to the battleground of Hungary? What did it matter that a battalion of Hungarians had been put into the field for nothing? In all haste negotiations were opened between Napoleon and Franz Josef. Franz Josef was ready to surrender Lombardy to Savoy. What else was to be gained? On the 10th July the Peace of Villafranca was concluded.

No one was indignant that Hungary had been cheated of her hopes. Only Count Cavour. He had bolder plans, and more far-reaching aims than Victor Emanuel. He wanted: a united Italy—for his king. The Peace of Villafranca seemed to him a disgrace; he felt a personal shame for he had pledged his word to the Hungarian Directorate. Cavour, the most important statesman of the Italy to be, resigned. For the third time Kossuth's action in Europe had brought about the fall of a minister.

But the Peace of Villafranca destroyed his greatest hope. All his work, his sacrifice, for nothing! "Gone, gone for ever!" Only Kossuth's cry of bitterness remained.

V

A Book of Job

"NOW I AM A SOLDIER. I SHALL NEVER AGAIN LET THE ARMY out of my hands." Thus Kossuth had written. Solferino, Napoleon's premature victory, had destroyed this dream. Solferino, a battle, a stupid battle! Not an inner law, but accident had ruined the magnificent scheme, the plan calculated with mathematical certainty. Accident! Even Franz Josef recognised it; wiser for his war adventure, he complained: "in every battle *le hazard* turns the scale." Kossuth shared the feelings of the defeated emperor, as he shared his defeat. Is this the end of everything? "There is nothing left for us to do but honourably to disband our legion and to take care of the personal insurance of the poor Hungarian lads who rallied to our flag." But even this was difficult; Napoleon had no intention of keeping his bargain which he had confirmed in a second audience with Kossuth on the 2nd July, after Solferino. At that time Kossuth issued his proclamation to the Hungarian army "from imperial French headquarters." Eight days later came Villafranca. What was Kossuth to say to his troops, "his army"? Kossuth wandered about Genoa, worried, burdened with this new problem, and still more harassed by his feeling of responsibility.

What was he to do? Mazzini had proved right, and not Cavour. Victor Emanuel thought only of his house and not of Italian independence. Cavour has resigned; let the "*re galantuomo*" enter reconquered Lombardy alone. Let him take the responsibility alone for compensating Napoleon with the cession of Milan, Nice and Savoy. Should Kossuth now link Hungary's destiny with Italy? He had no other choice. The common enemy must be fought in common. Garibaldi was still alive and undeterred. And Cavour, Italy's man of honour, comforted Kossuth by his confidence: "You and I, Signor Kossuth, will keep to our road, will we not? We two will accomplish what the Emperor of the French has not had the courage to complete. And, by God, we will not stop half way."

For a long while Kossuth studied the solemn face of this little man who had asked him for an interview at four o'clock in the morning. And from it he gained new hope. They had to stick together. Kossuth could well understand why many of his young legionaries were hurrying to Sicily to join Garibaldi in his march on Marsala. He felt more and more drawn to Garibaldi. Kossuth had meant to lead his "lads" with Italy against the enemy; let them now fight for Italy alone. But when the revolutionary government of Tuscany begged him to "lend his legion" he indignantly refused. "Gentlemen! We are no *condottieri* and our legion does not consist of slaves or mercenaries, but of free men, attracted to the Hungarian flag by patriotism."

Back to England! Back again to uncertainty, waiting and preparing, until a new hope beckoned. Kossuth had grown old. At sixty he had once more to take up this life, toiling for his daily bread, harassed by the perpetual anxiety what was to happen to him and his family. His sons were growing up, but his daughter Vilma was delicate. Would he at last be capable of making provision for their future? How long had he still to live? It was a marvel that his ailing body had borne him over the threshold of his seventh decade. He must put an end to the uncertainty of this daily struggle, he must find a profession at last. Hundreds of thousands had passed through his hands, the gifts of England, the contributions of America, conjured by the magic of his oratory. But not for himself! He had never touched this money. He had converted it into arms and munitions. The day before he left Italy the Emperor Napoleon, as a sop to his own conscience, wrote Kossuth a personal letter. "This time we cannot go any further. Tell Monsieur Kossuth how greatly I regret that the liberation of his country must be postponed. But I beg him not to despair, but to trust me and the future." Kossuth no longer believed his promises. The emperor had broken his word; he had only been enabled to win the war because Kossuth had kept his promise to overthrow the Tory government. His reward: the action on the Danube and the Theiss had been abandoned.

His reward? The Emperor Napoleon had thought of that. If he could not help the patriot Kossuth, he could at least aid the man. "I beg Kossuth to be convinced of my feelings of friendship and to dispose of me for his person and his children." Salvation! An official post? A salary or a pension for his impoverished ally? Was not this a way out in Kossuth's need? Kossuth's long life had always brought him to the verge of poverty, and over and over again the mighty had sought to cripple him by offers of money or position. His great adversary Metternich had tried in vain to bribe him; his faithless ally of 1849 tempted him with no greater success. Times had changed, but not Kossuth's character. The agitator Kossuth was still buoyed by the optimism of youth, the man turned sixty must surely tremble for the evening of his life. But his character was pride, and his life the development of that character. "When I reached this point in his letter," he writes, "I could not control my feelings. I replied to the bearer of the emperor's hand-written letter: Tell your master that the Emperor of the French is not rich enough to presume to offer Louis Kossuth alms. And Louis Kossuth not so abject as to accept them." And he added: "My sons will earn their bread by work."

Back to England therefore! Depression soon yields to the resolute will to work. Kossuth looked for hope; Cavour and Garibaldi gave him encouragement. Good news came from Hungary to the effect that Franz Josef's defeat had inspired his country with a new spirit; Kossuth himself speaks of an "awakening of the nation." The celebration of the centenary of Kazinczy, the resuscitator of the Hungarian language, was the occasion of a national demonstration. Hungary had found, thought Kossuth, a new "invisible, intangible, mighty agitator: public spirit." "Our country can rightly be proud of its young generation." The hope of reaching it, of again becoming its leader, kept him alive in his despair, at work in his disillusionment.

"Your voice has not died," wrote Baron Jósika to him. Let England again give the echo. Kossuth's *Essay on Hungary*, a brilliant exposé of the situation in his country, made its appearance in tens of thousands of copies. With consummate art he proved that his spirit was still unbroken; he affirmed Byron's words:

> "Streams like the thunderstorm against the wind
> Yet Freedom! Yet thy banner, turn but flying,
> Thy trumpet voice though broken now and dying
> The loudest, still the tempest leaves behind."

So Kossuth went on working. But Fate was stronger than he. The seventh decade of his life, at once the seventh decade of the century, had reserved for him all the torments of the

Inferno, disappointment and humiliation, the mockery of chance and the cruelty of a relentless "Too late!"

The hoisting of the Italian national flag in Sicily, the triumph of Garibaldi, had scarcely aroused new hopes, when the Directorate decided to transport the huge quantities of arms, bought with American money, from the port of Genoa to somewhere nearer the eventual theatre of war. An invasion into Hungary might be organised from the new independent principate of Moldavia-Wallachia—and Prince Couza raised no objection to the transport of arms across Roumania. Five ships carried this precious cargo to the East. But meanwhile the situation in Bucharest had changed. Couza was making overtures to Austria. In November, 1860, news arrived that the Prince had confiscated the munitions. With the utmost difficulty General Klapka who set off post-haste for Bucharest succeeded in getting the arms sent back to Genoa on a British ship. This immediately involved the British Foreign Minister, Lord Russell, in the affair. England was forced to dissociate herself from Kossuth and the Hungarian irredenta. The plan of operations which the Directorate had elaborated with Cavour collapsed. The invasion of Transylvania by the Hungarian army from Wallachia was frustrated.

Kossuth staggered under this fresh stroke of fate. He was further disquieted by the news from Hungary. After the outburst of young patriotism a new development seemed to have set in. It appeared as if the new generation had lost the desire to fight and were content to trot in double harness at the side of Austria. This coincided with the return to Pest of the man who had always been loyal to the theory of compromise with Austria, Ferenc Deák. Kossuth respected him, for he had been the only man who had never acted against his convictions. After the fall of the first Hungarian cabinet, he had retired to the country; now he had sold his small estate to the Countess Széchényi for an annuity and came back to Pest. He still remained on terms of friendship with his former comrades, but he was still true to his ideas. He too had aged; but he waited quietly until the time was ripe for the realisation of a compromise between the two neighbouring states. Gradually Bach's régime of terror in Hungary lost its impetus; defeated Austria needed a rapprochement with Hungary.

Meanwhile many of the former revolutionaries had returned home. No obstacle was put in the way of their return. Even Count Julius Andrássy had been permitted to come home. The emperor graciously restored his confiscated estates. Andrássy had been young when he had allied himself to Kossuth; Franz Josef pardoned the errors of his youth. Kossuth understood. But nevertheless the news was a hard blow; he had been deeply attached to Etelka's son.

Then one day Count Teleki informed Kossuth from Geneva that he was going away for a week. Teleki gave no hint as to where he was going. Why did he think it necessary to let Kossuth know? Was this an apology, a warning? The letter puzzled Kossuth. One day in December, 1860, a short notice appeared in *The Times:* "Count Ladislaus Teleki, a Hungarian emigrant, who arrived in Dresden with a British passport, had been arrested and extradited to Austria." This was a dreadful blow. Teleki was irreplaceable. His fate seemed sealed. Kossuth at once attempted to decide the British government to intervene; for both arrest and extradition were a grave breach of international law. Letters to Paris, letters to Hungary. Interviews with Lord Palmerston. Petitions, articles. Only in the small hours of the morning when the old man, pale and shaken with coughing, sank back in his chair, had he time to ask himself the question: What was Teleki doing in Dresden? What was the meaning of this mysterious journey, this sudden ending to it? Mistrust, the first suspicion against a friend, took hold of him.

How cruelly the news in the morning papers justified it! "Count Teleki has been received in Vienna by the emperor and has given his promise henceforward to be a loyal subject. Thereupon H.M. the Emperor granted him a pardon." Kossuth gave a cry. This was treachery. And for the first time a blow of fate had the power to paralyse his will. But his belief in human nature was too strong. He refused to believe the facts. It could not be true. It was an error of the paper. But on the 2nd January Touvenel, the Foreign Minister of France, informed him: "The Austrian Emperor sent for Teleki and said to him: 'You have been conspiring against me since 1848; I know everything, also what you are planning next. In spite of all I pardon you. You are a man of honour; only promise me that you will break off your relations abroad—and you are free.' And Teleki, deeply affected by the emperor's words, promised thenceforward to be a loyal subject."

"I am ashamed to face the daylight," exclaimed Kossuth. He had read Touvenel's letter. It was the truth. Teleki was lost—not only lost, but lost by treachery. Andrássy's return and oath of allegiance to Franz Josef had grieved him, but Teleki's disaffection destroyed all his hopes. This was the signal that the emigration was breaking up.

But there was yet more to come. Teleki, realising that he had fallen into a trap, shot himself in remorse. Hardly had Kossuth recovered from the shock of this tragedy when a new trial visited him. The one hope that still remained was a new revolution in Italy. The Peace of Villafranca could not last long. Cavour has been recalled by King Victor Emanuel. When Garibaldi, supported by the Hungarian legionaries, took Sicily, Cavour thought it was time to interfere. This was the moment to achieve the unity of Italy under the flag of Victor Emanuel. Now was the time for the Directorate to act, and to act quickly. An attack on Dalmatia by Garibaldi was planned for the spring of 1862. From there an advance on Hungary might succeed. Pulszky was convinced that Kossuth must go with Garibaldi and against Cavour. But Kossuth held with the strategist, he mistrusted the filibuster. So greatly had he changed. But Pulszky in Turin warned him. If Kossuth did not cut loose from Cavour, Pulszky threatened to leave the Directorate.

What a threat! And this, too, after Kossuth had lost Teleki. Kossuth, in an excitement such as he had never known, answered his most loyal friend: "Do as you please." These words, understandable in the bitterness of his disappointments, led Pulszky to break with Kossuth. Now Kossuth stood alone.

But this year of fatalities did not spare him. "There was no end to my afflictions," he groaned. The next blow was the most decisive. Cavour had recommended Kossuth not to forget the *nervus rerum* in his preparations for the invasion of Hungary. He would need money when he got there. Who knew that better than Kossuth, once Minister of Finance? But how dreadful was the memory of the finance campaign of 1849! Those journeys with that monster printing press, from Pest to Debrecen, from there to Szeged, always dependent upon Duschek who had so soon stopped the issuing of Kossuth notes. This time it was proposed to take their financial munitions with them. Cavour had provided money for the purpose. The new Kossuth notes were to be printed in England. This was done. A firm of lithographers, Day Bros., printed notes to a value of a hundred million kronen.

But ill luck pursued Kossuth's money. Even in his advanced old age in Turin he would be shocked by letters from compatriots who had been impoverished by the cancellation of the old Kossuth notes and now called on the old man with words of scorn to honour his signature which had given these notes validity. Now the millions of future money lay warehoused in the cellars of Messrs. Day. As yet they had no value; they were merely luggage for the journey when the invasion should begin. But meanwhile, by some curious chance, a specimen of one of these notes found its way into the hands of the Austrian Embassy in London. How this happened no one knew. But in any case the result was that Austria requested the British government to punish the printer of these notes on a charge of forgery.

And so in February an alarming danger threatened Kossuth. To be sentenced in London, that would be the end! But for once fate was kind. Lord Russell refused to comply, on the ground that there was not sufficient evidence to substantiate a charge of forgery. But though Lord Russell refused to institute a criminal action, there was nothing to prevent the matter being brought before the civil courts. And so the world was treated to the comedy of seeing Kossuth charged with forgery in a civil action. Who brought the case? According to the law no one had a right to bring an accusation except some one who was entitled to print banknotes for Hungary. And who was this? The Austrian Emperor. And so the action read: "Franz Josef, Emperor of Austria, King of Hungary and Bohemia *versus* Day Bros. and Louis Kossuth."

Kossuth had now no time for anything but the preparation of his defence. He was compelled to move into cheaper lodgings with his wife and his two sons. He had long ago decided to leave London where life was too expensive and go to live in Turin when the case was over. Then one day Prince Napoleon sent him a thousand pounds with instructions to make as much publicity out of the case as possible. But the costs of the action swallowed up the whole amount. In the first instance judgment was given against him. He appealed and lost. The Lord Chancellor's comment that Kossuth was a "thoroughly honest and exceptionally able man" scarcely made the pill more palatable.

But this judgment had one other result: a warning to the emigration to refrain from every conspiracy against foreign governments and not to plan armed expeditions against the allies of Great Britain while enjoying her hospitality.

The bank-notes were to be destroyed. At the last moment the question arose who was to defray the expenses of their destruction. The counsel for the emperor declared that they were willing. There were seventeen tons of notes. It took a fortnight to reduce the lot to ashes.

And so to Italy. In London Kossuth was afraid of poverty, and the strict surveillance of the police. Italy would not abandon her loyal ally. He removed with all his family. Vilma had been left in Pulszky's care some time before, as her lungs were seriously affected. What a joy to see his daughter again!

Before leaving England, he heard the news of Cavour's death. Another blow for Kossuth! Stroke by stroke fate was beating him to his knees. He had to hasten to Nervi. He found his daughter in the last stages of consumption. She died in his arms.

This was too much. Self-reproaches tormented him to the verge of madness. Like Széchényi, before his collapse, he believed that he could feel the hand of Nemesis. Therese never recovered from the death of her daughter; worn out, irritable, a burden, she dragged herself beside her husband to the funeral, and when they returned to their lodging in Genoa she broke down. Her grief undermined her health. Three years later she died, shortly after they had removed to Turin. His sons had grown to manhood and gone their ways. Now Kossuth was alone.

And then when all hopes seemed shattered by the blows of fate, suddenly dawned a new, a last great hope: the war of Austria with Prussia. In great haste the old guard, the Hungarian Legion, were called together, and Kossuth telegraphed to Berlin to ask if Bismarck would receive him. But Bismarck had just had to deal with Lasalle. He was not disposed to ally himself with a revolutionary, a republican. He refused. In feverish haste a Hungarian volunteer corps was put into the field at Görlitz. Numerous volunteers flocked to the national army.

Kossuth bit his lips. What did it matter how they treated him? Let Klapka gain the victory. When it was won, it was Kossuth Hungary would call for. Then Victor Emanuel's army was routed at Custozza, and Italy's proud fleet was wiped out by the Austrian admiral Tegethoff. Kossuth stood with the whole city all night long in the streets of Turin waiting anxiously for news. Then, three weeks after the beginning of the war, came the news: Königgrätz. The Austrian army under Benedek had been defeated. Vienna was at Prussia's mercy. Now surely the end of the monarchy had come. Now Hungary would rise, the legion of the loyal would march in. The old man wept with emotion. His day was drawing near. His Hungary would welcome him with rejoicing. . . .

Kossuth's short-lived jubilation was extinguished by the news of the Treaty of Nikolsburg. The war was over. Bismarck's genius had converted the victory into a swift and amicable peace. Kossuth's last hope was destroyed. He broke down and cried aloud. The loneliness of his room was more unbearable than ever. That night his hair turned white.

What now followed was only a ghastly epilogue. Franz Josef immediately summoned Deák and Andrássy. In December, 1867, the "Ausgleich" was concluded. And yet once more the old warrior with all his remaining strength hurled himself against the inevitable and almost succeeded in wrecking Deák's work of peace. In May, 1867, Kossuth addressed an open letter to Deák. He called him "friend"; for all the years of separation, the sufferings of exile had not impaired the feelings of friendship for the comrade of his youth. He implored him to see that the planned "Ausgleich" encroached on Hungary's rights every bit as much as Austria's ultimatum on the eve of Jellasich's invasion. And this at a moment when Austria was dependent on Hungary, when no shadow of compulsion forced his country to accept this compromise. "The role of Cassandra is ungrateful, I know; but I urge you to reflect that Cassandra was right." This letter was broadcast in Hungary in forty thousand copies. It was read in every county. Once again the voice of the great prophet found an echo in the hearts of his distant people.

Deák did not reply. His work was nearly completed. The die was cast. He sent Baron Wenckheim to the old King Ferdinand to persuade him to a formal renunciation of the Hungarian throne, so that Franz Josef might be legally crowned with the crown of St. Stephen. With a gentle smile the king signed. But as he handed back the paper with his signature, he said: "Do you know, my dear Wenckheim, to lose Lombardy and to be kicked out of the German Confederation, those are things that even I could have managed."

A new era was beginning. Kossuth knew it. What meaning had his life now? His day was over. Sadly he said good-bye to politics. He remained only a silent, exiled, lonely man. The amnesty had recalled the last fighters of the cause. Even

Pulszky returned home. Kossuth alone remained. The inflexible old man had no desire to see his country again—the country that had deserted him.

From that day on his letter-paper was edged with black. His clear sensitive writing was framed in this expression of mourning. Letters were now the last threads that linked him with his home. Letters, endless letters, kind, fatherly, full of counsel, prophecy and wisdom; they gave him the illusion that he was still indispensable. But he was so no longer.

In a letter to Virgil Szilágyi written on the 19th September of this year 1867, he bids the past farewell. This letter, too, is written on black-edged paper. "Now I no longer believe in the future. I am convinced of the superfluousness of all my exertions and in truth I wish for nothing more heartily than that I may be left in the loneliness of my mourning and forgotten."

VI

The Love of a People

THE ROOM IN THE OLD HOUSE BECAME CHILLIER; HE KNEW IT too well. The library grew till it almost reached the ceiling. He still went out whenever the sun shone, but duty kept him chained to his desk. His last money was spent; this protracted life had already lasted too long. He strove—was it for the last time?—to earn his bread by work. What if he were to write his memoirs? Would not the world respond to all his fights, experiences, the wisdom he had stored? But what did the world of 1888 care about the long-forgotten struggle of 1848! Forty years reduce the most living things to dust.

Eight years ago he had found a publisher who was at least interested in the recollections of the period when Kossuth had been implicated in Italian history. For a meagre pittance he wrote down two thousand pages of the past, laboriously wading through old notes and piles of documents. His plants had to wait; only in his hours of leisure could he return to the science which was life. It was a torment to him to steep himself again in the world of conflicts that he had quitted. And with the memories that necessity revived, the old desires came to life again; his ideas demanded once again to be put to the test of actuality.

How he had believed that he was still the terror of Austria! Yes, that was why he now entreated Charlotte Zeyk to burn his letters, for fear that she might get into trouble through her connection with the dreaded old man of Turin. But when the first volume of his memoirs appeared, his friends wrote him: "The Hungary of to-day no longer understands you." Had he been so blind? He was staggered. He ended the long work of two thousand pages with the words: "Perhaps they are right. And I no longer understand the Hungary of to-day." And reawakened by this two years' work, the hope was resuscitated that the present might crown his influence with a belated success. And if not now, then in the distant future. "The wheel of destiny rotates rapidly. The time may yet come when I shall be understood.

The years went by. It was five years since he had last seen Charlotte. His loneliness was now more trying. What remained of all the struggles of his life? Nothing, nothing. He alone was an isolated exile. His son often begged him to come to him at Naples; the old man refused. The roomy study in the Via dei Mille had become his home. And in his happiest dreams he thought that one day it might become a sentimental Mecca for his fellow-countrymen.

1889. Great internal conflicts were spreading in the Austro-Hungarian monarchy; those who lived in it felt that the internal peace was not assured. Once more the great conception of the Hapsburgs—the idea of welding together the peoples of the empire into a mighty and enduring state by the power of the dynasty—seemed to find its realisation under Franz Josef. Kossuth's Cassandra eye had prematurely scanned the horizon; no one believed him. But the disillusioned and the grateful looked to the quiet, proud house in the Via dei Mille as to some distant holy place. The peasant who was now free and owned his bit of land included the name of Kossuth in his prayers; to the growing generation he became a symbolical figure. His legendary personality held Hungary's millions together as a people.

The Paris World Exhibition of 1889 attracted all the world to the French capital. Turin was off the route taken by the special trains run from Hungary to Paris. But no Hungarian thought of undertaking the long journey without visiting the distant Mecca on the way. Every Magyar wanted once in his life to see the grand old man under whom their fathers had fought; the father of Hungary in whom they believed. Turin was suddenly overrun with hundreds and hundreds of travellers speaking the strange Hungarian tongue. The man in the street stopped to watch them; everyone knew; they were pilgrims come to visit Kossuth. And everyone knew the old man's habits; the hours at which he went out and when he returned home. Eight hundred men and women arrived with the first trains. Some of them went to fetch him at his house. A room had been taken for a banquet. The old man entered; their cheers were ready on their lips, but as he came into the room they were struck dumb. The old man's back was not bent; he held himself erect, just as if he were advancing to the rostrum of the Diet. He reached his seat and stood upright. He wished to make a speech.

He raised his arms slowly, as if with a great effort, in a gesture of blessing, a dim recollection of the day of Kápolna. He spoke. "So many Hungarians!" He managed to bring out the words and then burst into tears. He sat down. Silence. No one dared to speak. The Italian waiters tiptoed out of the room so as not to disturb the Hungarian visitors. But suddenly, behind the closed doors, they heard a clear, penetrating, ringing voice. Kossuth was speaking. Once, once more, he was speaking to these eight hundred as to his people. For they were his people, his people who had come to him at last. Let them who had come to him judge him. But this belated apologia, made voluntarily before the forum of the nation, unprepared, prompted only by the overwhelming emotion of the moment, became a manifesto. The aged voice regained the magic of the years of victory. He spoke for two hours. No applause, no cheers were enough to thank him. Eight hundred men and woman bowed their heads, as if they represented the whole Hungarian nation, in this the greatest hour of their lives.

Now he could die. But death does not come at bidding. Once more the eternal enemy held the torment of Job reserved for him. A subtly devised Austrian law permitted him to adopt Hungarian citizenship. He did so. On the 10th January, 1890, Lajos Kossuth ceased to be a Hungarian.

But the revenge avenged itself. The capital of Budapest, now one city, conferred upon him honorary citizenship. On the 19th September, 1892, his ninetieth birthday was celebrated like a Saint's day in all the towns, in all the villages, in the meanest cabin of the meanest shepherd. And strangely enough, as if History meant to teach the mighty that might is brought to nothing on the frontiers of sentiment, the Empress Elizabeth, the wife of Franz Josef, who loved Hungary, secretly telegraphed her congratulations to the old man.

Death still tarried. Kossuth was ninety-one. He sat freezing at his desk, with woollen rugs wrapped round his frozen legs, and worked. So the wife of the naturalist Otto Hermann found him on a visit to Italy. She writes:

"I returned home from Turin a week ago. I saw the great exile, bowed under the weight of his ninety-one years, bent over his writing-table; in one of his shaking hands he held a magnifying glass to his almost sightless eyes in order to be able to write the letters on the paper—for his daily bread.

The laborious work of the day, the fear that he will not have anything to eat to-morrow, rob him of his sleep. . . . And he works, works by the sweat of his brow, in order to have enough to eat.

This picture has haunted me day and night ever since; I can only think, and the thought makes me very sad, how we Hungarians might offer Hungary's saviour, Lajos Kossuth, the bit of bread he needs, so that he might have a span of rest, free from worry, before he lays his grey head upon his pillow in eternal sleep.

I only know one thing: I only know that Kossuth, in order to obtain this brief rest, is willing to separate himself from his splendid, valuable library. I am looking for generous hearts, ready to acquire this treasure for the nation, if the gratitude of a nation can really find no other way."

This letter appeared in the *Pesti Naplo* in October, 1893. Six months later, in March, 1894, the National Museum decided to purchase Kossuth's library. Five days later, on the 20th March, the old man collapsed, writing at his desk. That evening, shortly before eleven o'clock, he died.

On the 30th March Kossuth's body was brought to Budapest. The coffin of his wife Therese and his daughter Vilma went with him. They lay in state in the hall of the National Museum until the funeral on the 1st April.

The capital could hardly contain the people who crowded it for this occasion. The city was black with people. Special trains were run from all parts of the country. Tens of thousands walked to Budapest. The whole nation came together to pay their last tribute to the dead man. And for the last time the government in Vienna stretched out its hand against its adversary: the officers of the army were forbidden to take part in the funeral procession and the wearing of uniform was forbidden on that day. What did it matter? They put on mufti and mingled with the crowd.

Go into a tavern, go into a peasant cottage, anywhere in Hungary, and you will find, in a special place of honour, a picture of Kossuth; a picture from which generations have not separated and generations will not separate. And you will hear: "This is father Kossuth," and old peasants on the pusztas will whisper to you: "He still lives."

He still lives, like the few that History has used to reveal her meaning.

Index

E

F

G

H

I

J

K

L

M

N

O

P

R

S

T

V

W

Z